Superior, Nebraska

Also by Denis Boyles

Vile France

African Lives

Man Eaters Motel:
An East African Traveler's Nightbook

A Man's Life

Superior, Nebraska

The Common-Sense Values of America's Heartland

Denis Boyles

Doubleday

New York   London   Toronto   Sydney   Auckland

PUBLISHED BY DOUBLEDAY

Published in the United States by Doubleday,
an imprint of The Doubleday Broadway Publishing Group,
a division of Random House, Inc., New York.
www.doubleday.com

DOUBLEDAY and the portrayal of an anchor with a dolphin
are registered trademarks of Random House, Inc.

Brief portions of this book appeared in *The American Enterprise*
and on *National Review* online.

Book design by Donna Sinisgalli

Library of Congress Cataloging-in-Publication Data
Boyles, Denis.
Superior, Nebraska: the common-sense values of America's heartland /
by Denis Boyles.—1st ed.
p. cm.
Includes bibliographical references and index.
1. Social values—Middle West.   2. Voters—Middle West—Attitudes.
3. Middle West—Politics and government.   4. Middle West—Social conditions.
5. Political sociology.   I. Title.
HN79.A14B69 2007
324.977
2007027608

ISBN 978-0-385-51674-7

PRINTED IN THE UNITED STATES OF AMERICA

1 3 5 7 9 10 8 6 4 2

First Edition

This book is dedicated to

Oliver, Claude, and

Donald Boyles,

Superior Kansans

Contents

Superior, Nebraska

Introduction

Welcome to Superior

If you divided the great red sea of American voters that stretches from one blue coast to the other and stood on the dry ground in the middle, you'd be on the north bank of the Republican River looking down Central Avenue, the wide, dusty main street of Superior, Nebraska, population 2,055.

At the south end of Superior's main street are the Burlington Northern's tracks, along with a few rough warehouses and sheds and a liquor store with lots of warning stickers on it to scare away the kids. At the other end, a neighborhood of fashionable Victorian homes, all done up with new gingerbread and fresh paint. In between, the dime store, the Crest theater, three banks and a bunch of beauty parlors, antiques and appliance shops, a JCPenney's catalog outlet, hardware and gift stores, and a women's clothier—the retail district, with its constant churn. The old Git-a-Bite still has its sign up, although the café is long gone. Superior has a newspaper, parks, a pool, a library, a couple of supermarkets, a crafts shop, and the BPOE, the Benevolent and Protective Order of Elks, where many people go for Sunday dinners—"dinner" is lunch, in Superior—right after they attend one of the town's many churches. There's a motel up by the hospital and a *winery* outside town, but nobody seems to know what to think of that yet.

Every small midwestern village has its local claim to a wider fame— the sign on the way in tells you you're entering the birthplace of an astronaut, a politician, or a ballplayer. In the case of Superior, it's the town's recent and unexpected links to the entertainment business. Lew Hunter, a Hollywood veteran and a member of the Screenwriting Hall of Fame, grew up around Superior and has returned home. A couple of times every year—once in the early summer and again in the autumn—Superior's coffee shops and cafés are filled with people eating cheeseburgers but dreaming of Spago while attending classes at Hunter's Superior Screenwriting Colony workshops. And a former TV news producer from New York, Ben Sherwood, set his novel *The Man Who Ate the 747* in Superior,[1] which so endeared him to the town that they made him an honorary citizen and star attraction of the Lady Vestey Festival Parade—the annual community fair honoring a local girl named Evelyn Brodstone, who, before Sherwood and Hunter, had been Superior's most famous resident. A childhood chum of Willa Cather's, who lived upriver in Red Cloud, Evelyn led a very adventurous life for a girl who was a trained stenographer: she made piles of money, married an English lord, lived in a castle, and died in London in 1941 at the age of sixty-six—but not before giving Superior a bird sanctuary and a hospital.

However, to most people on the East and West Coasts, Superior is just another dot on the mysterious map of the Midwest, a place out there, somewhere off the right side of the aircraft. For decades—and especially during the last two presidential terms—people in small towns like Superior have been ignored or, worse, insulted by people from big cities who don't know much about the middle of America except how it votes, which is sometimes but not always Republican. Blue-state pundits have reviled people like the ones you see walking up Central Avenue as Babbitts and bigots, hicks and Jesus freaks. It's not just a lazy way of caricaturing people they don't know; it's a political weapon based on a century-old stereotype, and its use has been spreading since Reagan was president. Even the Midwest's liberals, eager to mimic elitists on the coasts, now think of their neighbors this way. They probably have to, since the only alternative is to grant them a little good faith, something partisans right and left find impossible these days.

The problem people in places like New York have with citizens of towns like Superior has to do with big-city assumptions versus small-town notions of community and government, self-reliance, responsibility, honor. The whole middle of the country seems to have produced a paucity of pretension and a bumper crop of civility. While those values are the ones that most Americans like to see in themselves, they're not typically the qualities that come to mind when you think about New York or Los Angeles, where rude pretension alone can be enough to make you famous.

But the Midwest's most valuable commodity of all is the common sense of its durable inhabitants. Too bad it doesn't come in barrels, because there's a huge reservoir of the stuff out there, and part of the goal of this little book with its innocuous subtitle is to help export some of it to places where it's desperately needed.

Superior sits near the apex of the giant arc made by the Republican River as it meanders through Nebraska and Kansas, circling the geographical center of America. Just south of town, past the ball fields, you can see farmers pausing on the highway bridge to watch the river go from trickle to torrent and back again, knowing that if the river stops, everything else will too. On the other side of the river is Jewell County, Kansas. And beyond all that is the distant, uninterrupted horizon—what some San Franciscans and New Yorkers may see as the endless flatline of a dying Middle America, but what people in Superior see as the place where heaven touches the earth.

Superior's just north of where my great-grandfather Oliver settled after the Civil War. It's where my grandfather Claude went to catch the train to go to fight in France in the First World War, and it's where my dad and two of his three brothers got their papers for World War II. All those boys survived the wars—one of them, Gerald, even survived Iwo Jima, which is like surviving twice. But it's also where two of those uncles of mine, Delmar and his little brother, Neal, died of emphysema after decades of smoking cigarettes while huffing wheat chaff in the cab of a combine. It's where my friend Bill Blauvelt has run the local newspaper, the *Superior Express,* since even before his dad closed the Sinclair station south of town, on the Kansas side of the Republican. As a kid around my age, Bill not only pumped gas under the big "Dino the Dinosaur" sign, but also rose to a near-mythic status, at least to me, late every June when he presided over his very own fireworks stand.

Superior is also the town closest to where I spent many of my most memorable summers growing up, sweating through the week from one Saturday night to the next. My Superior bona fides are tenuous and sentimental but sincere: My father had no interest in farming, which, when I was young, was a source of embarrassment and regret to me, because I thought Superior more than lived up to its name. On the other hand, he'd grown up during the Dust Bowl and had lost a five-year-old brother when the whole family was stricken with sickness, so maybe his Midwest wasn't quite as charming as mine. So we lived in Kansas City, and when we wanted to go home for Christmas or the Fourth of July or for a birthday or a reunion, we headed west on U.S. 36, aiming for the Republican River. Eventually, my parents moved to California, a place I never really liked, but my lucky break was that every summer, we'd go back home. And, later, when my folks couldn't go, they'd send me.

One summer, I rode out there with a couple of ladies in sundresses who were deeply concerned with making a rendezvous with a mysterious Navajo man in Window Rock, Arizona, during the big tribal meeting. Me and miles of Navajos! A couple of summers I rode the Union Pacific; once, when I was about twelve, as I vaguely recall, I fell for a nineteen-year-old girl who I was certain had designated herself my train-sitter. (In fact, my *very* clear understanding was that she'd pledged herself to me all the way to Grand Island—*then* I find her sitting next to some Pat-Boone–alike Baptist *seminarian* character in the observation car *at night* with her head *on his shoulder.* It took half of New Mexico and the conductor with his keys to pry me out of the washroom, not that it matters to me now, of course.)

This was all in the 1950s and early '60s, when the Midwest offered more rites of passage than a Freemason's handbook. I tried to hit them all.

At thirteen, I learned to steer my uncle's old Studebaker pickup down the treacherous loose gravel roads that went from Superior down toward Burr Oak, Kansas. The silhouette of the naked lady on the truck's knicker-knob is embedded in my brain as securely as if I'd encountered it head-on at sixty, which I nearly did more than once. Next to me, my cousin Terry—a year older, a little taller, and consequently full of himself—and next to the door, Uncle Neal himself, fresh out of the postwar air force. While I drove, they offered helpful suggestions in that white-knuckled but casual way that screams, "For God's sake, don't scare the boy!" I tasted my first beer—a bottle of watery 3.2 stuff—in a pool hall in Beverly, Kansas, and got in my first serious fight in a field near Burr Oak (with a kid named Davey who never seemed to have to wear shoes).

Far away, the edges of America seemed to spin faster than the still center of the country. Teenagers in New York and Los Angeles could listen to rock and roll all day long, if they wanted. But midcentury in the Midwest, there was only one rock-and-roll station audible on the Great Plains: the fabulous KOMA in Okla*homa* City. You couldn't get it until after sunset, but it was worth the wait, since twice a night the DJ read the location of every single Legion-hall dance in ten states. All you had to do to meet a pretty girl was get to one.

That I could spend a summer night parked out by the lake south of town listening to DJs on KOMA talk about kids going to dances in South Dakota, Kansas, and the panhandle of Texas made Superior seem like the center of everything, which it is.

In the middle of Superior stands the old Leslie Hotel, where I once had to paint the lobby green in exchange for a room after my grandmother tossed me and a couple of high school friends out of the house for smoking a cigarette in the attic.

We had driven out to Kansas from California right after high school graduation. Jim Wilde and Bob Wurster were both spending their late adolescence as folksingers, and I wasn't. After hearing me talk about Kansas for years, they finally agreed to come out and take a look.

It was an error. It's when I first learned that even if they go, people who aren't from there don't know what they're looking at when they get there.

Wurster, the acerbic president of our graduating class and Princeton-bound in the autumn, was especially unkind about the hot, dusty landscape, despite his own Nebraskan ancestry.[2] The day after we arrived, sitting in Granny's stifling attic, he wrote a little parody of Malvina Reynolds's "What Have They Done to the Rain." He called it "What Kansas Needs Is Just a Little Rain," and he sang it while Wilde sat next to the window smoking a Parliament and promising me that Granny, all the way downstairs, would never notice. He underestimated my grandmother's olfactory powers, refined by a lifetime of Protestant purity. She threw us out with thirty seconds' notice.

We didn't have any money because we had forgotten to get any jobs so we tried living rough in a field for a few minutes, until sweat bees and the hundred-degree temperature drove us to seek the shelter of civilization, which meant retreating to Superior.

When we got there, there was an American Legion game in progress down by the river. Wurster, a very handsome, witty, blond California boy, promptly chatted up a local girl, who got us the lobby-painting gig. We were given a tiny room to share, bath down the hall. The nights were short and the days were long, as they say, and slowly, slowly, the lobby went from a yellow-gray-beige to a truly lurid green.[3] "That's quite a change," the worried owner said when we were done. He was right. The lobby looked radioactive. He thought maybe the old color was better and, as we were leaving, started talking about painting it all beige again. Sometimes, change works that way. You ask for a little, but you get a lot.

But not when it comes to midwestern politics. Although the 2006 election saw a few Republican reverses and a rising, if still wistful hope by East Coast liberals that the plains might paint themselves blue, the red-blue paradigm has never meant to Nebraskans and Kansans what faraway coastal observers think it means.

For one thing, most of the people in places like Superior have a practical sense of politics. They know as well as the rest of us that America is at one of its crazy apogees of polarization; they see conflicting political beliefs turned into quasi-religious convictions with their own set of faith-based hatreds. In a recent speech at Harvard, James Q. Wilson talked about the intensity of the the current environment by distinguishing what we see now as something radically, dangerously different from traditional partisanship:

> By polarization I mean something else: an intense commitment to a candidate, a culture, or an ideology that sets people in one group definitively apart from people in another, rival group. Such a condition is revealed when a candidate for public office is regarded by a competitor and his supporters not simply as wrong but as corrupt or wicked; when one way of thinking about the world is assumed to be morally superior to any other way; when one set of political beliefs is considered to be entirely correct and a rival set wholly wrong. In extreme form, as defined by Richard Hofstadter in *The Paranoid Style in American Politics* (1965), polarization can entail the belief that the other side is in thrall to a secret conspiracy that is using devious means to obtain control over society. Today's versions might go like this: "Liberals employ their dominance of the media, the universities, and Hollywood to enforce a radically secular agenda"; or, "conservatives, working through the religious Right and the big corporations, conspired with their hired neocon advisers to invade Iraq for the sake of oil."[4]

As Wilson and many, many others suggest, the "disagreement" in national politics is actually a deep mutual revulsion made permanent on both sides by an assumption of moral superiority often based solely on party affiliation.

That's crazy, of course, and so that's not how it works in Kansas and Nebraska, along the Republican River or all across the Great Plains, where most people are Republicans but don't feel they stop being one even when they vote for a Democrat, as they often do. Meanwhile, there are people who live in places like New Jersey who wouldn't vote for a Republican no matter how shady the Democrat looks—or even admittedly is. A woman I know, an intelligent attorney who lives only minutes from Washington, D.C., once told me she would rather vote for a crooked Democrat than an honest Republican, that there is no Republican alive for whom she would ever vote, no matter what. This is more or less the position taken by the editorial page at the *New York Times*. People like her may be surprised to learn that voting patterns are far more sophisticated in places where people commute to work on tractors. For example, in some ways this book is just a casual, amateur political and anthropological shuffle along the course of a midwestern river. Yet in discussing a title for this book, I was surprised to be told that even mentioning the Republican River would put "some readers" off.

I guess you know who you are, but you sure aren't from Superior.

As I hope to show, the complications of prairie politics are maddening. I discovered this when I set out to write this book. I thought I knew the territory and that it would take a few months to poke fun at a few local liberal lunatics—but I discovered that I knew a lot less than I thought and that it would take much longer than that. I convinced my wife and my three very reluctant daughters that it would be pleasant to spend a few months in a quiet little town near the Kansas-Nebraska border, sponging off the ancestors, instead of going to our customary retreat in France.

But the place is sticky, and by the time I was finished and ready to go *a year and a half later,* my daughters were being trained by one of the top-ranked fencing coaches in the country and taking music lessons from a fabulous teacher from Fairbury, Nebraska, who had toured the world. They had become friends with all the knitting ladies in three counties, a concert organist, and an amazing young woman home from her opera studies in Milan. They had learned the basics of ballroom dancing from a teacher who emphasized the importance of the elbow and the smile and had cataloged part of the rather substantial costume collection at the local museum; they had studied chess for months with one of Anatoly Karpov's Russian friends; they'd indulged their passion for Gilbert and Sullivan and been reliably informed by local teens that it was socially unwise to put a functioning muffler on your pickup truck in small midwestern towns. One of them had joined the string section of a decent community orchestra. Another had written a novel.

Now we're all back in France, in a charming village, surrounded by museums, great food, interesting work, and beaucoup friends—and the whole family's furious at me for making them leave the Midwest.

Part One

Out Where?

Although we've spent much of the past few years living in rural Europe, I happened to be at our home in rural America—in Pennsylvania's corner of Appalachia, to be exact—sitting in an office repurposed (some say unconvincingly) from its previous use as a pig barn when I started this book. It was November 3, about four in the afternoon, the day after the 2004 election. I had spent a large part of the morning reading the news on the Internet and much of the afternoon talking on the phone about politics.

I had reluctantly voted for Bush. I thought that, like his father, he was deeply cynical, and I hated to hear him talk. I figured a president leading a nation into a very complicated war should be capable of a few Saint Crispin's Day moments without needing a fire truck and a bullhorn as props. The trouble was, John Kerry was all props and no play. He thought the country should swallow his "reporting for duty" jive and fall in line behind him and his weird zillionaire wife while they pretended to relive the anti-war movement's glory days and also, you know, save the poor and some seals. Every time Bush spoke, I and a thousand other apologists would immediately start trying to do his talking for him. But when Kerry opened his mouth, all I could hear was Country Joe and the Fish—except Country Joe was at least clear on the issues. It was stretching it, to me, to call Bush the best of a bad choice. But it seemed a snap to call Kerry the worst.

To most of rural America, however, including the Pennsylvania part, Bush was just fine. Aside from a brief conversation with Tom Morrall at the feed mill, there were no "moderate" phone calls. A magazine editor in Washington carefully prefaced his comments by saying, "I hope you're not a Republican." I told him I was an independent. He hesitated for a moment, probably calculating the difference between "independent" and "liar," then began complaining about the "moronic" voters who'd been seduced by homophobia and lust for war. I reassured him that I feared nothing *but* war. Another guy, a New Yorker who worked at an entertainment magazine, told me that somebody ought to look into all that vote rigging in Ohio and maybe Florida. From NPR I heard a groan of grief and disbelief sweep across America's blue states. The sorrowful incredulity raced across the water: A friend in Europe e-mailed me, demanding to know why the hell Americans had learned *nothing* from *Farenheit 9/11*.

But not everyone was depressed that day. Neighbors who'd long ago asked me to please stop making them into rural silage for "that crazy stuff" I write were in a good mood. The guy a couple of farms over called with an ag question but ended with a last-minute topic change: "Kicked butt yesterday, bud." A dairy farmer stopped by to gloat: "Hey, *that* was fun!" One fish-out-of-water New York Republican gleefully informed me that he'd spent the morning after the election on Manhattan's Upper West Side, "soaking up the gloom." My cousin Deb, an accountant, called from Mankato, a county seat in northern Kansas, just south of the Republican River. She had a question for me: "Hey, what happened to you guys in Pennsylvania?"

"Happened? Kerry got the Philly and Pittsburgh vote." The margins there had been enough to push the commonwealth into the Kerry column. Pennsylvania had gone to the Democrats by 100,000 suspect votes from the big-city precincts—about the same suspicious margin by which Bush took Ohio, next door.

"Well, that's no excuse," she said. "We've got K.C. and all these newspapers out here—but, heck, we're on top of the world!"

She obviously didn't read those papers—or scan the 'Net or watch TV—because, heck, it may have been the top of the world from where she sat

in Kansas, but in 2004, Kansas—and Nebraska and Missouri and Oklahoma and the whole rest of the middle of the country, and the southern
part, too, and also those mountainous regions, plus Alaska—looked a lot
like the bottom of the barrel, especially to those perched along the nation's edges.

But *especially* Kansas.

In fact, to a lot of easterners, the election defied comprehension. After
all, for weeks, months, *years,* hadn't the truth been obvious? Had all those
thousands of big media reporters, editors, and columnists, the best writers
in America, the best *minds,* just been wasting their time? Had they not
worked tirelessly—almost *selflessly,* really—creating a simple narrative that
was as easy to understand as the label on a bottle of Perrier? Left = tolerant.
Right = cruel. Howard Dean? ☺. Dick Cheney? ☹.

By now everybody should have been on the same page! In fact, the
whole effort had been brought to the level of art during the campaign.
Even the Boss campaigned for Kerry.

So why hadn't all those farmers gotten the message in 2004? Or, as
one British newspaper's headline whimsically pondered, "How can 59
million people be so dumb?"[1]

So at four in the afternoon I started typing this, what I hoped would
be an explanation of why Kansans and Nebraskans voted as they do. My
explanation wasn't going to be the only one, that's for sure: Over the
next days and weeks, the 2004 election would be "analyzed"—to put it
gently—by journalists, pundits, and ordinary left-wing types. Their incredulity blended with hysteria and spread until it was everywhere: cartoon maps of America with big inland seas of dumbness; Internet rants;
sociological studies. I was on the phone again, this time talking to a New
Yorker toiling in the sweatshops of the global lit biz. I mentioned the
59-million-dumb-people headline.

"Yes," she enthusiastically agreed, "that's what I'd like to know. Really,
the only reason I can think of that all those people out there vote like they
do is that they're *dumb.* Can there be another reason? Isn't what it comes
down to is that they're just *stupid*?"[2] By "out there," she meant that big

pile of red states filled with illiterates, Jesusland, the heart of political darkness.

As it happens, "out there" is a fairly precise measurement describing the distance from where you stand to where all knowledge disappears and all sense evaporates. A smart writer can double that distance: "The village of Holcomb stands on the high wheat plains of western Kansas, a lonesome area that other Kansans call 'out there.' " That's the brilliant first sentence of Truman Capote's *In Cold Blood.* It locates Holcomb, Kansas, not only *out there,* from the viewpoint of a *New Yorker* writer, which Capote was at the time, but *out there* even to a *Kansan.* That places Holcomb on another planet in another solar system, since as everybody from everyplace else knows, Kansas itself is already out there.

Of course, "out there" has pretty much always described my idea of where I came from and who I think I am. For sure, I always considered out there to be more home than the little house in Garden Grove, California, where my parents eventually moved—or, for that matter, that ex–pig barn office in Pennsylvania.

And here's something else: I've never thought of any of my relatives, all Out Thereites through and through, as stupid. In fact, when it came to the things that seemed to me to be useful measures of intelligence—putting stuff together, taking stuff apart, adapting one of these to improve one of those, knowing when to add some of that; really, all the lessons in applied physics a kid could drag out of a country workshop—I always assumed that a rural education, with daily life as its ongoing internship, was demonstrably superior to the one I received in crowded suburban schools.

That's largely why, when I had kids of my own, I contrived to find a setting for their childhood that was as close to out there as I could get, without, of course, actually going out *there.* Hence, that farm in Pennsylvania—only hours from Washington and New York, where I did much of my work at the time, and bought with sudden urgency (and my new wife's reluctant compliance) when we discovered we were going to be parents. Sixteen years later, I still hadn't found an entirely reliable drinking buddy, but the best meals were caught from the ponds and the kids lived the way all kids should live when they're young, with the big porch and the dock and without shoes, and acres of fields and woods, a pony, lots of sheep, a three-legged goat, a blind donkey named Jack, and the big empty pit out back where Daddy pours all his money.

Once, a magazine sent a photographer out to take a picture of me on a Ford 8N, a cute old tractor, along with some snapshots of my "farm" office. He marveled over its decor motif, best described here as the kind of rococo rustification you get if you don't pick up after yourself. His story was about a writer living on a farm. No wonder the magazine went out of business. Almost *every* writer outside Manhattan lives on a farm of some kind. Writers love to romanticize agriculture, whether it's wheat or petunias. I think it's a way of associating a frankly passive, obviously self-indulgent occupation with something more redeeming, since farming is definitely work and requires a certain set of practical skills. Writing—well, it depends. This is not new, of course. I'm sure most of us know by now that "writer on farm" equates to at least one hoax, and often two. A bunch of straw in an old barn and chickens in the yard don't make a farm, unless you've got the rural-philosophy beat for some big-city newspaper or magazine. You can't dress platitudes in overalls and call it philosophy, as I may have just shown.

Real farmers run agricultural businesses that live or die according to how much education and common sense are applied to a chancy enterprise that requires very long hours, the proper paperwork, some sophisticated economics, and a decent iPod to help you get through the hottest days. Actual farmers use phenomenally expensive, distinctly uncute high-tech equipment to farm thousands of acres, often from an office where they sit phoning their brokers, reading about the weather in other places, complaining about the weather where they are, and cursing the government with the rest of us.

But for the angry Democrats I talked to on November 3, 2004, and in the weeks afterward, *nothing* about out there made any sense. They knew what they knew, and they knew it with a certainty that defied argument. It never occurred to any of them that Kansans and Nebraskans would have been happy to vote for a Democrat—just not for one like John Kerry, thanks. From what I read in the polls, most Democrats now feel the same way. But back then, the only reason not to vote for Kerry was a conservative midwestern failure to make what Thomas Frank, in his best-selling book *What's the Matter with Kansas?*, called "certain mental connections about the world."[3]

Then, a mere two years later, a miracle! In 2006, places like Kansas were suddenly filled with geniuses. In the wake of the midterm elections, the *New York Times* ran an editorial imaginatively called "What's Right with Kansas."[4] It was the paper's celebration of "a major shift in the nation's heartland"—a geologically frightening concept, but to the *Times* an awesome moment borrowed from Darwin: "Kansas—lately considered the reddest of red states—emerged from the election as a bastion of moderation." Look at Kansas! Right out of the swamp primeval and into a new pair of shoes. There was more:

> The Democratic Party posted major gains, including some by former Republicans who switched parties. The moderate Democratic governor, Kathleen Sebelius, received a whopping 58 percent of the vote to secure her re-election. Three moderate Republicans holding statewide jobs also won easy re-election, two of them after beating back conservative challengers in the primary. And two of the four people elected to the House of Representatives were Democrats, a result that would have seemed inconceivable not too long ago.

Only if you believe what you read in the New York papers. Kansas may be filled with Republicans, but there's a reason why God put Kansas in the middle of the country. It's a political waterbed, sloshing one way then another, just enough to make everybody uncomfortable. Kansas already had one Democrat congressman, and until not long ago, it had had two, just like now. The place is filled with "moderate" Republicans who would be liberal Democrats anyplace else; Democrats who would be reviled anywhere east of the Mississippi or west of the Rockies; and libertarians galore, all of whom vote with cavalier disregard for party loyalty. The governor of Kansas has been a Democrat for thirty-three of the last fifty years—each time elected with the hefty support of liberal Republicans who'd much rather a Democrat than a conservative Republican. As a result, the state's supreme court, chosen by the governor without any approval process by the state senate or any other elected body, is populated only by liberal Republicans and Democrats. The subtitle of Frank's book is "How Conservatives Won the Heart of America." That may be true elsewhere, but not in Kansas. It's true that a mildly liberal Republican fought off an Oxford-educated conservative Republican challenger for the all-important post of state insurance commissioner, but then Kansas almost never elects a conservative Republican to *any* statewide office. "It's impossible for a conservative," former Kansas state representative Kathe Decker told me. "If you run a conservative [for statewide office], Democrats will vote for their candidate and 'moderate' Republicans will all stay home—or vote for the Democrat."

One of the rare exceptions (Senator Sam Brownback is the only other) came in 2002, when a pro-life candidate, Phill Kline, barely defeated a little-known Democratic opponent to become the state's attorney general. But Kline then spent his four-year term fighting with an antagonistic press and the state's "moderate" judiciary over abortion-related issues, and when his term was up, he was voted out and Kansas once again had an avidly pro-choice attorney general, as it always has. Of course, it was Kline's defeat that was the real inspiration for the *Times*'s discovery of Kansans' sudden political savvy. The *Times* may not know much about Kansas, but they know what they like.

In 2008, there's a fifty-fifty chance that the editors of the *Times* will once again find something the matter with Kansas—as there certainly must be with Nebraska, where 2006 didn't do much to change the political landscape. If the Democrats run another John Kerry, Kansas will glow a brighter shade of red and the editorialists at the *Times* will once again look down upon Jesusland and see signs of a certain type of renewal they will call "disturbing."

Transcript 1:
Superior People

I never have stopped bragging about the Midwest to friends who have never been there. Sometimes, I can still lure a pal or two out with the promise of good company and thick steaks. I had told my friend Harry Stein so much about the sagacity of midwesterners and their amazing barbecue restaurants that he decided to leave Manhattan and come out and meet some of them himself. He thought it would be good to combine the company and the steaks with a visit to Superior.

So, relying on Bill Blauvelt and my cousin Gloria Schlaefli for names and unaware of whatever political convictions, if any, these people may have had, I invited an interesting if not particularly large cross-section of townsfolk to lunch in Superior, and traded them a free meal for an hour or two with Harry and a tape recorder.

Do not confuse this with science. I admit the sample is small, but I was picking up the tab. Besides, to reach this level of representation for a similar sit-down in New York City, I'd have to buy lunch for about twenty thousand people.

Here's our table:

Bill Blauvelt. Owner and editor of the *Superior Express,* and one of the most respected men in the county. In addition to the *Express,* back before the Web Bill started a singles' publication for rural lonely hearts called *Country Connections,* through which he met his attractive, charming, and talented wife, Rita. For years, most of us who had known him forever thought Bill was a genius to have started a whole magazine just to find a wife, but he told me a few weeks before our lunch, "It was a commercial decision." It was apparently just a coincidence that Rita was among the first to send in an ad looking for an honest man. "She was letter number thirty-seven," he mentioned casually one day.[1]

Val Heim. Retired farmer, avid golfer, and, for a while in 1942, a White Sox outfielder.

Rich Nelson. Banker.

Pat Richards. Widow and grocery store owner.

Stan Sheets. Local amateur historian.

Stan: One thing I think a lot of people on the coasts don't understand about midwesterners is how independent we are. Most of us sitting here are the offspring of pioneers, and pioneers are pretty strong-willed people.

Pat: It's true, the independent streak is powerful out here. But, really, I don't think they give us much thought at all. West of the Mississippi, you just sort of drop off the face of the earth.

Stan: I think they kind of lump us all together . . .

Pat: Right. Not very bright, and not very interesting . . . *(laughs)*

Stan: You know, words like "provincial" and "backward" get tossed around a lot, but those things cut both ways. I remember back in 1947, I was back East, and was dancing with a girl from Wellesley College. I was wearing my cowboy boots, and she asked about the danger from Indians. I explained they're pretty well settled down by now.

Bill: I used to know a fellow in college whose family vacationed every summer in Colorado. And he told me they'd always drive all night, because to be caught on the western Kansas plains in the daytime was sure death, it was so hot. He had never been west of Manhattan [Kansas, home of Kansas State University] in the daylight, and he didn't have a clue what Kansas or Nebraska *looked* like, so I decided to bring him out here to Superior. On the way, I blow a tire, and he goes into a panic: "What's wrong, what's wrong? Are they shooting at us?"

"No, we just blew a tire."

"What are we gonna do?"

"We're gonna change it."

"Is it safe? Is it safe?"

So we changed the tire, and it worked out fine. The Indians never attacked, and nobody died of thirst.

Stan: The very term "Midwest" is confusing to people back there. If you say "Midwest" to someone in New York City, they're thinking, "Ohio." Nebraska? I don't know *what* we're supposed to be.

Bill: I was on a boat trip in the Bahamas one time and one night the fella across the table from me asked how long you had to stay with my company before you got to be promoted to New York City. He'd just been promoted there and was saying how wonderful that was. I said, "My company would never promote me to New York City, but I'd quit if they did." He was amazed; he just couldn't understand that.

Rich: No, he wouldn't.

Bill: It's not really so hard. I walked to work this morning. I like that.

Pat: And when you left home, did you lock your doors?

Bill: No.

Rich: I was back East not long ago, in New Brunswick, New Jersey, outside New York, and I'd go into the city with some bankers from Texas. One day one of these guys says, "You ever notice what happens when you try to have a conversation with someone on the subway?" I said, "What do you mean? They seem all right." He says, "I mean, how they'll never look you in the eye." So I started looking for that, and he was absolutely right.

Pat: I think that's self-defense—you don't want to bring anything into your life that day that might hurt you.

Rich: But can you imagine *living* that way?

Stan: Just knowing there might be people around you with criminal intent! In a rural community, there's not that same anonymity factor—and the criminals know that all those farmers out here have rifles.

Me: I think the setting makes crime—especially murder—even more threatening. *In Cold Blood* couldn't be about a murder in Brooklyn.

Pat: That's true. Here, everybody knows everybody. If you come to this community, your privacy is no longer entirely yours. But you are respected as an individual, and you can be sure the community will care about what happens to you. If you're ever in need, there'll be hundreds of people who'll step forward to help you.

Bill: To give some indication of the crime out here, and what's valuable: A few years ago, I was at the lake, and, as is my practice, I left some money and my driver's license unlocked in my vehicle. I came back, and the money was still there, but the driver's license was gone. *(Laughter)*. Evidently some young fella wanted to buy some beer.

Stan: It's flattering to you, Bill. They never steal my license.

Bill: Well, it was an older photo.

Pat: That's the thing—there's something deeply rooted about coming from the Midwest. We hang in there, we're tenacious. And we know how to work.

Rich: No question, that comes with the territory. It's second nature.

Bill: I started at two years old, literally. One day Granddad lifts me over the fence in the yard and says, "I need you in the garage to help me fix tires," and I was there every day after that. Val knows—he used to come in there and buy gas.

Val: It's true, I remember it well.

Pat *(laughing)*: Couldn't happen today—"child endangerment."

Bill: But, you know, it didn't do me a bit of harm. To the contrary, it gives you a sense of responsibility and importance in the world. They tell me that when I was six, and supposed to start school, I said, "Well, maybe in October, but we're too busy at the gas station in September." You really felt that the family would starve if you weren't there to help.

Pat: A lot of that is still alive and well out here. When our kids get up in the morning, they know there's work to do; you've got to put your shoulder to the wheel if you're gonna get by.

Bill: That's just a given. One time when I was ten, I was helping my dad tear down a barn a few miles away. There were just the two of us, and we had a truck and pickup, and we had to get back home. So he said, "Well, son, I'll take the truck and you take the pickup." And I did, no problem.

Pat: More child endangerment. But that sort of thing gives kids a sense of identity in the family, and the understanding that they're important. I'm not sure that's as true in other parts of this country. I have a niece who worked for a while in New York City, and she said that, in her experience, employers were glad to get kids from the Midwest. They speak well, they're respectful, they're mannerly, and they get their work done.

Rich: I don't doubt it.

Bill: You hear on the news last night that they had a coyote in Central Park?

Stan (laughing): That made the news, did it?

Rich (laughing): I hate to even estimate how many dollars it cost New Yorkers to catch that thing. Probably involved several municipal departments.

Stan: Instead of one farmer with a rifle. . . . You want to talk about the difference between people on the coasts and people here, that's it right there. I know you can't have people shooting coyotes in New York, but I mean the principle of just taking care of things on your own. They pretty much believe government should handle everything. From cradle to grave.

Bill: It's easier here to see how the money gets wasted, and the incompetence, and the red tape. I had a personal experience lately that highlights that. For the past couple of years, I've printed envelopes for a couple of government agency offices, and the arrangement has worked out very well. They've been delighted, because my prices are so much better and my service is so much faster than what they're getting elsewhere. Well, I delivered some to them the other day, and afterward they called and said, "We're sorry, but we can't buy any more envelopes from you. We have been reprimanded pretty severely because you're not a General Services Administration contractor and we have to buy our envelopes only from them."

Rich: That's government for you.

Bill: So I went on the Web to see what it would take to become a GSA contractor, and it turns out you have to sell a minimum of $25,000 a year before you can even be considered, and *then* you have to give a kickback on every order to the General Services Administration. And you have to be willing to accept orders of any size and do a series of reports—some annually, some quarterly, whatever. And you have your affirmative action reports, your this, your that. I suspect that even if I was willing to do the $25,000 a year, they wouldn't accept us. We're not a union shop, we don't have any minority employees . . . we don't have a very large minority community. So we're out of it, even though we're cheaper and better.

Stan: And I don't see how anyone could *not* see that kind of thing as a problem? But it seems like a lot of people in other parts of the country just don't. It looks like common sense to us, but they simply accept it as normal and natural.

Pat: Well, you know, we talk about why we in different parts of the country don't understand each other better—maybe that's the wrong question. There's a book that subdivides the United States into nine distinct regions, each with its own unique culture and ways of looking at the world. Culturally, they're almost as different as the nations of Europe. Why should people from New York or Boston appreciate our ways, or vice versa? Do you ever hear the French or Italians wondering why they don't have more in common with the Germans or the Danes? We're just different, that's all.

Return of the Part-Time Native

Here's the story of a guy who grows up in Kansas, goes to the big city, becomes a writer, then comes home again and tells everybody in Kansas how stupid they are.

Obviously, this is not me. No, the subject in this particular case is a man named Harrison George; the time is the early 1930s, and in the Midwest, the dust is still settling on houses, cars, and trucks.

George is a member of the politically furious class. An early adapter to the new radicalism of the Industrial Workers of the World, by the time we meet him, he's a busy party apparatchik shuttling between assignments in California and New York. His line, not surprisingly, is journalism. When he finds himself passing through his old home state, he steps off the Santa Fe long enough to grab a quick lunch at one of the Harvey House restaurants that dot the main line. As he eats, he ruminates about the sorry state of Kansas, making a mental note or two for later use.

George isn't a completely unknown hack. He had made a name for himself in the wider world as one of several Kansas-bred Communist heavyweights. I understand that "Kansas Communist" may seem like an impossibly dissonant concept, like an underseat air bag; Kansas is where common sense is supposed to grow wild and where small-town American values adhere to the state's image like bugs on a windshield. Even "Kansas liberal" has a curious ring to it, which is perhaps why the local press never uses the term, "moderate" being the preferred euphemism.

But at the time, Kansas Communists were not at all uncommon. For example, as Harrison George was lunching in Kansas, the Communist Party USA was being run by Earl Browder, nominally a typewriter repairman from the Sunflower State. He was part of a circle that included the famous Trotskyite James Cannon, who came from Rosedale, and L. E. "Louis" Katterfeld, who, with Kansas City's Gertrude Harmon, was present at the birth of the Communist Labor Party of America (later the CPUSA) in 1919. Before moving a little farther west in the state, Katterfeld went to a long-vanished country school in Cloud County, just south of where I'm sitting now.

For all these people, and for reasons that still resonate, the Kansas association was not just a mere biographical note but an important credential; a "New York Communist" made sense to people reading about a movement that seemed to be dominated by urban easterners and by the foreign-born. Midwesterners must have seemed more authentically American. As *Time* noted in a 1938 cover story on Browder, the party's leader was born in Wichita, "and he never lets . . . his public forget it." One of Browder's more memorable slogans: "Communism is Twentieth-Century Americanism." Dutifully noted *Time*'s anonymous correspondent, "His life is an American biography."

Of course, the same could be said of you, me, and hundreds of millions of other Americans, but I suppose what *Time* meant was that Communists were Americans, too—and who could be more American than a guy from Wichita?

Like Browder, Harrison George wore the mantle of Kansas hard-toiler with pride. His story was that he had been born in a dugout—a one- or two-room hole in the ground with a roof—near Oakley, Kansas, in 1888. "That little spot of homestead on the Kansas prairie where my pioneer mother bore me is more sacred to me than the Stock Exchange quotations on U.S. Steel Common or American Can Preferred," he wrote in a 1937 pamphlet called *This 4th of July.* His self-portrayal as a son of the sod was rich in supporting detail: George smoked a corncob pipe and spoke with a pronounced prairie twang, but while it's quite possible that he was indeed a hardscrabble kind of guy, Whittaker Chambers later reported that he was a typical "middle-class American revolutionist."

By the time his train stopped in Kansas, George had been in the Industrial Workers of the World, edited the IWW newspaper, done time for sedition during World War I, been put on trial by the party for trying to lead a Communist putsch, and married Comrade Browder's sister. He'd written a column for the *Daily Worker* called—in solidarity with the Loyalists in the Spanish Civil War—"Red Sparks by Jorge" and had gone to China and to the Philippines, working to start Communist movements there. His convincing cover: kinky health nut—a real avocation, as it happened. To meet the needs of Filipino workers, George had started a small chain of enema-therapy clinics offering colonics to the masses. Over the years, he'd also written a very tall pile of propaganda pamphlets, containing the sort of class-warfare bombast that still sounds familiar today:

> [Capitalists] demand that jobless workers starve by the millions rather than for the rich to pay taxes sufficient to expand the W.P.A. and insure the wives and babies of workers against slow starvation, disease and death!
>
> They . . . do *not* love this country. They love their stocks and bonds. Only the workers and the toiling farmers and hard working small business men, and professionals and intellectuals who struggle for progress now love this country.

But the George opus that holds the greatest interest for us at the moment is the one that had its beginnings in that Harvey House restaurant by the Santa Fe tracks, a 1938 essay for a college review, *Kansas* magazine,[1] entitled—what else?—"What's the Matter with Kansas?"

First, it's useful and important to note that loaded question was not coined by Harrison George (or, obviously, by Thomas Frank). It was appropriated from an old cowboy saying by William Allen White, the legendary editor of the *Emporia Gazette*, whose essay of the same name appeared on his paper's front page on August 15, 1896.

White's piece also spoke to the politics of the day. However, for White, the title was explicitly ironic, intended to demolish the Populists, then on the loose in Kansas and elsewhere, who were spreading a message of improvised socialism and advocating inflation as a means of reducing agrarian debt—and who were warring with the Republicans, whom White supported. His point was that Kansans knew exactly what they were doing, politically and otherwise.

But the particular objects of his scorn were those condescending outsiders who oozed contempt for the values of Kansans. "Go east and you hear them laugh at Kansas," he wrote, in a passage that might have been composed yesterday. "Go west and they sneer at her. . . . Go into any crowd of intelligent people gathered anywhere on the globe, and you will find the Kansas man on the defensive. The newspaper columns and magazines . . . are now filled with cartoons, jibes and Pefferian[2] speeches."

It is brilliant people like these, he continued, in mocking respect, who will tell you we need more men like themselves, men who

hate prosperity, and who think, because a man believes in national honor, he is a tool of Wall Street. . . .

That's the stuff! Give the prosperous man the dickens! Legislate the thriftless man into ease, whack the stuffing out of the creditors and tell debtors who borrowed the money five years ago when money "per capita" was greater than it is now, that the contraction of the currency gives him a right to repudiate.

Whoop it up for the ragged trousers; put the lazy, greasy fizzle, who can't pay his bets, on the altar, and bow down and worship him. Let the state ideal be high. What we need is not the respect of our fellow men, but the chance to get something for nothing.

. . . Let's drive all the decent, self-respecting men out of the state. . . . What Kansas needs is men who can talk, who have large leisure to argue the currency question while their wives wait at home for that nickel's worth of bluing.

White concludes by repeating the question, this time in utter seriousness: "What's the matter with Kansas?"

Then, for those greasy fizzles who still may not get it, he provides the answer: "Nothing under the shining sun."

White correctly assumed that his readers shared that view. By the turn of the century, White and the citizens of Emporia had already had more than their fill of lectures from people who thought there was something very wrong with Kansas.

Only fifty years before, "Bleeding Kansas" had suffered as the proto-battleground of the American Civil War—a conflict that erupted in the 1850s, when, as we shall soon see, lots of other people decided to tell Kansans what to do. In 1896, this stuff was still living memory to a generation of Kansans, and White and many, many others had grown tired of being portrayed as small-town rubes with pinched spirits and narrow minds by Populist rabble-rousers and by cynical political slicks.[3] And, in fact, this is exactly the caricature drawn by George in his clever essay, in which White's ironic question was first turned into a condescending indictment.

George began by recalling that day in the trackside restaurant, especially "the miserable two tiny cuts of bread, not half the size of one's hand, set before me. There they lay, silent and anemic spokesmen of what's the matter with America. Tell-tale symbols of what's the matter with Kansas. And that is: Capitalism." The reason for this injustice, George observed, was as simple as Kansans themselves:

> The farmer has been deceived by countless schemes and schemers, who allure him with promises of what he wants, but without telling him that it is impossible before abolishing capitalism. Indeed, they solemnly warn him against such "outlaw" ideas.

As a political sell, both George and the apparently progressive editors of *Kansas* magazine must have known the essay wouldn't do much to sway the minds of Kansans. While a lot of leftists were *from* Kansas, there weren't a lot of them actually still *in* Kansas.

But that wasn't really the point, anyway. As these things go, the object was to confirm the political instincts of those who were already part of his constituency. George's essay may have appeared in *Kansas* magazine, but he understood that his readers were people living much more enlightened lives far, far away from the Sunflower State, even if only mentally; George was simply appealing to their overweening sense of virtue and superiority. After all, did anyone seriously think there was anything *right* with Kansas? Just look at the miserable slices of bread on your plate!

In the wake of the 2004 election, Thomas Frank's version of *What's the Matter with Kansas?* was widely lauded in the media as prescient and insightful. In short order it became the accepted point of view for those struggling to understand how so many people could have voted for a guy as obviously dim as George W. Bush when they could have voted for the brilliant junior senator from Massachusetts.

It turns out, according to Frank, that Harrison George had been right all along: It's stupidity that does it. Indeed, with its portrait of conservative midwesterners being so thoroughly blinded by the pyrotechnics of cultural warfare that they're unable to make those "certain mental connections about the world" and so keep voting for social conservatives when they could be voting against the dark forces of capitalism, his conclusion is nearly identical to George's seven decades earlier.

Those who were repulsed by the choice made by voters in Kansas in 2004 loved the book.

And what's not to love? *What's the Matter with Kansas?* is a pleasure to read. It features every Democrat's favorite devils engaged in a familiar narrative (clever, deceitful right-wingers playing on the moral vulnerabilities of the unwashed). Nor have the more dogmatic partisans of the left ignored the secondary narrative of Frank's book, in which he is no kinder to centrist Democrats than he is to Republicans: He punishes what was once the "party of Roosevelt" for its failure to reach out and embrace "the class language that once distinguished them sharply from Republicans"[4] and for lending support to the image of liberals as a latte-drinking effete elite by, among other things, drinking lots of lattes.[5] His apparent belief that the Democrats would have won if they'd only become fluent in all that class-language business and run *even more* to the left seems to work better the farther from Kansas and Nebraska you get. For example, while many would suggest that this theory is contrary to the experience of most leftish politicians in the United States, Canada, and even Europe, it does seem to be working in Bolivia, for now.

Of course, most of his readers in New York and San Francisco won't understand that. They presume that because Frank is from a place called Mission Hills, Kansas, he wears the halo of native wisdom.

In fact, Mission Hills, that most luxurious of Kansas City neighborhoods, is only marginally in Kansas at all; if it weren't for those big country clubs on its border, the place would be in Missouri. Mission Hills has been represented in the House by a Democrat, heavily supported by local liberal Republicans, since 1999. While Kansas is, as in so many things, in the middle of America in terms of per capita income, in Mission Hills that figure is almost five times greater than the state average: the per capita income of the thirty-five hundred residents is just under $100,000.[6] In 2003, there were exactly zero violent crimes in Mission Hills. Some readers sense that this may have somewhat shaded Frank's big picture. As University of Wichita historian Craig Miner[7] put it to me, Frank "knows a lot more about Mission Hills than he does about Garden City—and Mission Hills isn't Kansas." Not that Frank hides any of this at all; it's not his fault if his readers are unable to make sufficient mental connections about Kansas to be able to see it.

One of the book's observations about the Kansas side of Kansas City is that the malls—well, they just aren't what they used to be. Also, the neighborhoods surrounding Mission Hills, where, judging by anti-conservative voting patterns, the lingo of class warfare is understood loud and clear, are filled with rusting cars, rottweilers, and "No Trespassing" signs.

Mission Hills is immeasurably more swank than the part of Kansas

City we lived in when I was young. My old neighborhood was called Welborn. It's not there anymore. It's buried beneath a layer or two of Wyandotte County's Democratic sprawl. Although I don't remember doing so, maybe I played in those very rusting heaps of metal while dodging runaway rottweilers. After the war, my parents had moved into a small mobile home parked next to my great-grandmother's house, and they picked up a little extra money for a few years by running an icehouse and a fireworks stand at the local feed store. I had my first memorable meal in Welborn—eating rat poison I found behind my great-grandmother's sofa and then being held upside down under a faucet.

Actually *neither* neighborhood really has much at all to do with the rest of Kansas. Kansas City is home to people who watch major league sports, attend huge universities, and work for global corporations. The rest of the state gets by on American Legion games, college and high school football, and jobs that mostly involve agriculture, no matter how tangentially.

Nevertheless, playing on the general coastal ignorance of the heartland—as well as the assumption that something *is* the matter with Kansas because . . . well, because it's so very, very Republican—Frank's book became a point of reference and a message of hope for those who had never been to Kansas and who certainly had no intention of ever going.[8]

There are lots of things Frank gets right, as I think most Kansans would agree. Do they think Frank is right that Kansans—like other Americans—play a little game with themselves when they enter the voting booth? *Sí.* Do they think old-money Republicans are keeping those troublesome conservatives in check? They do. Do they sometimes put moral principle ahead of their own economic self-interest? Yes. Do they think that they understand perfectly well that in voting for conservative Republicans to solve social problems like abortion and gambling and school prayer they're voting for candidates who invariably will be stymied by liberal Republicans and Democrats and not be able to deliver on their promises?

Well, of course they do.

But I also think that they worry that Democrats just might deliver on *exactly* what they promise. After all, there's a reason why even smart people voted for George Bush, a man whose rhetorical style is best suited to a pickup truck window, instead of John Kerry, a man who was clear and erudite in most of what he had to say. They simply liked what Bush said badly more than what Kerry said well.

In 2006, the argument was a different one. And in 2008? Well, you never know. The state GOP is a mess and nobody shoots a foot faster than a congressional Republican. After all, Vermont used to be safely Republican, too.

You Are Not Here

To many coastal Americans familiar with travel to once-exotic locales, driving across their own country is more daunting than, say, safariing across the Masai Mara. Kansas, Nebraska, one Dakota or another—none of them seem to have much charm as a tourist destination. In fact, the middle of the country is perceptible to most American coastal dwellers only around election time, when they perceive it dimly and suspiciously.

The same assumptions that others make about the Midwest are, of course, also made by midwesterners who live in the big inland cities—Chicago, Omaha, Kansas City. A recent *New York Times* op-ed piece written by a man from Omaha about Nebraska is more or less a typical example: "It's big: over 77,000 square miles (about 10 percent bigger than the six New England states combined) and 450 miles wide, roughly the distance from Boston to the District of Columbia. . . . Large parts of Nebraska are arguably in trouble. The dismal statistic that trends lower, year after year, for many of these struggling counties, is population."[1]

That's the takeaway many easterners have on places like Nebraska, too: It's really big and nobody's home. It's true that as farming practices have changed, some small towns have become even smaller. The urban assumptions underpinning the "dismal statistic" have infected even some small-town residents who, often compelled by their own bitter pessimism, see their village and their way of life in some sort of downward spiral. When that happens, the first thing they jettison is common sense, the very fuel that sustains them. The *Times*'s op-ed writer was from Nebraska's biggest city, and while he normally may be an astute observer of topics farther afield, he spoke for many urban easterners and midwesterners when he looked at the consequences of farm consolidation and the technological revolutions changing global agriculture: "A cynical futurist might see mega-farms, owned by global corporations, and farmed by armies of robot combines, controlled by global positioning satellite technology from offices in Omaha."

Well, call me a cynical futurist, but that sounds *excellent* to me, especially if the object of the ag game is to grow lots of healthy, cheap eats so everybody has supper. Food is a valuable product. City folk might find lunch more picturesque when it's grown organically by people walking slowly behind mules, but that's about as realistic as expecting all American motor vehicles to be made by philosophically inclined shade-tree mechanics in the backyards of rural Michigan. Farming is not gardening on a grand scale. It's an industry, like building SUVs. If more efficient farming means more nutritious food for more people for less money, who—other than an inefficient farmer hanging on to his federal supplements or a romantic city dweller hanging on to his pastoral sentiments—is going to say that's *bad?*

I happen to agree, however, that a culture cut adrift from a respect for agrarian values—as complex as they might be, given a global market—is lost in the woods. But one of those values is efficiency, so many midwesterners might advise those who want the Midwest to flourish in bucolic splendor as in days of yore to just rent a U-Haul, move out there, plant some boutique crops, join the Rotary, and pitch in. Beautiful little towns, charming main streets, very inexpensive housing, idyllic summers, big lakes, and boats out the wazoo—it's all yours! You can do almost anything you want in that part of America, including grow designer wheat. Just *go* there and make something happen.

And if you do, you won't be alone. Blue-state folks amazed that a town that in 1960 had 1,000 people in it now gets by on 700 should probably remember that the exodus from small towns in the Midwest pales compared to what's happening in their own neighborhoods. It takes far less to turn around the population drift in Concordia, Kansas, a lovely town of 5,400 that loses a couple dozen people every year, than it does to save most big cities, where just one of the dismal statistics that trend lower, year after year, for many of those struggling cities, is population. In the forty years between 1960 and 2000, according to the Census Bureau, Chicago lost 600,000 people, Boston lost more than 100,000, Washington, D.C., lost 200,000, Detroit lost 700,000, and Philadelphia dropped a half million; in 2004–5 alone New York City's population declined by 21,500—about four Concordias. Large parts of America, from Boston to Washington, D.C., are in trouble, and not just because cities are losing population. In the same forty years between 1960 and 2000, meanwhile, the population of Nebraska grew by 300,000, while Kansas picked up as many new citizens as Philly lost. Other Middle American states did even better: There are 11 *million* more (legal) Texans now than there were in 1960. It costs a lot of money to get into farming these days, but not nearly as much as it costs to get into a house in most parts of Los Angeles.

Philadelphia may have lost a quarter of its population, but the place still seems kind of crowded—both to commuting Philadelphians and to visiting midwesterners, almost all of whom have at least a functional knowledge of New York, Philadelphia, San Francisco, Chicago, and other blue enclaves—not only because these cities are the America of TV and movies but also because most of these people have been to the East more than once. My grandfather used to tell his tales of Times Square, 1918, the way only a farmer-turned-soldier from Burr Oak, Kansas, could tell them. My grandmother lived through many losses in her life, but few as memorable as the one that took her prized hat off her head and sucked it out the window of the train she was riding east to New York City at about the same time. Eighty years later, that hat was still on her mind.

Almost every day, marching bands or drama clubs or debate teams or high school graduating classes board buses in Kansas or Nebraska or Oklahoma and end up in Washington, D.C., or Boston or Pasadena.

What does Nebraska get in return? Provincialism, ignorance, and conde-scension from the *New York Times.* Since the invention of buses, none has ever carried a bunch of inquisitive New York City students to Alma, Nebraska—and it's too bad for them.

The front yards of Kansas roll on mile after mile, crossing an invisible border to become Nebraska or Colorado or Oklahoma. It's a very big-picture landscape unfamiliar to many Americans, for whom the heartland of their own nation can be strange and even terrifying. For them, Middle America is unknown territory, not just mapwise but mindwise, with only the most basic of stereotypes to use for navigation. For those for whom the nation between St. Louis and Vail is a blank space, it must seem there's a moral primitivism loose in the land wholly at odds with their ex-perience of the world, a place made civilized only by populating it with the imaginary men of *Brokeback Mountain,* handsome lads who dress for cows but look at sheep, or by a bit of electoral unpredictability, as in 2006.

This is not new. In the nineteenth century, publications like *Harper's Weekly Journal* and *Frank Leslie's Illustrated Newspaper* churned out lurid stories of the exotic outback to big-city readers eager to read accounts of Indian war battles, army scouts, poker murders, train robberies, and other high-plains exploits. To Bostonians and New Yorkers, these tales of unciv-ilized, mysterious mid-America were almost as horrifying as they were ex-citing; for decades wily showboaters like Buffalo Bill grew rich by selling the whole shebang to city slickers. A half century later, Truman Capote was canonized for doing the same with *In Cold Blood.* While he captured the essence of the high plains at midcentury, the complexities he reported were largely ignored. His book was beloved not for its sophisticated nu-ance but for confirming in the minds of readers the flat and banal evil of America's mystery plains. Happily, air travel has placed one blue coast next to the other, with only a nap to separate them. What a relief not to have to drive through Nebraska.

But the cold truth is, even people who travel that way now travel blind if all they can see are their stereotypes. They're certainly missing something. Something as big as America, and it's different from how it looks in the papers.

For those heading west to Kansas, allow me to recommend our U.S. 36, one of the country's oldest highways, and one of its more colorful. It starts, as close as I can tell, just north of the golf course in a little Ohio town called Uhrichsville, before disappearing, after 1,414 miles, near Deer Ridge Junction, five miles west of Estes Park, Colorado, in the Rocky Mountains National Park.

U.S. 36 is a great ride, flirting here and there with I-70, but for the most part going its own way. For the family on the slow go, it's not a bad teaching aid: The kids in the back will get a great demonstration of how architecture and geography morph on the run west, every mile reflecting its own history, taking you deeper and deeper into the great red sea, surfacing only to access the ring roads that typically surround the little blue atolls of cities like Columbus and Indianapolis, where machine politicians cling to power by relentlessly milking the goat of urban discontent, then heading straight across the red belly of Illinois, a state made blue only by Chicago's voters. By the time you hit Missouri, you're on a boy's own highway and crossing the Mississippi in Hannibal.

Actually, until just a few years ago, the river bridge at Hannibal was a spindly two-lane iron thing—slightly worrisome at midstream but completely beautiful. The highway dumped you right into downtown Hannibal, where Samuel Clemens's family lived for ten years, until 1853. The captains of the local industry here are invented characters—Tom, Huck, Becky, Jim, Aunt Polly, the Injun—and as a result, every building of a certain age has been pressed into service as the site of something from the book or the residence of some character that never actually lived anywhere except at the dendrite end of Clemens's fabulous hair.

But Mark Twain is a long time dead, and as a result the annual fence-painting contest sadly does not result in anyone's actual fence being painted, which would have been much more in keeping with Clemens's vision. Instead, whitewash is slapped on eight boards nailed together in the middle of the street, tourists cheer, and a valuable point about hucksterism is lost—even while another about midwestern kindness is made. Not long ago, traveling 36 with my wife and three daughters in a minivan, I broke down in Hannibal on the weekend of their big Harley get-together—kind of a mini-Sturgis, but not mini enough for a guy in a minivan with a wife and three daughters. The place was packed with weekend bikers. I managed to find Murphy Motors' service manager at home. He came down, unlocked the place, took in the minivan, and gave me a loaner in which to make my getaway. "At least this will get you out of town and down the road," he said, pointing westward and into 36's rolling hills.

Missouri is the home of the Y chromosome: No other state in the Union provides their citizens with access to every Class C firework known to man, and loved by many. This spectacular bounty is sold at gigantic, supermarket-sized retail boxes perched along the highway and surrounded by cars filled with sleeping women parked in front of huge "No Smoking!" signs. This is shopping for guys: nothing but explosives arranged in rows like a not-very-Safeway. Push a cart (built-in baby seat included!) down the rocket aisle, with everything you need for that backyard moon shot, from toothpick-sized bottle rockets to missiles the size of Tom Cruise. This aisle is nothing but stuff that makes painful noise. This one is box after box of crackers, from teensy little pops to mini-bombs strong enough to rule out a pro bowling career for a pyrotechnician fresh out of luck. What beautiful wrappers are created by the Chinese—and so poetic! Some sound like the names of Oriental paintings: Night Blossoms, Golden Lady, Moon Raindrops, Blooming Flower. Some sound like ex-wives: Midnight Banshee, Whistling Witch. The best sound like strippers: Ruby Storm, Jasmine Star, Angel Rack.

After a couple hundred green, undulating miles, 36 leads you to another bridge, this one across the Missouri River, where you're given two last-chance options: north, to the cheesy casinos in St. Joseph, or south, to the rich suburban malls of Kansas City. But for the undecided or the persistent there's a third choice, right down the middle: the lane marked simply "Kansas." It hangs over the road like an emergency exit. If Truman Capote wrote highway signs, it would read "Out There."

That center lane takes you away from the river, right through the obvious speed trap in Elwood, and in no time you're looking at Troy (Pioneer Days in September), then the Wal-Mart on the bend in the highway at Hiawatha (museum with forty windmills; ice-cream social in June), and on into America's huge heartland, passing county seats every thirty miles or so as if they were standing still, which they are. U.S. 36 is an almost-straight line across the northern tier of Kansas counties—Brown, Nemaha, Marshall, Washington. Between every town, scores of hand-painted signs— "Choose Life: Your Mother Did," "Abortion Is Not a Choice," "It's a Child Not Tissue"—say in big, bold letters things people wouldn't say aloud in most places in Manhattan unless they were being, like, ironic. The highway follows, very approximately, the route used by the Pony Express. Life-sized silhouettes, cut from sheets of steel, of riders leaning forward over their saddles appear on distant hilltops. They're all going your way, straight across all those side roads leading from one story to another. Just south of Hiawatha, for example, is Powhattan, home of the Kickapoo Nation and the Kickapoo Nation School "Warriors" (a name offensive to those who think it's offensive to Kickapoos). Buy a souvenir and see the authentic Kickapoo accountants banking the tons of money they're raking in from their Golden Eagle casino.

By the time you cross the Republican River the first time, you realize you're a long way from everywhere—and not just geographically either. It's drier here, harder, more austere. When I was younger, I used to ride the western part of this highway while reading, then rereading, Hamlin Garland's *Main-Travelled Roads*. Garland's fiction is filled with people for whom leisure is unknown and for whom disaster was as common as sunshine and never the stuff of drama. Everywhere out here is the sense of make-believe permanence, of unsentimental enterprise surrounded by heartbreaking necessity, a willingness to tear down as quickly as you build up, since the object of the game is survival. Your traveling op-ed writers may have missed a grim truth about the Midwest: It's been hard times out here since time began. Here it is already in the 1880s:

> He came at last to the little farm . . . and he stopped in sorrowful surprise. The barn had been moved away, the garden plowed up, and the house, turned into a granary, stood with boards nailed across its dusty cobwebbed windows. The tears started into the man's eyes; he stood staring at it silently.
>
> In the face of this house the seven years that he had last lived stretched away into a wild waste of time. It stood as a symbol of his wasted, ruined life. It was personal, intimately personal, this decay of her home.
>
> All that last scene came back to him: the booming roar of the threshing machine, the cheery whistle of the driver, the loud, merry shouts of the men. He remembered how warmly the lamplight streamed out of that door as he turned away tired, hungry, sullen with rage and jealousy.[2]

It's the shock you feel when you pass through a place where once you bought pop and prayed for girls but where now cattle crowd through the holes cut into the walls of the broken buildings of a falling-down town. The dusty, grim realism of Garland's stories seemed to me to be just as well suited to the Kansas-Nebraska border as to his "middle-border" farther north, in the Dakotas, since out here, as everyone knows, the true borders run north and south—you've got rivers, and then you've got mountains. Everything in between is however many states you need: Those east-west borders that stack neatly atop Oklahoma until you get to Canada mean nothing to God (unless you count State U. football loyalties as religion—and many certainly do).

The slope away from the great central rivers of the nation is barely perceptible on U.S. 36. But it's there, gently shaping the floor of what Fort Hays State University geologist Mike Everhart calls "the oceans of

Kansas."[3] Forget ideology. It seems that what once divided the country was a huge inland sea some six hundred feet deep. To drain the plains it was necessary to raise the Rockies, a place-shifting process that lifted the flat floor of the sea a half mile. The elevation at the eastern end of Kansas is about 1,100 feet; the elevation at the other end is 3,700 feet.

It's a landscape as purpose-driven as Wall Street's: You can see how people might find charm in a place like Missouri, with its Twain-right towns, its woods and lakes and, in the south, the gentle mountains. But the hard plains on this stretch of 36 don't look easy. Nobody comes this far unless they mean agribusiness.

Before you know it, you're passing Courtland and Formoso; my father was born in Formoso; his grandparents, Oliver and the formidable Fannie, are buried in Courtland. Then Mankato, then Lebanon—the geographical center of the forty-eight states—then Smith Center, then Phillipsburg, Norton, Oberlin, and St. Francis, where I once saw a series of spidery twisters along the distant northern horizon, above the Kansas breaks, fingering crazily down from the clouds, like the latex glove of God. Then, at last, 36 disappears into the Rockies. You really are way out there now.

Midwestern Scale

For a very brief period—roughly the half century between 1870 and 1920—the flow of America's growing population defied gravity and spread from the rivers up toward the Rockies. Railroads, farms, and towns appeared on the featureless maps—only to immediately give way to the slow runoff of people and businesses.

There are modern analogies to this kind of speculative, uphill optimism. In the 1990s, huge, overproduced Web-based "communities" popped up anywhere there was a T1 line. I worked for a while as the editorial director for a couple of these, back in the days when nerdy salesmen-turned-CEOs would collar you just before an IPO and with a straight face say, "I'm going to make you rich." The assumption behind these sites, I was always told, was that if you gave people everything they needed, if you built a solid online community with lots of "stickiness," people would never go anywhere else. Because why should they? Once an AOL portal dropped them down onto your little patch of the Web, they'd know they were home virtually.

Railroads were America's first T1. A century or more before the first dot-com, developers—including the railways themselves—convinced everybody that if you built a community next to a railroad track, filled it with libraries, banks, schools, churches, restaurants, Masonic temples, and bars, all you'd have to do was kick back and wait for the 7:13 from Chicago. People would get off the train, fill up your town, and never go

anywhere else. Because why should they?[1] For a minute, it worked beautifully. Then, in the 1890s, came the first big economic collapse and all
those town builders realized that the problem with having a railway
nearby is that the same trains that come to your community also leave it.

Depopulation isn't a new thing in the Midwest, but it does create
some interesting special effects. For example, as cities and towns are re-
duced by circumstance to a bare minimum, the individuals left behind
grow larger and larger. In places like New York and Los Angeles, there's
one citizen for every one hundred square yards or so. In midwestern
states like Nebraska and South Dakota, there's a guy for every ten *acres,*
give or take, so if you want to rub shoulders with your neighbor, you'll
have to drive to do it. The old joke about a farmer being a man outstanding in his field works differently out there, because as anyone can see it's
no joke at all. It's just a normal way of looking at a man and at a field.

Understanding the optics of the Great Plains is essential to understanding how to look at midwestern politics and the rationale behind
their prevailing political values. For scale determines everything about the
relationship between people and government. You'd think that when the
distance from here to there is no longer measured in feet or blocks but in
miles or hours, you'd feel a little smaller; and, indeed, that may be the
case when you're flat on your back on a patch of grass wondering about
the meaning of life and all that.

But it isn't at all the case when you consider the scale of a single man
or woman to a village or town. When you travel from Mankato's West
Street dead north to my grandfather's old farmstead, twelve miles away,
there's a long, empty stretch of gravel, and when you get to Granddad's
old place, you'll find my cousin Bryan. He's hard to miss because he and
his wife, Jan, are about the road's only residents. So should the barn catch
fire, old Bryan could do what they do in Queens or Mill Valley and call
the fire department and ask the government to send out a little *help!* in
the form of a fire truck. But if he did that, he'd only be talking to himself,
since he's the fireman, and the township fire truck is already parked out
back.

The distance between citizens and the messy lasagna of layered impersonal bureaucracy that makes life possible in the blue cities is nonexistent in the heartland, where being the "government" is something most people see as an unpleasant but necessary personal obligation. Bryan's older brother, Marvin, was very greatly annoyed when he had to take his turn as city councilman in Burr Oak, that microscopic (pop. 274) village a few miles away on White Rock Creek, near the Nebraska line. Marvin spent "two years talking about cracked sidewalks" (he speaks slowly), followed by a three-year term on the board of the local bank, before he could get back to full-time farming. "It was grueling," he told me.

There may not be much separating many Kansans from government, but that's not to say there's any shortage of the stuff. In every corner of Kansas, you have a school board, a county government, a few city governments, and a bunch of township governments—nearly four thousand local government units in all, and all providing "services," such as administering a truly annoying set of liquor laws, that often duplicate one another, some in counties so small you could evacuate the entire population by just calling a cab, if there were a cab to call, and a phone. It's the one aspect of nineteenth-century overdevelopment that won't go away; owing to the Populist eccentricities of Kansas's history and the pattern of settlement, it's been like this since day one.

"In the 1880s and '90s, when the population was rising quickly, there were a lot of farms out here. I mean, you could make a living on a quarter section [160 acres] in those days," Keith Roe, a former state representative from Mankato, explained. "You needed lots of smaller counties because you had to be able to get to the county courthouse in a day. But," he said, "that's all changing now." Not fast enough for some.

Most of the resistance to political consolidation is from the sheriffs and other county employees who are worried about their jobs, some of it is due to rural fears of losing out yet again to the cities—and some of it is due to simple legislative inertia. While some counties, like Jewell, where Roe and many members of my family live, consolidated city and county offices and law enforcement functions years ago, they had to go to the legislature for permission to do it. Every single attempt at consolidation requires a legislative act. Conservatives who don't have worried rural constituents resisting change push for consolidation, but as Kansans have learned, it takes time, money, and a lot of patience for government to make itself go away.[2] Plus, all that personal bureaucracy is expensive, even though nobody makes much working for little townships and water districts.[3] In some places, there's more government than there are people to be governed, so out here one person wears many bureaucratic hats. However, almost all of them look like ball caps with feed company logos on the front.

Take Cuba—the one in Kansas, a town settled by Czechs where the population is just under 250 (from an all-time high of just over 300), and where the man-to-government scale has been thoroughly documented for more than three decades by *National Geographic* photographer Jim Richardson. One of his best illustrations of Cuba's tax dollars at work is a photograph he calls "City council fixing the sidewalk"—or, as he described it to me, "the antidote to *What's the Matter with Kansas?*"

Taken in 1977, the photograph shows three guys looking at a puddle of wet cement and says approximately ten thousand instructive words about the relationship between taxpayers and government in red-state America. When the photo was published in *National Geographic,* the caption read, "Mayor Larry Hinkle, at right, convinced fellow citizens to help him pour a sidewalk, all for a couple of beers."[4]

The guy behind the wheelbarrow is Steve Benyshek, who told me he became mayor the day Hinkle, a schoolteacher, walked in and said, "I quit—*you're* mayor." The sidewalk repair, he told me, wasn't an unusual situation. "It was an easy job—a one six-pack job." It seems all city projects undertaken during the Hinkle-Benyshek administrations were measured in terms of beer consumption. When the "city man," who was the only full-time municipal employee—in this case, Mike Knox, the guy on the left with, okay, the beer in his hand—had something that needed to be done, he'd round up the mayor and the president of the city council and escort a few six-packs to the job site. They'd look it over, and after a

couple of cold deliberations, the city government would spring into action. "Now the senior citizens' center floor, *that* was a two-*case* job," said
Benyshek, who served five terms as mayor and for his trouble was paid
around a hundred dollars a year. The city government—that would be the
mayor, the city man, the president of the city council, and the three city
council members—finally had to pass an ordinance that, while not exactly forbidding a beer assessment for work to be done, did require the
work to be done *before* the beer was actually consumed, "because, well,
you know."

Cuba, like many small towns, hires a chap like Mike Knox every year
to do fix-it jobs around town. When Benyshek was mayor, back in the
1980s, the city man made around five hundred dollars a month. His job?
"He's the city man—the 'works department.' Electrical, plumbing, street repair, you name it, it's him," said Benyshek. The toughest part of the mayor's
job was hiring a good city man. "You learned real quick to have respect for
somebody's mechanical aptitudes. If the city man didn't know what he was
doing with, you know, plumbing, then it was cheaper just to sub it out."

One year, Cuba got a new city man, who, it was discovered one frigid midwinter night, didn't actually know much about how the city's water system worked. You only have a few moving parts: a well to feed an underground tank, a pump to lift the water up out of the tank and into another tank on a tower, and gravity to fill your toilet bowl every time you flush. Normally, water in the small municipal systems used by towns this size is kept in motion—in Cuba's case, flowing back and forth between the thirty-thousand-gallon underground tank fed by the city well and the big fifty-thousand-gallon tank up on stilts in the center of town with "CUBA" painted on it—the reason being, as everyone with common sense knows, moving water won't freeze as easily as still water. "But if you *don't* know that," Benyshek recalled, "you just fill up the tank and wait until you need more." One night, mid-January, twenty below, "we lost water pressure all over town. I knew right away what it was. We had a fifty-thousand-gallon ice cube." In seconds the entire town went dry, and not just Sunday-in-Kansas dry either.

Local governmental authorities immediately brought in "a lot of beer *and* whiskey" and built a big tent around the tower scaffolding, then parked a truck with a propane heater on it inside the tent, while emergency water was provided by an old centrifugal pump from the early 1900s. As town residents began taking turns to keep the pump running twenty-four hours a day, the municipal employees opened the beer, poured the whiskey, lit the giant propane heater, and waited. God was merciful. "We finally got a warm day and the water started going again," said Benyshek. The propane and the beer? "Well, they really didn't do that much," he admitted. Not long after that, a woman ran for mayor and won. Of course, one of her first acts was to abolish the beer system.

You wonder why the citizens in places like this have so little respect for big government? The towns of Burr Oak and Cuba have far fewer residents than a typical residential block of Manhattan. Yet the citizens of Burr Oak and Cuba have to meet many of the same civic demands that all of New York City meets: Somebody has to run the schools, pick up the trash, plow the snow, patch the roads, fix the sidewalks, make the arrests, and throw away the key—all while holding down a real job. There's a park in Burr Oak, for example, several churches, a bank, a school, a museum, a small library, a mill, a little grocery, a bar, a very good café, and some small businesses. Same thing in Cuba. Every bit of it requires the infrastructure of government in order for Burr Oak and Cuba to continue their delicate existence. Because government is seen as a necessary nuisance and not as a source of power or money (with the exception of the education bureaucracy, to which we'll turn later), there just isn't a political caste in these little towns, certainly not the way there is in Boston or San Francisco. Every citizen in places like Cuba not only carries the expense of local government but also provides the labor and expertise to make government work well enough to get from one year to the next. Imagine running the city of, say, Newark, New Jersey, on a part-time, spare-change, cost-of-materials basis.

To maintain their tiny town's park and other civic attractions, the residents of Cuba hold their annual "Rock-a-thon" to raise money. "Usually, it's a marathon in most cities, but not everybody here can run," Richardson told me, referring to the area's large elderly population. "So it's a Rock-a-thon"—seven straight twenty-four-hour days of riding a rocking chair right there on Main Street. "This way, everybody can be a part of it." Over the last twenty-five years, Richardson estimated, the Rock-a-thon has raised between $300,000 and $400,000, more money than could have reasonably been harvested from local taxpayers.

Burr Oak, like Cuba and most other small towns up and down the Republican River Valley, has just one full-time employee. Everybody else working for local government is a casual. If you want to visit the Burr Oak parks and recreation department, talk to the teenager with the summer job cutting the grass around the town's swing set and slide. He's it. Just as the women serving lunches in the café are two-thirds of the local school board and the guy running the welding shop is the highway department. Next year, they'll all change; a couple of people will move away, maybe somebody new will show up, and in any case life will carry on.

Even in bigger towns on the Republican River, such as Concordia, you walk past a street repair site and you'll hear, as I did, one of the workers call out to a pedestrian, "Hey, would you call my wife and tell her I'll be a little late?" The pedestrian just nodded, gave a little wave, reached for his cell, and kept walking. At the motor vehicles office in the Cloud County courthouse, a guy named Jeff will spend a day trying to help you figure out why Maryland is still looking for you for that parking ticket you got twenty years ago, even though you paid it at the time. Lynn Scarrow, Jewell County's treasurer, told me a funny story about people who came from someplace else, bought a house, and stopped in his office to ask the county to send somebody around to see how much of it was up to code. "I just laughed," he said.

Quite simply, out here rural government is a do-it-yourself project, which is how it started in this country two centuries ago. So while it's efficient and well run, mostly it's extremely minimal. The inhabitants of what was once this giant inland sea understand the realities of this kind of scale instinctively, both from experience and from common sense, and that understanding of what government should be and how it should behave is pervasive in red America. A few days after Hurricane Katrina struck New Orleans, a woman named Lisa Mikesell stood up in her church in Concordia and suggested using an empty nursing home for New Orleans flood victims. That was in the morning. By the afternoon, the place was swarming with people cutting grass, mopping floors, getting rooms ready. Word of mouth and an announcement on the local radio station—not government involvement, of which there was none—did the trick. "Some of these people, we didn't even know," Mikesell told me when I stopped by late that night to drop off a few supplies. She was exhausted—but the place was ready. "The Red Cross said they might be here by two this morning," she added. (They never arrived; the Red Cross found most of those bound for Concordia places in shelters farther south.)

In America's bluest precincts, meanwhile, calling for government help is as normal as calling for pizza. Got a fire? Call the fire department.

Got hunger? Call WIC or some other human services–type office—or, if you've got the money, call a Hunan Wok–type carryout. All this stuff, provided by a faceless government and other people you really don't know at all, is a blue-state way of life. In the most populous parts of America, "government" is a conceptual thing, an invisible machine that keeps urban life ticking. You're allowed to pay for it, but you're not allowed to get in the way of it.

For years, I lived near the corner of Lexington and Twenty-eighth Street in Manhattan. Every time a truck rolled along Lex in the middle of the night and hit the permanent pothole halfway between my place and Twenty-seventh Street, the sound of steel banging against steel echoed up and down the avenue, while I clung to the cheap chandelier. I called the pothole hotline on Monday mornings. This went on forever; the pothole (or another exactly like it) was there when I moved away. If I had wanted to fill the pothole myself, I'd have been arrested; I wouldn't have been able to do the city's work if I had wanted to, and certainly nobody from city hall came around during lunch hour and asked me to pitch in filling the thing, or to do any of the other things that needed to be done to keep Manhattan ticking.

In fact, I could have lived my whole life in Manhattan and never once would I have had to perform any of the tasks associated with the survival of the city, beyond paying my giant taxes. Every night, I ate dinner with friends who told me how uncomfortable they felt every time they left Manhattan. They meant they missed their friends and their jobs, of course. But I think if they were anything like me, what they really missed was the feeling of living lives that were richly, deeply upholstered to protect them from the hard realities of what is, after all, a precarious, unnatural existence on a big granite rock surrounded by cold, cold water.

The Republican River

The topographical chart showing the Republican River Valley is a battle map. In addition to corn, wheat, and milo, the river also irrigates a bountiful harvest of interstate judicial fights over rights and agricultural policies; the landlocked states through which it flows are engaged in a perpetual war over water.

The Republican rises in a far corner of Lincoln County, Colorado, slips across the northwest Kansas border near St. Francis, then arcs gently across southern Nebraska, where it passes through Willa Cather's hometown of Red Cloud. It reenters Kansas in Jewell County, south of Superior, and cuts across the northeastern quadrant of the state, ending as it joins the Smoky Hill River to form the Kansas (also called the Kaw) River. See the top map on page 56.

In other words, if you spill your beer in Lincoln County, Colorado, where it's really needed, it will eventually end up in New Orleans, where it's not needed at all.

The rivers meet just outside Fort Riley's Grant Gate. Where most American towns have a smiley-face sign welcoming you to "The Home of Happy People," Fort Riley, the home of the 1st Infantry Division, the Big Red One, has a huge water tower on which is painted three words that let you know you're a long way from Pleasantville: "America's Warfighting Center." You can park just outside Grant Gate, cross the busy road leading into the fort, and pick your way through the brush and trees to see the exact point where the Republican ends.

Finding where the Republican River starts, however, is a little trickier. I'd been looking for the spot for most of a morning, and finally found myself in Flagler, Colorado, at about twelve-thirty in the afternoon. The whole town was closed—even though "Open" signs were everywhere. The few shops were locked, and so were the library and the city hall. Only the post office was open. A woman standing in the middle of the main street chatting with a friend explained that everybody was home eating lunch. Except for the post office, it was like a workday in Italy.

The postal clerk looked at my map, but couldn't figure out where the river started either. "Maybe over toward Arriba?" she suggested.

Maybe. So I finally drifted back down to the interstate, to the co-op gas station–pizzeria, and annoyed some people—a big, extended family from the look of things—eating lunch. We all looked at the map again.

"I think it's over toward Greggs," someone said. "Probably Greggs is what you're looking for."

I studied the map closely. "Greggs?"

"I'm Gregg," said Gregg Lukenhimer, smiling. "Try going south about six miles or so. You'll cross the Republican a couple of times. It's dry." And so I did and it was. I drove six miles down a dusty gravel road into rolling, treeless grasslands and never was sure I'd finally found the exact spot. I tried the same stunt later from Arriba and got the same result, but without the Gregg. I finally decided to ask the Colorado Department of Natural Resources. I received an e-mail from Ken Knox: "It is difficult to identify the exact location of the Republican River headwaters due to the flat topography and the point of flow origination changes in response to rainfall or other precipitation events," he wrote. "For descriptive purposes, the headwater of the South Fork of the Republican River begins on the northern high plains of eastern Colorado, approximately 3 miles south of Arriba, Colorado."[1] See the bottom map on the following page.

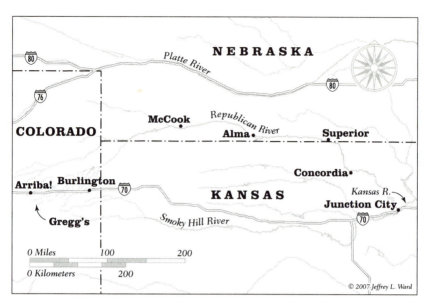

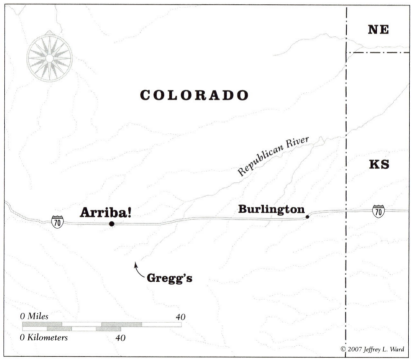

———

Wherever it starts, it doesn't run for long. The Republican River is only about 550 miles long. And while it wasn't named for the GOP—it took its name from the "Pawnee Republic," a description early traders gave to what they thought was the tribal structure of the original residents—it does provide an irresistible cartographic trope for grand theorizing about midwestern political and cultural values. Every single one of the nineteen counties through which the Republic flows voted overwhelmingly for George W. Bush in 2004, and in even greater numbers than voted for him in 2000. A Democrat may sneak in every now and then, but along the Republican River what you have mostly is lots of Republicans.

The Republican's no longer a little Big Muddy, the way it was when I was small. Back then, you could wade and play in the Republican. The Republican loved to flood and did so with regularity, as every old-timer loved to recall. There were major floods in 1870, 1906, 1935, and 1951.

The floods of 1935 were the most spectacular. Twenty years later, they and the Dust Bowl they so rudely interrupted were still the daily topics of conversation in towns all along the river. In the space of only twenty days, four floods swept through the valley, the biggest one a killer surge following a storm that dumped twenty-four inches of water in six hours between Flagler and the Kansas line. "We'd had five years of drought before that flood," Mrs. Verylron Williams told me one afternoon when we were sitting around a table in the municipal museum in McCook, Nebraska. "And then, after it, we got another five years of drought. So over the ten-year period, we got average rainfall. We just got it all at one time." What she remembered most, she said, was "how hard it was to believe something could come so quickly and be so terrible."

She was fifteen at the time, the youngest by far of four girls, and the only one still at home on the farm—"right on the river"—outside Culbertson, where the river makes a slight feint to the north, just west of McCook.

"It had been raining for weeks," she said. At first, it seemed like a blessing, dampening the huge drifts of dust and grit that had been blasting across the prairie for years, daily reminders of Depression and drought. But the rain didn't stop and then the river rose and then the ground became saturated, and her mother warned her father that water was starting to flow across the flat surface of the earth, not just down the gullies and washes. Verylron started out to take care of the livestock and watched, shocked, as the river snatched a group of calves. "Then," she said, "it came for the cows, too."

By five in the morning of May 30, 1935, the river was at the door of Verylron's parents' home. "I was sleeping upstairs when Mother and Father came to get me. They said, 'We have to go now.' But when I went down the stairs, the water was already in the house. We waded through water up to here"—she indicated her tiny waist—"and got up to a neighbor's. It was on top of a hill. There were already nine people there. Then right after we got there, a man came riding up from the south and said he couldn't go any further, so that made thirteen of us."

They were on the highest ground around, so the small group thought they might be safe. But suddenly, as they watched, a wall of water eight feet high roared down the valley. The flood's increase caught them by surprise and sent them sprinting across the farmyard. "You had to run if you were going to stay out of it," Mrs. Williams said.

By now, the river was rising uphill in some places at ten miles per hour or more, faster than most men can run. Houses, cars, wagons, barns, sheds, livestock, people, whole towns washed past them. The group dashed from the farmhouse to a barn and finally up to a granary. "It was the only building bolted to its foundation," she said. "It was just a little building with a wall dividing it down the middle." The water followed. "So we all climbed up into the rafters, the men on one side and the women on the other." It was about eleven in the morning.

Her perch was next to a small, shuttered opening where a window had once been. Looking down, she could see the river slowly climbing the walls. They all knew that if the water rose high enough to reach them, there would be no place higher to go but heaven. From time to time, one of the rafter clingers would ask her to open the shutter and take a look. She would open it a crack and peer out across the valley. "It was like an ocean," she recalls. By then the river was four miles wide, and the plains had become the turbulent sea they had been long, long ago. Below her, the little wooden building swayed and groaned. One wall went, then another, leaving behind just the timber frame to which they all clung desperately. "We just didn't know what we'd do if the water went any higher."

But it didn't, and at eight the next evening they came down out of the rafters and into the mud. When they finally went back to their farm, the house had floated "a block or two" downstream. For farmers already hard hit by calamity after calamity, "it was complete devastation," she said.

"It must have been like New Orleans," I said. We were meeting a few weeks after Hurricane Katrina had struck the Gulf. "Did Mr. Roosevelt send some help?"

She looked at me as if I'd just put on a stupid party hat. "Oh goodness, no! The government? We never even thought of that. We just went back to work."[2]

The summer of 1935 was a disastrous weather year elsewhere in America—including Florida, where on Labor Day one of the strongest hurricanes on record struck the Keys and wiped them clean, killing more than four hundred people. But in the American Midwest, the Republican River flood was the big deal, permanently changing the towns, jobs, and lives of the people who lived there. As another farm woman, Bernice Haskins Post, recorded in her memoirs, "Yes, The Flood. I had lived on the river bottom all my life [and] I have no desire to write this story. To those who were victims of the flood, no words are adequate to describe it. To those who see the valley now, or read about the flood, it is hard to realize what the flood did."[3]

The river had been a problem since forever, of course, and after a little more of this sort of thing, two vast reservoirs were finally built in Nebraska: one, Swanson Reservoir, is near Trenton; the other, Harlan County Lake, when full—which is never—stretches from the Republican stronghold of Alma to the Democratic redoubt of Republican City. There's another in Colorado, and several more in Kansas. It's the kind of government activity locals understand. "We needed the government for *that*," said Mrs. Williams. "We can't do things like that by ourselves."

Whole towns are submerged at the bottom of some of those reservoirs. You can take the main street in Wakefield, Kansas, for example, and head east toward downtown—but you'll never get there, because Wakefield's old downtown is under Tuttle Creek Lake. The town museum has pictures of what you've missed (including several floods): a town settled by English people whose stout little Anglican church was rescued from the rising water and much of whose population descends from a boatload of orphan boys rounded up off the streets of London in the 1870s and sent to break sod and put down roots in Kansas. A former Kansas governor, William H. Avery, lives just north of town.

Over time, the network of reservoirs has expanded, until it now stretches into Colorado. Today, the river's cycles are regulated fairly well; local floods, like one in Scandia in 2003, are still a problem, but farmers and small towns siphon a steady living out of the Republican all along its course as it trickles through prairie grasses and wheat fields until it joins the Smoky Hill to form the Kaw.

Aside from the reservoirs, for most of the way, the Republican, the Smoky Hill, and the Kaw rivers are what Karl Mueldener, who runs the Bureau of Water for the Kansas Department of Health and Environment, described to me as "pretty native—pretty much the way they have always been, very pretty."

This natural beauty lasts until the Kaw reaches the discharges of the only two areas in Kansas that voted against Bush in 2004: the faux–New England college town of Lawrence—home to the Kansas chapter of the Sierra Club, the Kansas Green Party, the Friends of the Kaw, Save Our Kansas River, and the Kansas Wildlife Federation—and Kansas City, at the Wyandotte County Line, just inside I-435, where the river finally loses in sewage, dredging, and levees whatever's left of its wholesome upstream charm. "From that point on, the river is like a half-pipe," Mueldener said.

Gone with the Wind

Two of the largest towns on the Republican—McCook, Nebraska, and Concordia, in Kansas—have populations of 7,700 and 5,400 respectively. I should say "had," since this is the agricultural heartland, and that was last year; every year twenty-five to fifty people in both places pack up and leave. It doesn't seem like a lot, but the population decline actually started not long after the towns were founded—Concordia in 1866, Mc-Cook sixteen years later—with the cycles of agrarian economic collapse and recovery that have swept the region since the 1890s.

In fact, that these towns continue to exist at all, with their schools, churches, and libraries, speaks to the remarkable sense of optimism with which they were built. For most citizens, that optimism remains. Still, there have always been those who saw things more darkly—or, perhaps, simply more realistically. Perceiving the economy in collapse almost as soon as the paint was dry, they moved on farther west or went back to their eastern hometowns. A second population boom never happened, but for more than a century, through one cycle after another, the slow, painful drip-drip of resignation, sometimes becoming a rush before slowing again, continued on.

It continues now. The last great economic disaster hit in the early 1980s, as a consequence of bad agricultural policy, high interest rates, tumbling commodity prices, and a collapse in land values. By 1985, the entire Midwest was languishing; the oil boom skidded and crashed in

Oklahoma and Texas, and agriculture took a beating in states farther north. I'd see it on my periodic visits. Closed cafés and stores—even big places that always had that sense of near-institutional permanence, like the Dreilings store and the JCPenney in Mankato, all closed. Farm bankruptcy sales outnumbered church services in some places. Main streets that had held on through decades of tough times yielded as this latest wave of depopulation swept the region.

Concordia is typical. One of the toughest jobs in town these days belongs to a fifth-generation Concordian named Kirk Lowell. A reformed farmer with a colorful habit of avoiding obscenities by using absurdities instead ("My cow!" is an apparent favorite), he is the director of the local economic-development bureau. That is perhaps the most thankless job in Cloud County, Kansas. He's charged not only with raising a crop of opportunity in rocky soil—that is, reviving the main shopping district, the four blocks along Sixth Street—but also with holding back the coyotes of pessimism that in every small town greet new ideas with howls of derision and charges of mischief.

Far better than any distant bureaucrat, he knows what's at stake. In the mid-1980s, when Concordia started suffering, Lowell suffered too. At the time, he was working for his cousin Brad, the owner of the local newspaper, trying to sell ads on a deserted main street. "You were in the middle of the farm crisis and you had a lot of closures downtown," Lowell said. "We had seventeen, eighteen empty storefronts on Sixth. I called it 'Tumbleweed Alley.' I used to say you could commit suicide by laying down in the middle of the street on a Saturday, but you probably wouldn't die until Monday. My cow, there were just *no* cars."

Same story in McCook, if somewhat less colorfully told: In the 1980s ag disaster, said Muschi Mues, a German-born artist who arrived in the McCook area in 1972, "farmers were hurt, yes, but it was the main street that had the hardest time. When I came we had a men's clothing store, two women's clothing stores, shoe stores, all kinds of stores. But then . . . it was just sort of dead."

Mark Graff is president and CEO of the McCook National Bank. Its big, brick-solid building on the town's main street, Norris Avenue, provides a not-so-subtle hint that come hell or high water—and both come calling from time to time—the town will somehow survive. A native of McCook, Graff refused to go as far as Mues. "We never quite *died*," he told me. "But it was bad." Even the Keystone Hotel, a 1920s project of a local Kan-Do Club to stimulate downtown business, gave up welcoming newcomers and instead became an old folks' home before finally closing completely.

To urban dwellers, the population density of the high plains is bizarre, even frightening. The fact that it's necessary to drive thirty or forty miles or even more between towns is dizzying to people whose sense of these distances is experienced as commuters. In Los Angeles, forty miles equals a long time in tight traffic. In Nebraska or Kansas, it's just a couple of commercial breaks on *Rush Limbaugh*.

It's been two decades since the last great ag-economic crisis, and while some towns have failed, plenty of others are today getting by quite nicely, thank you. Genna Hurd, the codirector of the Center for Community Economic Development at the University of Kansas, told me there were plenty of small towns facing problems today, but she had an ambition to study the high plains towns that are actually growing "for no good reason." It might not take a study. Maybe some people simply enjoy living in places like these pretty, uncrowded, safe, and reasonably priced small-villes. Besides, living in small-town Nebraska or Kansas isn't exactly camping. The nicer the town, the more people want to live there, of course; ugly, unfriendly towns tend eventually to blow away, like huge chunks of downtown Detroit.

And, of course, change doesn't always mean disaster, demographically. In fact, often change is necessary for improvements to take place. Not long ago, lots of people were sure that when the steel mill closed, Bethlehem, Pennsylvania, would become a ghost town. I used to own a condo in Bethlehem, on Main Street. I bought it just when gentrification was setting in; I wish I could afford to buy it back now. Thinking the plains will be completely depopulated because of a changing economy is the same kind of thinking that has pronounced cities from Seattle to Baltimore dead.

Few have been as exhaustive in their civic obituaries of small rural towns as the *New York Times,* which has pronounced the expiration of the Midwest many times, once at length in a melancholy series called "The Vanishing Point: Life in the Emptying Great Plains."

My favorite in the series is the profile of Reydon, Oklahoma,[1] a map speck near the Texas border, where, as you might suspect, "the plows of depopulation and decay slice through the Plains"; where miraculously "a turtle crosses Main Street unscathed"; where reporters harvest insights like this one: "To make it in Reydon, people rely on one another", and where paradoxes sometimes even seem to be fueled by 'shrooms: "Empty roads and pickup trucks are a common sight around Reydon."

The reason for all this overwriting? It seems Reydon "is running out of people"! Evidence that the plow of depopulation and decay sliced through Reydon is in the numbers: In forty-three years, from 1960 until 2003, the number of residents dropped from 183 to 166. Get those seventeen people back from the dead and all the turtles on Main Street would be well-scathed for sure.

"Bonds among families and neighbors supply the economic energy that used to come from small farmers, big employers, government offices, Main Street services and stores and, ages ago, streams of new settlers," the *Times* reported. What the—? None of those things were *ever* in Reydon, Oklahoma. There hasn't even been a *liquor store* in Reydon for half a century. Thousands of square miles dotted with Reydon-sized hamlets is a terra so wildly incognita that editors of big-city papers don't know what they're looking at even when they send reporters to go see it.

So maybe it's not very surprising that curious ideas about what to do with this part of the world keep getting generated by people for whom a turtle crossing a main street unscathed is New York news. Many of these people are academics, of course, professors who read stories about dwindling populations and big, empty fields. They look at maps and charts and what they see is a vast, empty canvas upon which their creative vision might be finger-painted.

Among the most strangely imaginative of these ideas is the one put forth by Deborah Popper and her urban-planner husband, Frank, a pair of professors from Rutgers University, in New Jersey, who in 1987 famously championed the "Buffalo Commons" concept.[2] Their idea: The best thing to do with the Great Plains was to return it to the Manufacturer. Just let the grass grow and let Buffalo eat the grass. It seemed a timely proposal; the economic collapse of the mid-1980s was just ending, and prairie towns were envisioning a future made bleak by recent events. Looking back on the proposal in 1999, the Poppers wrote:

> We conceived the Buffalo Commons in part as a literary device, a metaphor that would resolve the narrative conflicts—past, present and most important, future—of the Plains. In land-use terms, the Buffalo Commons was an umbrella phrase for a large-scale, long-term restoration project to counter the effects of the three cycles. We wrote that in about a generation, after the far end of the third cycle had depopulated much more of the Plains, the federal government would step in as the vacated land's owner of last resort.

One academic's literary device, however, is another family's home-town. So no matter how nuanced the Poppers' proposal was, it was received by most midwesterners with the sort of insincere smile specially reserved for people who come from the coasts to the middle of the country, look for a Starbucks, and then start every sentence with the phrase, "What you ought to do out here is . . ."

> As we traveled the Plains, it became clear that we did not control the meaning of our metaphor, nor did anyone else. For some the Buffalo Commons was only about bison, for others about wildlife in general, for others about raising cattle to more closely mimic

bison behavior. The metaphor might mean getting the people out of the region, encouraging their coexistence with wildlife, or promoting economic development based on wildlife. People variously interpreted the metaphor as a general assault on their way of life, an evocation of a fabled past, a vision of a feasible future, or a distillation of what they were already doing. Many Plains people intensely disliked the commons portion of the metaphor, associating it with collectivism and lack of choice, but even so the strength of their reaction helped achieve some community-building.[3]

Implementing the Poppers' project, and bringing a sense of control to the metaphor, is the apparent goal of the Great Plains Restoration Council, where Frank Popper sits on the board. The GPRC is a "multicultural, multiracial non-profit organization building the Buffalo Commons step-by-step by bringing the wild buffalo back and restoring healthy, sustainable communities to the Great Plains. . . . The Project will rescue prairie animal nations out of the current emergency-room situation."[4]

In April 1990, the Poppers showed up in McCook to explain to the citizens of the town their good idea about the prairie animal nations. It's hard to overstate the disinclination midwesterners had to accept the Poppers' idea—or how quickly environmentalists and think-tankers quickly claimed and adapted it for their own purposes. In McCook, the "community-building" reaction was to launch the Buffalo Commons Storytelling Festival every June "just to thumb our noses at the Poppers," as eighty-two-year-old festival cofounder Mary Ellen Goodenberger explained to me. What started as a modest local storytelling and morale-boosting session now fills the town's old Fox Theatre and other venues. People come all the way from New Jersey to hear musicians like Jay Ungar and Molly Mason as well as cowboy poets and storytellers.[5]

There's no shortage of Popper-type plans, usually advanced by organizations with clumsy but evocative, romantic-sounding names like "The Wildlands Project's Heart of the West Wildlands Network" campaign.

Among the WPH of the WWN's goals: stopping oil drilling in Wyoming and "assisting Utahns in the assimilation of naturally recolonizing wolves into Utah, through science-based planning and education." Okay. More wolves, less oil. Bonus for Democrats: less Utahns, too.

The latest greatest idea is from a team of seemingly mad scientists led by C. Josh Donlan, a biologist at Cornell University. Donlan's idea, published in *Nature,* is "Pleistocene re-wilding" of the Great Plains. Step one: turning feral horses and Bactrian camels loose in the backyards of Kansas and Nebraska in order to replace the species scientists say were killed off by those rapacious invaders from Asia some thirteen thousand years ago.[6]

And that's when the fun starts:

> The second, more controversial phase of Pleistocene re-wilding could also begin immediately, with the maintenance of small numbers of African cheetahs *(Acinonyx jubatus),* Asian *(Elephas maximus)* and African *(Loxodonta africana)* elephants, and lions *(Panthera leo)* on private property. Many of these animals are already in captivity in the United States, and the primary challenge will be to provide them with naturalistic settings, including large protected areas of appropriate habitat and, in the case of carnivores, live prey. . . . The obstacles are substantial and the risks are not trivial, but we no longer accept a hands-off approach to wilderness preservation. Instead, we want to reinvigorate wild places, as widely and rapidly as is prudently possible.

Cheetahs! Of course. That's what they need out there. Drumming up support for his idea, Donlan explained to NBC News his idea for a "vast ecological park in the Midwest with free-roaming carnivores, free-roaming elephants, and the other large biodiversity that we once had." This sounded more Jurassic than Pleistocene to many midwesterners. Donlan, writing in *Slate,* seemed aware that there could be some pushback from the locals:

Sure, the costs and risks of bringing back the megafauna are significant—they include angry ranchers, scared passersby, and unanticipated effects on other plants and animals. But without rewilding, we settle forever for an American wilderness that is diminished compared with just 100 centuries ago. And in the event of global climate change that affects Africa in particular, or economic and political strife there, we risk the extinction of the world's remaining bolson tortoises, camels, elephants, cheetahs, and lions. Safari trip to Texas, anyone?[7]

Been done. Most of my friends gave up their Pleistocene re-wilding just after college, but about fifteen years ago, when I was writing a book about lions, I spent a long day with a guy who ran a "safari ranch" near Houston.[8] His plan was like Donlan's, I guess, but with a private-enterprise twist that gave a more humane ending for circus lions released on pension. He bought them when they got too old to roar convincingly. Then he'd re-wild them on his two thousand acres of savanna-like Texas prairie, where the largely toothless beasts would find some shade and go to sleep. Then a guy, maybe a dentist from New Jersey or New York, would ride up, poke his head and his rifle out of the sunroof, and shoot the thing. Only cost a few thousand. Making the skin into a nice rug for the doc's office, that was extra.

It's not quite clear how Donlan's cheetahs and lions are going to go down with the GPRC's prairie animal nations already suffering in that emergency-room situation of theirs. There are also a few prairie humans in actual bedrooms across the region to worry about—those would include the "angry ranchers" and "scared passersby" Donlan dismisses. Professor George Packer from the University of Minnesota told a reporter that the problem he sees with Donlan's plan is that "once [lions] have figured out that humans are food they will go into houses and drag someone out of bed." So, okay, there's that.

When I told Bill Blauvelt about the Pleistocene re-wilding idea, he told me about the circus lion that got loose someplace a few miles north of town not long ago. "They asked me if I wanted to go up and take a picture for the paper. I said, 'No, thanks.'" Bill allowed that it might be more interesting to re-wild Ithaca, New York, where Cornell University lives.

Donlan, the Poppers, the defenders of the prairie animal nation, the Wildlands Project's Heart of the West Wildlands Network enthusiasts—none of these are the first people to take a look at the big, open, extremely unpopulated expanse of Kansas and Nebraska and decide that the people living there have it all wrong. And they won't be the last. Along the Republican River, people have been listening more or less politely for years to the big plans visitors from deep blue precincts have for the Midwest. Since the 1850s, Kansans and Nebraskans have been told where they should live, where they should work, and, especially, how they should vote so many times it just doesn't matter anymore. They know that when city people start asking questions like "What's the matter with Kansas?" the last thing they want to hear is William Allen White's simple answer.

Transcript 2:
Superior People

Pat: I read something on the Internet this morning—I think it's been making the rounds—about a terrible Category 5 blizzard last winter in North Dakota, and how the neighbors came out and helped each other, but no one in the rest of the country paid any attention. No FEMA, no nothing. No one shows up to report it. And I really do think that's part of the midwestern mentality: When it's good, we share; when it's bad, we share and help each other out. When there's a disaster in one of the coastal areas, we all rally, but *(laughs)* I don't see anyone rallying to North Dakota.

Stan: Probably because they think nobody's there.

Bill: No one that *matters. (Laughter.)*

Pat: When the blizzard was coming, the front of my grocery store was lined with expensive pickup trucks, all with engines running while people ran inside to get a few things, and they know no one's gonna jump in and take it.

Rich: Of course not. It wouldn't even cross anyone's mind.

Bill: You rely on people to do the right thing; it's just the way things are. Like, for instance, there was the time four of us got into Alliance late at night and couldn't get a motel room, either there or in Valentine—no place in the inn. Around midnight, I go into a convenience store to see if I can buy an air mattress to sleep in the bed of the truck, and there's this railroader in there. Never saw him before. But he's headed home and he says, "I've got a spare bedroom, and we can set up a tent in the backyard. A couple of you can sleep inside, and the others in the tent—I'll leave the back door open. Just let me call my wife and alert her you're coming home with me."

Pat: Oh, of course—men volunteer their wives all the time. *(Laughter.)*

Bill: But I just don't know if that would happen in a lot of other places in this country? We have friends from Delaware, I've been to their house, and they have a whole series of locks on the front door. Well, they came to visit us here, and one day we're sitting in the living room, and there's a knock at the door. My father calls, "Come in," and in walks someone we've never seen before. I tell you, these people are scared to death—they can't believe we just let this stranger walk into the house. *(Laughs.)* It was just someone looking for directions.

Stan: My family got here in 1934, the Dust Bowl era. The dust would fly by so heavy you couldn't see across the street. And, of course, those were also the Depression years. And, boy, how people helped each other then!

Pat: There was no other way. There might've not been much else, but people saw to it no one starved. Everyone had eggs for breakfast—

Stan: —and a new pair of overalls in the fall to go to school in—

Pat: —and there was always flour for bread. Farmers never lacked for that.

Bill: I was at a church potluck in Lincoln, Kansas, not long ago, where people brought all kinds of good things to eat. And one older gentleman said, "I remember one potluck in the 1930s where we had only two things to eat, cottage cheese and chicken. Everybody brought what they had at home, and that was all there was."

Stan: We fed a family of five on six dollars a week. *(Laughs.)* And if some stranger knocked on the door and walked in, we'd have fed him, too.

A Local History of Democrats

To recap: One of the many conclusions most people reach about places like Kansas without actually going there is that somebody's political party reveals their place on a left-right spectrum that seems to have only two positions, like a light switch. "Republican" means conservative. "Democrat" means liberal. In many parts of the country, that's simply quite true. There are not many conservative Democrats in Manhattan, for example, and while the number of admittedly liberal Republicans is still significant in many parts of America, they're a dwindling number, holding on to power in places like New England, California, and New York City by being more practical and palatable in their politics than their rivals.

But in the Midwest generally, and specifically in Kansas and, to a lesser extent, Nebraska, the situation is a little different. There just aren't many Democrats around. The result is a confusion of the tags most of us use for convenience. *In Kansas and Nebraska, you have the same range of ideological beliefs you have anyplace else, but you have them all shoehorned into one party.* There is a Democratic Party—at the moment, more active in Kansas than Nebraska. (At the Nebraska State Fair in 2005, the Republican booth was jammed, despite its enormous length. The Democrats had a booth, too: two lonely guys in an empty corner handing out pamphlets extolling the virtues of hemp.) But it doesn't matter. In both states, Zell Miller Democrats aren't particularly unusual, and the Kansas GOP is a living museum of Rockefeller Republicans. Liberals with good ideas are as welcome out here as anyone else—and far more welcome than any thoughtful conservative ever would be in New York or New Jersey. Bob Kerrey, a midwestern liberal Democrat, was governor of Nebraska for four years before serving two terms in the Senate. Kerrey was forthright in his views: He voted against the flag-protection amendment and the Defense of Marriage Act and was always a reliable vote on the left. But Nebraskans were impressed by his Medal of Honor from Vietnam, his instinct toward smaller government, and his personal charm, not to mention his whole-hearted support of farm welfare. Workmanlike Ben Nelson, the Democrat currently representing Nebraska in the Senate, is at least as conservative as Chuck Hagel, the Republican, who amuses voters with his eccentric ego and his lunar political views.

In Kansas, the former Republican Party state chairman, the mildly conservative Tim Shallenberger, who was soundly defeated by liberal Democrat Kathleen Sebelius in a 2002 gubernatorial election, thought that with his help the GOP could change. By 2004, for the first time ever, conservatives held positions of administrative power in the party hierarchy. Liberal Republican politicians, finding themselves out of power for the first time in fifty years, began defecting to the Democrats more and more.

This shift is probably overdue. Shallenberger, who left his post when his term ended in 2006, told me that until recently the state party "actively campaigned against conservatives." He cited the example of a former Republican Party chairman who left the GOP to work for a group agitating for same-sex marriage. So-called moderate Republicans had all opposed the Kansas Marriage Amendment. It failed to clear the legislature when it was first proposed, and only an outcry from the grass roots overcame stiff liberal Republican opposition in the house. Conservatives were finally able to get the thing through and out to the voters for their overwhelming approval in 2005.

It was a rare victory for the conservatives. These middle states are as divided as the rest of America, but out here, liberal Republicans and their Democratic allies have generally held sway.

————

In fact, Kansas, to easterners the reddest of all red states, actually resembles France more than anyplace else. For the last half century or so, France has been ruled by an elite class of people who are graduates of one of the country's *grandes écoles.* The grandest of them all is the *École nationale d'administration*—the ENA. Its graduates are called *énarques,* and virtually every member of the French ruling class—right or left, government or industry—is one. They are far less interested in party loyalty or in ideology or in "values" than they are in protecting one another's interests. The result is political cynicism, popular disenchantment, and the widespread corruption of institutions and even of individuals. Even "moderate" French commentators have described them as a cancer of French political life. The recent election of Nicolas Sarkozy as president is partly attributed to voters' rejection of traditional elites.

The *énarques* of Kansas are "moderate" Republicans, the men and women who for generations have run banks, country clubs, law firms, newspapers, the state's vast educational bureaucracy. Their necessary allies and ideological kinsmen are the Democrats, and their foils are the state's conservatives. For most of the twentieth century, these red-state *énarques* have tossed power back and forth, always keeping it well over the heads of leaping, troublemaking right-wingers. Lately, as the conservatives have mounted a major challenge to wrest control of the Republican Party away from the state's ruling class, most left-wing Republicans have switched parties and run as Democrats to avoid facing defeat in a Republican primary. This causes them very little discomfort. In fact, the only plausible majority in Kansas politics comes from combining "moderate" Republicans with Democrats. Just ask Jim Barnett, the Republican candidate for governor in 2006.

Barnett, a smart, genial, but little-known state senator and physician from Emporia, had a crowded Republican primary battle, an invisible campaign, and a dysfunctional political party to deal with. As Doug Mays, the former speaker of the Kansas house, reminded me, Kathleen Sebelius's win wasn't a surprise to anyone, except possibly the *New York Times.* "Most, if not all, incumbent governors [won in 2006]," Mays said. "She was not opposed in the primary, and was able to raise millions of dollars for her general election campaign. Potential first-tier candidates, myself included, saw this coming nearly a year before the election. That left lower-tiered challengers like Jim Barnett. In a good year nationally, he could not have won against incumbent Sebelius."

Mays's pronouncement notwithstanding, Barnett's campaign in Kansas was consistent with all the problems that have been faced by all statewide Republican candidates if they are even slightly right of center, as was Barnett. Moreover, it's also a preview of all races to be run by Republicans in the future: As Barnett told me, "The breakdown of the Kansas Republican Party [between right and left factions] is a huge problem. This isn't new, but the reason Republicans have difficulties is because they are disunited. So there are always primaries." Barnett had faced a crowded field himself. "In the primaries, you must run a conservative campaign, because that's how most of the party votes. But then, after you win the primary, you have to campaign as a moderate. It's not easy to do both of those things successfully."

Also complicating the state's Republican future are the three factors that Barnett says have done most to change state politics recently. All of them, of course, involve money.

"First," he said, "the gambling industry has had a major impact on our elections, with lots of money coming in to get people elected who will help gaming interests.

"Second is the money brought in by Stowers and his people and the embryonic stem-cell interests." Barnett was referring to a Missouri billionaire named James Stowers, founder of the Stowers Institute for Medical Research in Kansas City, who flooded the 2006 election with cash. Stowers spent as much as $30 million in Missouri (under the banner of The Coalition for Life-Saving Cures) and, according to one state legislator, at least another $12 million or so in Kansas to defeat candidates who might oppose embryonic stem-cell research. Stowers targeted local and statewide political races and was successful in both states. Missouri senator Jim Talent, a

Republican who opposed Stowers's ambitions, was defeated and a bill to allow the research was approved in Missouri. Kansas will follow suit. In both states, the political fund-raising hit record levels and almost all of it targeted people like Barnett.

"Third," he said, "and maybe most important to Kansans, is George Tiller's direct impact through money given to campaigns, mailings, issues ads." Tiller, to whom we will return shortly, is the operator of one of the country's few clinics specializing in very late-term abortions. His money is everywhere in Kansas politics.

"All of this has caused the Republican party to split. We also had [former] attorney general Phill Kline's race focusing on abortion and we had the influence of the war in Iraq. I think 2006 was a bad year to have 'Republican' behind your name. I don't think any Republican could have won here." Kansas, in other words, might as well have been New Jersey.

All of this is great news to the Kansas political establishment—and especially to Democrats, like the state's current governor. While Kansas has had a lot of Democratic governors, few have been so well-connected outside the state as Sebelius.

The daughter of former Ohio Democratic governor John Gilligan, Sebelius married into one of Kansas's "moderate" Republican political dynasties. She's supported by Emily's List, is wildly pro-choice, and generally shares most positions espoused by liberal Democrats everywhere. Some cynics have observed that even her hairstyle is a replica of John Kerry's famed gray helmet. She entered the 2006 campaign with $2 million in the bank and then added to it by receiving far more money from Republicans than did Barnett, the Republican party candidate.

Actually, the real news in 2006 was that Sebelius didn't get *more* than 58 percent of the vote, since she is, by most accounts, a popular governor. Not only does she enjoy the complete support of "moderate" Kansas Republicans, even previous Republican governors, such as Bill Graves and Mike Hayden, have gladly joined her administration. Her new lieutenant governor, Mark Parkinson, had been, until just before the 2006 election, an influential Republican and chairman of the state party from 1999 to 2003.

He replaced another ex-Republican, who had been Sebelius's running mate in 2002.

So what's going on here? Actually, a lot less than meets the eye. Or, to put it more precisely, pretty much the same thing as when a Republican is elected governor in places like Massachusetts, California, or New York. Voters cast their ballots in statewide races with a different mind-set than they do in national contests, based on very different, and more parochial, concerns. As I write, Republicans control the New York state senate. Big deal. Indeed, in many ways Sebelius resembles no one so much as New York's charmless George Pataki. Her political style—almost reactive, prone to making secret deals on sensitive issues,[1] but given to highly publicized platitudes about the importance of things like car seats for kids—is calculated, above all, not to alienate significant numbers of voters and to give the state's press, by default extremely well behaved and docile, as little to write about as possible. Sebelius stands firmly for the politics of Muzak, she understands the Midwest's deep, deep aversion to confrontational politics, and she stresses her ability to deliver smooth, worry-free government. The conservatives, meanwhile, just *stress* and they worry everybody, what with their shrill, awkward questions about abortions and all.

It is in presidential and senatorial races that, to the consternation of liberals, Kansans show their true colors, which generally tend toward the scarlet. The Republican parties of Kansas and Nebraska may be heavily influenced by "moderates," but in 2000 and 2004 they both backed Bush, and he won the states overwhelmingly. It's as hard to find a MoveOn.org Democrat outside the university town of Lawrence and Kansas City as it is to unearth a card-carrying NRA enthusiast at Zabar's deli on New York's Upper West Side.

Kansas's ruling class has lately come to agree on most things helpful to the cause of inflating the government they so actively control. For example, Democrats and liberal Republicans alike support big, expensive school systems and buckets of tax money to support them, and they both have a generally amenable attitude toward most social issues, especially abortion and gambling. But the thing these ruling moderates agree on most heartily is their shared hatred of conservatives. It's not a casual hatred, either. They actively despise them, and the feeling is mutual.

The realignment of the party is something conservative Republican strategists like Kris Van Meteren think is a very good thing—even if it also apparently portends more losses for future Republicans. The state's been Republican so long, he told me, the party has become fat and slow. It's short on ideas and long on a sense of entitlement, and, he claimed, it can no longer field exciting, energetic candidates. Once, it was the party of bankers. Now it's the party of laid-off bankers. Or, as Van Meteren understated it more succinctly, "We've gotten lazy."

"In 2006, the state Republican Party acted like it was 1972," he said. "They raised very little money for our candidates. They mailed out a couple of flyers and a fund-raising letter or two and that's it. Instead of ripping the Democrats, the party's chairman [Shallenberger] attacked *conservatives* for being divisive."

The state's highest office has been occupied by a series of easily forgotten Democrats, with occasional moderate Republicans popping up from time to time. Over the years, the effects of this kind of stranglehold on power have become increasingly evident. For example, the Kansas Supreme Court is one of the most activist in the Midwest, and perhaps in the nation, because Kansas has never elected a conservative governor—and has no legislative confirmation process—so no opportunities for giving the court ideological balance (or even representation) have ever presented themselves. The closest Kansans ever came to electing a conservative governor was in 1991, when they voted in Joan Finney, the merrily eccentric, populist Democrat who shunned the statehouse Democrats and instead preferred the company of Native American lobbyists and affable legislative Republicans. Her taste in justices wasn't as idiosyncratic as she was, though. Today, the court is seen even by some otherwise sympathetic journalists as a nest of political cronies. While this situation is no doubt pleasing to the state's liberals, many feel it's probably not the best way to ensure widespread respect for the state's judiciary.

Meanwhile, conservatives have managed to keep themselves on the fringe largely because their outrage, no matter how justified, discourages discourse and offends many Kansans' sense of propriety. It's difficult to run on a social-issues platform anywhere, since the lines are drawn, the issues are personal, and the only possible movement of opinion is upward, toward greater volatility. But most people just aren't that pissed off about social issues—in fact, Barnett told me he thinks that when it comes to things like partial-birth abortion, "People hear a little about it on TV, but they don't really believe it"—so, despite the surprise of the *Times,* even very liberal Democrats are routinely elected in the most conservative districts of Kansas and Nebraska, so long as they aren't overtly liberal or overtly Democrats. This phenomenon was discovered in 2006 by Democrats far from Nebraska and Kansas, but it's been practiced out here for half a century.

In most rural areas, voters don't want to be reminded that by reelecting the same old moderate or Democrat candidates, they're voting to support policies they may find objectionable. At least they're electing a familiar face, which is better than voting for people they find annoying even if they're right. In a part of the country where everyone knows everyone else, being annoying is a much greater liability than being wrong.

So while most Democrats wouldn't dream of campaigning as Democrats, once they reach Topeka, they join a generally well-disciplined caucus guided by a Democratic leadership that chooses its battles wisely. When necessary, moderate Republicans, free of the burdens of party loyalty, join in to thwart the conservative Republicans' agenda, an agenda that is stuck in frustrated thwartedness.

Conservative leaders in Kansas keep saying the electorate is with them, but the party isn't. That's true—but only up to a point. As critics charge, the Republican Party in Kansas is largely an irrelevancy, so ineffectual has it become after generations of single-party sloth. Saying you're a Democrat in Kansas is saying something. Saying you're a Republican says nothing—in Kansas, practically *everybody*'s a Republican. Meanwhile, conservatives are often frustrated with each other, for much the same reason:

Everybody's a "conservative," too. But some of them are more libertarian than conservative; others are small-government conservatives; some are only interested in pro-life issues; others are driven by fiscal concerns. Sorting all this out can get pretty noisy: One careless statement by a conservative with a perfectly reasonable point of view is sufficient to merit the "pro-abort" label or worse, if that's possible. Incremental victory is often not in the conservative playbook, so recurring defeat often is. Without a unifying leader or two—or even a friendly op-ed page—when conservatives are confronted by a common, cohesive enemy, as they often are, their response is sometimes so bombastic, unpleasant, and diffuse that it completely fails to inform, let alone persuade. So they lose again. This leaves them angry and vulnerable. I knew a man who knew a man in Ireland who forced his parents into the attic until they'd agree to sign over the farm to him. The parents could be heard screaming as far away as the village. The situation outraged the neighbors. They marched on the house and shouted at the boy to release the old folks in the attic. But the boy just came out into his front garden and told the neighbors to bugger off, that it was no concern of theirs. This made the neighbors even angrier, so they threatened to call in the Garda, at which point the man's parents climbed down out of the attic, marched out into the front garden, lined up behind their son, and joined him in telling the locals to go to hell. Kansas conservatives are the people in the attic. But there's nobody out front.

All of this frustrates activists like Van Meteren. He looks at states like Missouri, where there is a real balance between the parties in terms of registration, where Republicans mount vigorous campaigns and sometimes win, and he sees in the defection of liberals a long-term advantage for Kansas's conservative Republicans. "People don't want bitter politics, but they do want a good debate on the issues," he said. "To have that, we need to have a little realignment and let Democrats run as Democrats—not as Republicans."

Running as a Republican, no matter where your loyalties lie, is a regional habit shaped by a history that started about the same time Kansas itself started—in the mid-1850s, as the nation was descending into civil war. There were no Republicans when the Kansas-Nebraska Act of 1854 was passed as part of a plan designed, so its cynical sponsors maintained, to save the Union. Two soon-to-be states were carved from the vast Nebraska Territory with the expectation that they would maintain the delicate balance between North and South: Nebraska would enter the Union as a free state, Kansas as a slave state. The catch was that this meant repealing the terms of the previous arrangement, the Missouri Compromise of 1820, under which slavery would have been barred in both territories. The solution: the magic words "popular sovereignty." If Kansans wanted slaves, argued the Democrats who held sway in Congress, then they should be able to have them. So put it to a vote, they said. It was Kansas's first exposure to the libertarian formulation—unless, of course, you were a slave, in which case it was just more slavery.

There were several immediate consequences to the act. One was the formation of the Republican Party as an explicitly anti-slavery party, which made it almost certain that the political divisions in the country would be irreconcilable.

Another was to make Kansas the first battlefield of the Civil War. "Bleeding Kansas" was soon a byword and a rallying cry for those on both sides.

Free Staters, as those who opposed slavery in Kansas were known, held a clear numerical advantage in the territory, but in short order pro-slavery Democrats began flooding into Kansas from neighboring Missouri. They were determined to ensure another slave state by stuffing the ballot boxes, then going back home to Missouri. This soon led to an eruption of spontaneous violence that shook the nation to its core, with real fighting breaking out all along the banks of the Missouri River and deep into the hills of Kansas.

Even as Republicans met to organize a national party, Free State Kansas partisans organized to defend the territory against pro-slavery incursions from Missouri redoubts and from Democratic towns on the Kansas side—Atchison, Leavenworth, Shawnee Mission, and Lecompton. The pro-slavery faction spawned local guerrilla bands with Klan-like names including the Sons of the South and the Blue Lodge.[2]

Operating from Topeka and other, smaller towns, the Free Staters brought in plenty of outsiders of their own, including twelve hundred New Englanders, armed by Horace Greeley and other anti-slavery leaders, and including radical firebrands like John Brown and James Henry Lane, who were ready to take up arms to abolish slavery not just in Kansas or Missouri but everywhere. These were regarded by the Democrats with the kind of special loathing reserved only for those enemies who would presume to occupy a higher moral perch.

But it was impossible to stanch the tide of "border ruffians" from Missouri. Indeed, in a vote held in 1855 to elect a territorial legislature, at one polling station a mere twenty of the six hundred who cast ballots were found to be legitimate Kansas residents. As a result, the Kansas legislature was delivered safely into the hands of Democrats. As Samuel J. Crawford, who would soon become governor, wrote, "Proslavery people resorted to every means, fair and foul, honest and dishonest, to establish slavery in Kansas. . . . [they] swarmed across the border into Kansas and committed crimes most brutal and barbarous. They came in squads, companies, and regiments, and . . . elected citizens of Missouri as members of the [Kansas] Territorial Legislature—a Legislature, the majority of whose members committed perjury when they took their oath of office . . . and enacted a code of laws for the territory of Kansas by taking the statutes of Missouri [which permitted slavery] and striking out the words, 'State of Missouri' . . . and inserting in their place the words, 'Kansas Territory.' "[3]

In the wake of the vote, violence spread. As a pair of Democratic administrations, those of Pierce and Buchanan, presided over national policy and lent support to local pro-slavery forces, the opposition, operating as militias with names like the Free State Army of Kansas, gathered public support and fought pitched battles across the territory.

In 1858, a new referendum was held, and the decidedly anti-Democratic result gave Kansas a political compass that pointed the way for a century and a half. When Kansas finally joined the Union in January 1861, on the eve of the Civil War, it was as a free state, passionately embracing Lincoln, the Republican Party, and a deep commitment to end slavery. As Crawford later put it, "From start to finish, it was a red-hot fight, with justice, humanity, and the heavy artillery on the Republican side."[4] In the Civil War that followed, Kansas would lose more men per capita than any other northern state.

While "Bleeding Kansas" is not really the grist of most American kids' education,[5] it certainly is in Kansas, where every child learns that the Civil War was previewed in Kansas. The state's seventh-grade curriculum requires that Kansas children be able to "analyze the importance of 'Bleeding Kansas' to the rest of the United States in the years leading up to the Civil War." They learn about the Kansas-Nebraska Act; about Brown and Lane and about Quantrill's raid on Olathe and Lawrence, where the pro-slavery men burned newspaper offices and ransacked homes. They're told what happened to anti-slavery Republican senator Charles Sumner after he delivered a scathing speech called the "Crime Against Kansas" attacking the Democrats and "the harlot, Slavery." He was beaten nearly to death by a furious Democratic congressman.

It took Sumner nearly three years to recover from the attack, but in Kansas, the Democrats never did.

"The events of the 1850s" had a big effect on Kansas," historian Craig Miner explained to me when I asked him why there were almost no Democrats on the property. "I think you'd have to say [Bleeding Kansas] is one big reason." Out here schools teach kids about Roosevelt and the New Deal and LBJ, Martin Luther King and civil rights but they're also taught about a homegrown conflict that was not only a shooting war but also a political one. It involved Republicans facing off against Democrats. And no one is sorry that the Democrats lost.[6]

That what it meant to be a Republican—or a Democrat—was permanently fixed for so many generations by events in the 1850s may strike many as absurd, but given the issues involved, at least it's understandable.

What's far harder to grasp is the degree to which much that's followed has only served to reinforce that political affiliation and to put off until now the emergence of Kansas Democrats as a serious political force.

True enough, Republicans were briefly voted out during the Dust Bowl years, when the New Deal offered the prospect of better times. Even Alf Landon, a native son, couldn't carry Kansas. But by 1940, Kansans had turned away from Roosevelt. "You know when things really went wrong for us?" eighty-five-year-old Mitchell County Democratic Party central committeeman Charles Hackett asked me after a local party meeting. "With Roosevelt. When we needed government help, he was fine. But when we didn't, we were left with all that government red tape and regulations, telling you what you could and couldn't do. That was no good. Farmers hate to be told what to do."

As a result, in 1940 Kansas went for Wilkie—and for every Republican after that with the exception of 1964, when Kansans, along with the rest of the country, bought into perhaps the most famous and successful Democratic fear campaign ever and voted against Barry Goldwater so the kids in the front yard wouldn't get nuked.

Even Truman, from just across the river in Missouri, couldn't break the Democrats' losing streak, perhaps because few in Kansas identified with him. As Kay Thull, a lifelong Democrat from Cawker City, told me, if it hadn't been for Truman's involvement with Thomas Pendergast and Kansas City's corrupt Democratic machine, he would have remained an Independence haberdasher.[7] "We knew all about Kansas City and Pendergast. We didn't want to be identified with *that,*" said Thull.

After Truman came Eisenhower, a legitimate Kansan, a son of Abilene, a solid, middle-of-the-road Republican, and a genuine military hero with a style of governance that appealed to Kansans' general disdain for political theatrics—although his use of federal troops to end the racist policies of southern Democrats fit nicely with the way Kansans felt the world should work.

Nothing has fundamentally altered Kansans' formal political affiliations during the half century since. Until recently, the extremist rhetoric from both sides in the ideological civil war that's taking place in the country to-day has left Kansans—and midwesterners in general—happy to be a long way from places like New York and San Francisco. That's all coming to an end, however, as conservatives, who draw a parallel between slavery and abortion, lambaste "pro-aborts," while liberals scream about "crazies" and "fundies." None of this convinces anyone, of course.

Real moderates are becoming as rare in Kansas politics as they are elsewhere in America, not least because of the way the word "moderate" has been repurposed by an unthinking press for use as a lead pipe with which to bash all conservatives. This is done with a mugger's sense of expediency by creating a category that associates all conservatives with the most extreme among them. In the newspapers of Kansas, there are only moderates and conservatives. All conservatives are extremists, according to this formulation, but no moderate is liberal, no matter how extreme they may be in their "moderation." You'd think "liberal" wouldn't need a euphemism; Nelson Rockefeller lived a long and politically happy life as a "liberal Republican." Why can't half the Republicans in Kansas?

The answer, at least in part, lies in the Protestant schism between evangelicals and old-line denominations, the latter clinging tenaciously to the banner of "moderation" as a way of demonstrating moral superiority over their fiery, often conservative brothers and sisters—and in doing so, granting credence to the idea that the L-word has become politically untenable, presumably because it carries the baggage of failed policies. The rest of the answer may be found in the importance of not admitting how extreme some "moderate" positions really are. Like most Americans, Kansans are happy to vote for nice people who say nice things. And what could be more inoffensive than moderation?

The press is always the essential co-conspirator in this kind of fraud. Only in the newspapers of Kansas can somebody be described as a "moderate" because he or she supports all or part of an agenda that includes gambling, higher taxes, bigger government, more centralized power, bloated education budgets, and unrestricted use of what is euphemistically called "a certain type of late-term abortion procedure"—the kind that shocks the ostensibly liberal populations of countries like France, Germany, and others in the European Union, where such things are seen as not just illegal and a violation of common sense but disgusting (and where other "moderate" causes in Kansas and Missouri, especially embryonic stem cell research, are seen as morally indefensible, too).[8]

In Kansas, all you need for a late-term abortion is five grand, a complaint about feeling "depressed," a wink, and an appointment with Dr. George Tiller, whose clinic in Wichita has been targeted by critics such as Fox News's Bill O'Reilly for performing "hundreds if not thousands" of partial-birth abortions every year. Women (and girls) in very advanced stages of pregnancy from all over the world fly to Wichita to call on Tiller, since most of the rest of the planet frowns on the grisly procedure. Not Kansas, where on average a perfectly viable fetus is killed at least once a day. The state's taxpayers even subsidize flights to the Wichita airport.

Clinic opponents claimed that Tiller was conducting late-term abortions by abusing the health-of-the-mother provision in Kansas law; right-to-life workers compiled lists of cases where late-term abortions were provided with little or no supporting evidence to suggest that the mother's health was in danger at all. Anti-Tiller activists worried that when girls ten, twelve, and fourteen were brought into the clinics for abortions, they were being returned to the same circumstances whence they had come—and that, barring the miraculous, the mere presence in an abortion clinic of a twelve-year-old was a pretty sensible indication that child molestation had taken place. State law required careful reporting, but Tiller's clinic had stubbornly denied attorney general Phill Kline access even to records that had been redacted to protect privacy, thus ensuring that it would be abortion providers who were the targets of the probe, not their patients. Nevertheless, reporters and editors (some of whom harbored a very deep personal dislike of Kline, who was sometimes the butt of journalists' private jokes) relentlessly pursued a narrative that portrayed Kline as an extremist bigot fueled by religious zeal and bent on stripping clinic patients of their privacy.

Although Kansas law notionally forbids post-viability abortions and requires monitoring of cases involving children brought to the clinic for abortions, there's no mechanism for enforcement of the law because there is no effective means of accountability. Therefore, nobody knows for sure how many children are given abortions in the clinics. The state's abortion providers simply refuse to meet the reporting requirement. Trying to force them to obey the law, of course, is what led to the ouster of Phill Kline.

Tiller sometimes manages to outrage the citizens of Wichita: the death of one teenager with Down syndrome who was given an abortion in her twenty-eighth week was the basis for a massive local petition calling for a grand jury investigation of Tiller,[9] but aside from unusual cases like this, there's virtually no press coverage of this kind of excess. Sebelius did manage to raise even a few "moderate" eyebrows when she vetoed a bill requiring health inspections of clinics. The legislature passed the statute after a TV news item showing rats infesting a Kansas City clinic was broadcast.[10] "The place was so filthy you wouldn't want your sister to go there," one statehouse journalist told me later.

Kansans knew all this; before the 2006 election, the right-wing airwaves were filled with news about Tiller, Sebelius, and the abortion mess in Kansas. The intended beneficiary of all this fulmination should have been Kline, who was locked in a struggle with a man named Paul Morrison, the district attorney from Thomas Frank's old neighborhood in Johnson County. Morrison was what you might call a moderate extremist: He had been reelected four times as a Republican before he switched parties to run as a pro-choice Democrat. Morrison benefitted from Tiller's effort to direct hundreds of thousands of dollars into campaigns to defeat Kline in 2002 and 2006.[11]

To the delight of Kline supporters, Fox News's Bill O'Reilly attacked Tiller as if the man were a stinky French cheese, and radio talkers joined in to support Kline in his uphill battle. The attention encouraged conservatives but left everyone else in the state stubbornly unaffected. For the most part, it was just another case of people telling Kansans what to do. Although it rarely made the press, most Kansans surely knew that George Tiller was one of the most powerful political donors in the state; they knew he had forked over hundreds of thousands of dollars that had eventually found their way to campaigns like Morrison's and Sebelius's. And they were convinced that Phill Kline was just snooping in his demand for medical documents he said he needed to investigate child rapes and late-term abortions that he suspected may have been performed illegally by Tiller and others—even if the documents had been redacted to ensure privacy. In fact, most people also assumed that girls way below the age of consent had been in and out of Tiller's and other clinics, only to be sent back to wherever they came from, no questions asked. And everybody knew that Morrison seemed to believe that what went on between a teenage girl, George Tiller, and a poisoned needle injected into a nearly born baby was nobody's business. They didn't need the national media to point all this out, and they didn't need Bill O'Reilly telling them what to do. It was embarrassing. Besides, everybody in Kansas also knew that Phill Kline had run a shrill and desperate campaign and had responded to the personal attacks on him by making similar attacks on his opponent, and not doing a very good job of that at all.

So the voters got to decide. What they decided, by a large margin, was that if the choice was Phill Kline or Tiller and his abortions, they'd take the abortions, thanks. To some, it was Kline himself and his earnest focus on moral issues—"A little too intense?" is how one sympathetic conservative legislator tentatively described it to me—that put people off. To others, it was what they saw as a pomposity distinctly alien to Kansans who really didn't like having to call Kline "General" in order to have a conversation with him. To former speaker of the Kansas house Doug Mays, it was "a couple of huge blunders on Kline's part"—including a very clumsy attempt at mudslinging. And to yet others, Kline was just mean—a mostly unfair image hugely amplified in the press, but one that carries weight in a part of the country where the politics of outrage don't always go down well. It takes some doing, however, to lose a "mean" contest with a late-term abortion doc. How had Kline done it?

In an interview, I found Kline to be witty and clever. But it was an image that never left his office, apparently. Kline infuriated not only the local press corps, some of whom loved to tell insulting stories at his expense, but also his political adversaries, not only because of his dogmatic conservatism but, one suspects, because of his lengthy, complicated, yet extemporaneous defenses of his views. When *Esquire* magazine sent a writer out to nail Kline on his anti-abortion opinions in 2005, all the guy could do was run paragraph-long quotes of stuff Kline said between bites at dinner. Kline assiduously shuns the empty-headed Bush-speak all journalists and pundits hope for when they quote conservatives. When asked a question, he stubbornly avoids producing yet another sound bite; instead, he offers a full-course meal. For example, when I asked him about the liberal state supreme court and its affection for making laws on behalf of the state legislature, he said, "The challenge is deep-rooted in the failure for us to teach, learn, understand, and apply some basic principles of governance in a culture that even denies that there are principles worth protecting." Right. But . . .

"In a culture of moral relativism, everything is pragmatic and therefore the foundational principles and the importance of those principles is lost in the immediacy of the moment," he continued.

In 2006, Morrison swept not only the usual blue precincts around Kansas City and Lawrence but counties all across Kansas, including ones where Democrats hadn't won an election for years. Suddenly, it seemed the range was filled with donkeys.[12]

Thus did Kansans finally earn the praise of the *New York Times.* Gone was the mortifying gloom that came with all those liberals wondering what was the matter with Kansas, anyway? Kansans had finally made those "mental connections" that critics said were supposed to result in benefits, somehow.

But it's just a moment. Another one's on the way: In a state as divided as Kansas, there'll be something the matter again soon enough. Despite the *Times'* claim, the 2006 election wasn't "a major shift in the nation's heartland" at all. According to some conservatives, the Republicans' best candidates for governor didn't run.[13] Barnett campaigned broke, and many thought Representative Jim Ryun's defeat was long overdue. Ryun wasn't exactly a charismatic figure. In fact, one of his opponents told me in confidence that "his best campaign events were the ones he didn't attend." Most conservatives don't expect the congressional seat to remain with the Democrats for long.[14] Surprisingly, the Fourth Congressional District, held by Todd Tiahrt (who defeated nine-term Democratic incumbent Dan Glickman in 1994), seems unlikely to revert to the Democrats soon.

The biggest defeat for the Republicans was the one most Republicans apparently wanted most: the ouster of Kline. The gains made by Democrats cost them millions of dollars: Kline was outspent two to one by Morrison, who raised more than $1.25 million, and the issue-oriented campaigns for things like abortions and embryonic stem cell research that were linked to the Sebelius-Morrison effort piped in many millions more.

The composition of the statehouse wasn't appreciably altered; a handful of seats changed hands, but the new speaker, a plainspoken man named Melvin Neufeld, is a blunt and controversial conservative who was once angrily accused by his opponents of "blackmailing" another house member in trying to secure a vote. (The charges were thrown out.) He seems to have engineered many liberal Republicans out of the influential leadership posts Doug Mays, Neufeld's predecessor, had permitted them. Mays's kindness to GOP liberals was a mystery to conservatives, some of whom thought he was acting out of a perhaps naive sense of fairness, or a real fear they'd bolt and join the Democrats to form a majority. Mays told me he preferred to be as tolerant as possible, something he said he learned from his mentor and predecessor as Speaker, Tim Shallenberger.

So the *Times's* endorsement of Kansas notwithstanding, nothing much changed in Kansas in 2006. The pendulum that had swung a notch to the right, now swung a notch to the left. It's the twenty-first century, after all, and Kansas, as always, is in the middle.

Transcript 3:
Superior People

Stan: People wonder why we elect so many Democrats in this part of the world. Well, it may sound strange to those from outside, but out here Democrats and Republicans can be almost identical on the issues.

Rich: Look at our senators—we've got a Democrat [Ben Nelson] who acts like a Republican, and a Republican [Chuck Hagel] who acts like a Democrat. So you look at the person as much as the letter after the name.

Bill: What that also means is there's not the same level of partisan animosity you find in other places. I've been a Republican all my life, and I think most Republicans would think I'm a pretty fair Republican. But the two Democratic county commissioners are both farmers, and a few years ago, when the Democratic lieutenant governor was out here campaigning, it was milo season. One of the commissioners said, "Bill, we've got to be in the fields, harvesting milo. Will you take her around and introduce her to people?" I don't think they gave a thought to the fact that I was a registered Republican—I just didn't have any milo to cut that day. (Laughter)

Pat: Basically, you vote for someone who shares your values.

Rich: Exactly. Some of us are bothered a lot by some of the things we see happening these days—all the latchkey kids with both parents

working, rising divorce, declining education, all the junk that you
see when you turn on the television. To me, that's one of the
biggest differences between the thinking here and on the coast. It
seems like people there aren't quite as concerned about those
things. They think conservative values are boring, they lack color,
they lack *pizzazz*. I even read an article that said that for a lot
of people, integrity is not an issue anymore. Well, I sure think it
still is.

Stan: I'm with you all the way on that.

Pat: I guess we do come across as conservative—which, for the most
part, we probably are. Fundamentally, most of us have deep
conservative values. But on an issue-by-issue basis, a lot of people
would be surprised at how liberal some of us are. Take the issue of
gays, for instance—the image in some parts of the country is
probably that if you're gay, you'll be shot if you come here. It's
not true at all. There's a lot of sympathy and understanding and
compassion for gay people in our neck of the woods.

Rich: Even those who hate the practice, they have compassion for the
individual. And you can run down a whole list of issues—we think
our views are the compassionate ones. Because to our way of
thinking, they're the ones that make for a better life for children
and families, a stronger economy, a better world—

Pat: Take the issue of illegal aliens—

Rich: Which as far as a lot of liberals are concerned, you're not even
supposed to call them. You're not allowed to call the thing what
it is.

Pat: I think most of us are kind of torn. Because you do feel for these
people . . .

Rich: On the other hand, how much are they costing us in social
services?

Stan: But they're also giving back. They're buying things, paying
taxes—

Pat: And taking service industry jobs that Americans don't seem to want.

Stan *(laughing)*: If we made them citizens, and they got stuck with as many taxes as the rest of us, then they'd be sorry.

Rich: The whole multicultural thing is part of it. If they really wanted to *become* Americans, and made sure their kids learned English and our history . . .

Stan: That's right, then there'd be a lot fewer objections. Because a lot of them already have a wonderful work ethic.

Bill: They sure do. I remember one year we had a booth at the fair, and a little Hispanic boy, maybe ten or twelve, used to come down every day for the helium balloons we were giving away. So after a while, I start objecting to how many balloons I'm giving to the kid, and he says, "Listen, I run the ring-toss game at the carnival, so you come up and you'll be a winner." So one night I have a little time, and I wander over to the carnival and find his ring-toss booth. He looks up at me and shakes his head no. The next day he comes down and says, "I saw you last night, but I had to be careful—I had customers. You come down when I have no customers and you'll be a winner." *(Laughter.)*

Stan: There's a kid that's gonna go far in this world.

Pat: If he works hard.

Snapshot: Prairie Companions

Like many people my age I have a résumé deep in political folly. After a high school career as a Republican, I became an English major—a surefire way to avoid future employment while justifying an embrace of economic policies designed to perpetuate unemployment forever. I edited an underground newspaper, sold ads to head shops, and started a local SDS chapter (the then-private university I attended flatly prohibited SDS chapters, however, so we called ours "Apple Pie"). I marched on Washington lots of times, and not just because my girlfriend at the time was a resident of George Washington University's famed "superdorm"—137 floors of women, stacked![1] I helped other guys get arrested. I think I went to a Zappa concert, and I *know* I went to a Youngbloods concert; I dug the Fugs. I was clean for Gene, then betrayed by Bobby. I served nearly ten years' active duty as a poet. I have always thought I knew the seductive appeal of righteous despair.

Then I was invited to the annual meeting of the Mitchell County Democratic Central Committee (2004 results: Bush 2,600, Kerry 700, Nader 25). Me and seven other people in a bank's community room in Beloit, Kansas. Plus one late arrival, the youngest guy there, in his late thirties. Old business: cash on hand, two hundred dollars and change. New business: "We're going to turn Kansas blue," Fred Karlin told his Democrats. Everybody agreed. The obvious solution: a fund-raiser! In less than a minute a plan was made: a cookout in the park where a George Foreman Grill would be auctioned to the highest bidder. Attention turned momentarily to missionary work. The guy in his thirties asked, "What are the chances we can get younger people involved? I mean . . ." He looked furtively around the table. "Well, you know, I mean people my age." Everybody laughed, and the business part of the meeting ended. Then I was invited to ask questions.

"This is Kansas. Why are you all Democrats?"

I expected the synaxarion of Democratic saints and their causes and something about justice for the workers of the world. But they all said they were Democrats because their parents had been Democrats, mostly the New Deal variety. "Here's a story," Karlin said. Then, looking around the table, he asked, "Should I tell him the story?"

Everybody said no.

"Okay, I will. When my grandfather was dying, he called everybody to his deathbed and said, 'I've been a Democrat all my life. But I'm converting.'

" 'Why?' everybody asked. 'Why would you do that?'

" 'Because,' he said, 'when I go, there'll be one fewer Republican left alive.' "

We all smiled.

"Have you read *What's the Matter with Kansas?*" committeeman Charles Hackett asked. "He really lets them have it, doesn't he?"

I agreed. "He does. Did you read the book?" Pause. "Well, what do you think of his advice to Democrats?" We all briefly discussed the class-warfare angle. "Think you'd do better if you ran to the left?" I asked.

Startled looks. A double barbershop quartet of Democrats replied in absolutely perfect unison: "No!"

A big, affable man in a T-shirt and shorts said, "The problem is, people back there"—he gestured vaguely in the direction of the East Coast—"they think that because we're Democrats, we don't go to church, that we don't believe in God. Hey. We're pro-life. We're not agitating for gay marriage. We don't go for *any* of that stuff."

The others all nodded.

So Frank's wrong on that? You should just skip the social issues and focus instead on economic issues?

"I'd say Mr. Frank's way wrong on that one," said another man.

"What we do think is that people should be easier on each other—spend a little more when we have to help out other people," said Karlin. "That's what I was taught, anyway."

I missed the fund-raiser in the park—but not the election results. In 2006, Mitchell County went bluish, backing both Sebelius and Morrison—but also the conservative Republican congressional incumbent, Jerry Moran.

The fact is, when it comes to "values" issues, economics, and national defense, most Kansas Democrats cross-dress as Republicans. Very few Democratic candidates even use the word "Democrat" on their signs and flyers. No one seems in a hurry to see whether or not 2006 changed that. "Why give people a reason to vote against you?" asked Kansas house minority leader Dennis McKinney.

From a very heavily Republican district himself, McKinney votes pro-life, pro-gun, and supported the amendment to the Kansas constitution that prohibits gay marriage. Another Democratic legislator—in fact, the most liberal member of the state senate, according to Doug Mays, the former speaker of the Kansas house—state senator Janis Lee, explained it to me this way: "On my signs, no 'Democrat' and no donkeys. It's just not worth it." Instead, she pounds pavement and presses flesh. Five or six years ago, when I was holed up in a little house on the northern edge of Mankato to work on a book, Janis Lee came by not once but *twice*. I saw her more often than the guy next door.

In the Midwest, most nonurban Democrats know that the only way they can win anything is to run just slightly left of the conservative Republican candidate, thus capturing "moderate" Republican votes. In fact, many don't bother with the D-word at all, registering and running as Republicans. Bill Light, an extremely affable—and extremely "moderate"—state legislator from a very rural, conservative southwestern district, told me one night over a beer that the first thing he did when he decided to run for the legislature was to change his registration from Democrat to Republican. "It would have been pointless to run if I didn't do that first." Another "moderate" leader in the statehouse, Ward Loyd, told me on the house floor that even though he often votes with Democrats, he ran as a Republican because, he said, otherwise "I'd lose."[2]

The problem of what it means to be a midwestern Democrat has only intensified as the country has become more sharply divided. Ted Kennedy, Barbara Boxer, and Hillary Clinton may speak for the national party, but they don't sound much like anyone from around here, where people hate talking politics, even with their politicians. "That Josh Svaty! I'd vote for him," said a cousin of mine who will here go nameless. This was one afternoon after he'd met a very young, very liberal Democratic state representative from Salina at some rural organization's annual get-together. I rattled off Svaty's support for one liberal policy after another. "Well, what I mean is that I'd vote for him if he'd keep all that to himself," he clarified. "He's really *funny!*"

Where Kansas Democrats have Josh Svaty, the rest of the country has cutups like Patty Murray and Harry Reid. "We'd do a lot better if it weren't for [the national party]," McKinney told me one day, standing in front of Dan's lunch counter in the Topeka statehouse. I had just watched him guide his Democratic house caucus with a light touch through a day of education funding. All around us were John Steuart Curry's fantastic murals, showing, among other things, a really furious John Brown on the rampage.

The Kansas statehouse was in the process of being restored. An acre or so of ugly blue paint had been removed, and scaffolding and hardware were everywhere, confounding the efforts of Dan, who is blind, to find his way around the building. He's missing something, because the result is stunning: rediscovered huge painted ceiling panels running around the house chamber and, above the transoms, the emblazoned names of famous Free Staters and proto-Republicans. These keep watch on McKinney's forty-odd Democrats who huddle together for safety along one of the room's walls, off to the speaker's far left.

"The national party just makes it a lot harder for us," continued McKinney, who also noted the contrast between the civility he finds in Kansas politics and the ugliness coming out of Washington these days. "In southern Europe, the Serbs and Bosnians still hate each other over atrocities that occurred over 700 years ago," he wrote not long ago in a Dodge City newspaper. "But these atrocities were no worse than the crimes committed by pro- and anti-slavery forces in eastern Kansas and western Missouri from 1856–1864. Why was our country able to rise above this, while others persist in hatred?"[3] You would answer this question one way if you were a faithful reader of the *San Francisco Chronicle*. You'd answer your own question this way if you were a Kansas Democrat like McKinney: "[Because] we regularly reaffirm our Christ-taught values of love and forgiveness. Second, we regularly affirm those values and ideas that make democracy work. We work hard to instill these values and ideas in our children."

To use the word "Christ" in public, an eastern liberal would have to be hitting his thumb with a hammer. But McKinney is popular in Kansas precisely because he reflects local values so accurately. The national party "has a lot more to do with New York than it does with Kansas," he said. Not surprisingly, he is sometimes mentioned as a potential candidate for governor.

It's certainly true that voters in Kansas and Nebraska are far more unpredictable than voters in, say, New Jersey, where apparently no shame is too great for voters to bear so long as they get their Democrats in office. Articulate, wry, and honest, McKinney's a politician who seems to his many supporters to live the beliefs he preaches. I myself was more than a little surprised when out of the blue he brought up the guy a cousin of mine was dating when she interned for him several years ago; he wanted to be sure she hadn't married him. "He was kind of . . ." He wrinkled his nose. But she hadn't, and McKinney was visibly relieved. And weren't we all.

Many blue-staters readily dismiss Democrats like McKinney for putting so-called social issues ahead of what people like Frank perceive to be their economic interests. But aside from the fact that most of these "economic interests" have little to do with the actual lives of midwesterners, such a view vastly underestimates the importance of values in all people's lives. In fact, what's truly bizarre is the assertion that people should be comfortable voting for candidates who *disregard* the social issues they hold dear.

Part Two

The Modern Main Street

For those who actually live out here, the concerns that interest most people don't have a lot to do with national politics. From Fort Riley to Gregg's place out there in Colorado, the issue that compels attention most is water, which is related to weather, which impacts agriculture, which determines income and the profitability of local businesses, which greatly affects schools and other government services. Invariably, the recipe for midwestern success is simple: Add water.

As I write, the plains are in the midst of yet another drought (or another year of one very long drought) and, again, farm policies, including those that often have nothing to do with rainfall and barely qualify as "policies" at all, given their arbitrariness, are in flux. This year, more farmland will be taken out of production and put into conservation programs—but it's just another way to write the subsidy check.

Malthus was wrong. The problem isn't too many people; it's too few trains. Less than a mile from where I sit is a huge elevator where summer after summer the wheat harvest overflows capacity as farmers arrive with semi loads of the stuff, dump it, and collect the check. My cousins Doug, Kurt, and Joe all still go out and help harvest wheat from Texas up to the Canadian border, and another cousin, Todd, drives the trucks that carry the grain; last year, Doug came back after spending a couple of hours sitting out an Oklahoma rainstorm talking with retired general Tommy Franks about the best way to mount an attack on a field of red wheat with a combine. Franks happened to own the next farm down the road.

Anyone can be an expert these days, but if you want to talk to somebody who knows *exactly* what he's doing, talk to a farmer. Anybody who's still operating a profitable farm in America in the twenty-first century is demonstrating far more expertise than a bushel of focus-group facilitators. Spend a few hours with Joe in the cab of his combine and he'll tell you exactly what it costs when he misses a turn by a couple of inches. Douglas's brother Bryan swears that if the government would just get out of the way and let farmers do what they do best, the whole planet could be fed by Kansas. Maybe that's a bit of hyperbole—and the global farmers' market isn't quite that simple—but even now, with completely nonsensical ag regulations in the way, there aren't enough railcars on the planet to be able to cart away all the wheat grown here, and even if there were, there aren't enough ovens in hell to bake it all into bread. One bushel of wheat contains more than a million kernels and yields more than seventy loaves of bread; in Kansas alone, even with all those acres out of production, farmers grow enough wheat every year to make thirty-six billion loaves. The Burlington Northern Santa Fe and the Union Pacific practically have to plow their way through the mountain of wheat in thousands of places like Concordia, but don't ask them to stop; national railroads don't like getting into the grain-toting business, with its wild seasonal fluctuations. Smaller regional railways, such as the Kyle here in Concordia, try to move the stuff, but it's an overwhelming task. And besides, move it where? Who needs *more* wheat who isn't in Chad?

So the wheat just piles up higher and higher. The surplus is now so predictable and permanent that last winter, the Concordia elevator built a metal shelter over the mountain of wheat. It's shaped like a mountain. If history is an indicator, soon it will be a range of mountains, and given time, maybe skiing will finally come to Kansas.[1]

It's a similar story farther west on the Republican River, in McCook, Nebraska. Although the annual grain harvest is more likely to be reflected in the price of beef than it is in wheat mountains, lots of people in western Nebraska pay close attention to the minute fluctuations of the commodities market and the economic health of the ag sector. But few people follow it with the avidity of the merchants whose shops line McCook's Norris Avenue as it stretches up the hill from the river and the train station, where Amtrak still makes a stop.

The street was named for a favorite son, maverick senator George Norris, who moved to McCook shortly after the town was founded, in 1882. Among Norris Avenue's eclectic assortment of architecturally interesting buildings one finds a surprising variety of businesses, including a yarn shop, a clothier's, a CD shop, and, rarity of rarities, an independent bookstore. There's Sehnert's Bakery, run by a family that has been in the baking business for five generations, "all the way back to Germany," Matt Sehnert told me. Next door is his Bieroc Café, where touring folk acts perform regularly. There are gifty sort of boutiques on Norris Avenue, an art gallery, antiques shops, offices, and Bob Longnecker's jewelry shop.

Mike Ford, a garrulous upmarket cooking supply merchant, followed his passion to Norris Avenue. "I sold agricultural chemicals for years," he said, "but I always wanted to be a gourmet chef. I sure wasn't going to open a restaurant, though. So I opened this." Ford coined the term "on the bricks"—Norris Avenue is paved with the things—to describe Main Street activities on the radio.

As we talked in his shop, customers came in for wedding registry lists and to buy packages of gourmet coffee and twee biscuits. Ford showed me a thousand-dollar espresso machine. "I sell these, believe it or not," he said, pouring me a stiff one. "Seven years here and I've been in the black since year one. I can't complain."

A rural resident without complaints is an oddity, I suppose, but finding one on a small-town Main Street is just bizarre. Out here, the shopping area is usually called the "business district," but sometimes the term drips with bitterness and frustration. In every small midwestern town, Main Street is a retail tundra, one of the country's most fragile economic environments, where harsh conditions mean potential extinction is always a billing cycle away, and where strange and wonderful businesses sprout up like genetically modified flora. I once rode out to McCook with my cousin Marvin in a yellow semi loaded with cows, taking them to the Heartland Cattle Company, a "heifer development and research center" run by two very smart women and a guy named Gail. Ranchers from all over the Midwest bring their heifers to Heartland, where the animals' ovulation cycles are put in sync—a tremendous advantage to a herd manager. These kinds of businesses just don't exist in other places, for obvious reasons, but out here they form an extremely valuable component of local economies, giving them a durability that often exceeds that of a Main Street widget shop.

"Main Street is not an easy place," Milan Wall, codirector of the Lincoln-based Heartland Center for Leadership, told me. While small prairie villages like McCook, Nebraska, and Concordia, Kansas—the major market towns along the upper reaches of the Republican River—are still slowly recovering from the last hard time twenty years ago, other small towns are slowly dying despite a fairly buoyant agricultural economy. "It doesn't take a lot to make things harder," Wall added.

A lot of people in cities far away will give you a short-hand explanation as to why Main Streets have failed in so many places out here recently. They'll talk ominously of a gray-and-red Arkansas-bred disaster that descended upon America's defenseless communities like a swarm of economic locusts, leaving once-idyllic small towns empty and broke. They'll tell you it's called Wal-Mart.

As it happens, both McCook and Concordia have a Wal-Mart. A Supercenter, no less. And the one thing those merchants on Norris Avenue have in common is that most of them opened for business long after Wal-Mart arrived in town.

It's hard to be a fan of Wal-Mart. Unless you work there and own stock, it's not the kind of place that inspires loyalty easily. One reason why blue-state people don't go to Wal-Mart, and why some red-state types wish there were an alternative, is that sometimes just visiting a Supercenter can be a melancholy, radically purgatorial experience. As soon as you walk through the door, a giant blower blasts you, as if you are being deloused. Inside, the place looks like a massive welfare office with shopping carts; there are people in there shopping in their *pajamas*. Huge pallets of stuff clog passageways, and warehouse workers come at you with more, shoving you off into a pile of rubberized boots next to some plastic shoes featuring genuine leather uppers made in the exotic Orient; everything is cheap, and something about the whole place suggests that corners were not only cut, they were hacked, chopped, sliced, and torn. All men's clothes are made by George or Dickie. Does Wal-Mart really think "plus-sized" women will feel good buying clothes marked "Faded Glory"? And where's the hardware guy to tell me how to use a thingie? This surely is what the East Germans had in mind for retail.

Plus, wandering aimlessly in a midwestern Wal-Mart Supercenter is like looking into the midwestern sky at night: you realize you're part of something much bigger than anything you can understand. It's not particularly comforting to know that the sheer size of the company is a reflection of how vast the middle class is in America. In just Kansas and Nebraska, two of America's most rural states, the numbers are staggering: Wal-Mart employs more than 30,000 people out here, paying most of them nine or ten bucks an hour—much more than most Main Street retailers—along with a benefit package that can deliver as much as five dollars an hour more for full-time employees. In just these two states, the company collects more than $283 million in sales tax and pays more than $37 million in state and local levies; it pays nearly $3 billion to 1,650 Kansas and Nebraska suppliers and, according to company figures, by doing so helps create another 71,000 jobs and who knows how much more tax revenue and other jobs as a result. Big numbers. Wal-Mart measures dollars the way China measures Chinese: by the billion.

Nationally, the stormy campaign against the retail giant is a caricature of Democratic politics, the result of a perfect confluence of elitist disapproval of working-class taste and blatant union self-interest. Far from

McCook and Concordia, many blue-state politicians score points by beating up on the supposedly voracious company. These rants have almost no significance in most of the Midwest, where concerns about Wal-Mart have nothing at all to do with class warfare or chumming for unions or a dislike of Wal-Mart aesthetics, if you'll pardon the oxymoron, and everything to do with local economics. In smaller, more conservative communities, where politics is blogless but deeply personal, growth and the things that compel it are much more volatile topics. In that respect, Wal-Mart is a hot issue on Main Street.

In McCook, as in Concordia, the Supercenter is one of the biggest employers, giving retail jobs to people who otherwise might not have jobs at all, especially after the closures that marked the 1980s collapse. The McCook Supercenter employs around three hundred people; when McCook National Bank's Mark Graff tried to total the number of retail employees Norris Avenue supported in its pre-Wal-Mart days, he couldn't top two hundred, and none of them would have made what a comparable Wal-Mart employee makes. Yet nothing makes blue blood boil like the havoc the wealthy see Wal-Mart wreaking on their Rockwell-perfect fantasy of small-town America. Gone are the friendly general store, the cheerful grocer, the haberdasher, and the dressmaker. In fact, so firmly implanted is this view that even people who live in small towns like to believe it, since it explains their nostalgic melancholy—never mind the fact that these Platonic emblems of village businesses vanished long before Wal-Mart showed up.

Maybe a cozy Main Street preservation strategy would make sense if the average household income in places like McCook were $71,300, as it is in Marin County, where Main Street environments, faux or real, are usually the priciest places to shop and eat, and where Wal-Marts are forbidden. But in McCook, the average household income isn't $71,300. It's forty grand less: around $31,100. At the moment, according to company figures, there are more Wal-Mart Supercenters in Nebraska (25 for 1.7 million people) and twice as many in Kansas (41 for a population of 2.6 million) than there are in California (21 for 33.8 million). The reason's simple. In places like McCook, unlike San Mateo, people *need* a Wal-Mart.

And, ironically, nobody needs Wal-Mart more than the Main Streets in the rural areas of the Midwest. As many McCook business leaders will tell you, to understand modern midwestern Main Streets, you have to understand how Wal-Mart fits in, since every food chain has a big predator perched at the top. Yet people who would gladly loose lions and tigers on the Great Plains recoil at the very idea of unleashing a Wal-Mart or two out here. They fear that given the right conditions, Wal-Marts might reproduce like retail bunnies—big, meat-eating, bloodsucking vampire bunnies.

And so they do. In fact, as middling-sized rural communities in Kansas and Nebraska have shrunk, ninety-two Wal-Mart Supercenters, discount stores, "neighborhood markets," and Sam's Clubs have moved into the void left by departing merchants, aggregating the lost inventory of hundreds of evaporating small hardware stores, groceries, and variety stores. This isn't just a midwestern phenomenon, of course. Small, independent merchants everywhere are swimming against the retail current in America these days.

Nevertheless, there is generally high anxiety the first time a small community hears the words "new Wal-Mart Supercenter"—as there should be, since for most small towns, a new Wal-Mart means that everything that has characterized a community's commercial life for a century—including business failures caused by market loss—will almost certainly change. If you're a small-town merchant running your gadget shop the way your daddy did and his daddy did, your kids will be looking for a new line of work faster than you can say "cheap Chinese gadgets," because Wal-Mart will be selling exotic Hunanese versions of your gadgets for less than it cost Doubleday to have me type the word "gadgets." Those small merchants still clinging to life when Wal-Mart shows up either disappear almost overnight or make big changes in the way they do business.

Wal-Mart arrived in both Concordia and McCook in 1985, back

before the retailer was regarded as quite the beast so many think it is to-day. Twenty-odd years ago, the company still carried the faint aroma of Arkansas, with all its "Made in USA" signs and smiley faces. The original Wal-Marts were about the same size as other discounters and carried much the same merchandise. In the mid-1980s, "Wal-Mart didn't have the con-notation it has now," Graff observed. "They weren't the empire builders people make them out to be now. It was just another discount store."

There certainly was no surge of alarm when Wal-Mart arrived in Concordia. "One day," recalled Concordia's Kirk Lowell, "there was a big sign [on an empty retail box in a small strip mall] out on the highway that said, 'Wal-Mart—Coming Soon.' That was it."

Except it wasn't. Wal-Marts don't just show up. How the company sites its stores is mysterious to most of us, but even more so to those who find one in the middle of their town. I remember when a Wal-Mart opened on the highway that runs near our Pennsylvania farm. Most of the county's residents figured the thing had fallen off the back of a truck. "Never thought I'd see *that*," my neighbor Keith Dibert told me after he made his first visit. People in McCook must have felt the same way: Wal-Mart? Here? There must have been a mistake. But of course Wal-Mart's market research is peerless. Down there in Bentonville, they don't often throw darts at a map and hope for the best.

For Concordia, as for McCook, there was something both lucky and freakish about Wal-Mart's appearance. It was like a scene from *The Gods Must Be Crazy*. In both towns, standard-issue gray-and-red forty-thousand-square-foot boxes—the kind of building Wal-Mart now calls a "neighbor-hood market"—seemed to fall from the sky and change everything. Their inventory of cheap hardware and plastic laundry baskets hit some local re-tailers harder than others. Many of the smaller stores that sold that kind of stuff, mostly locally owned variety stores and the like, had already closed because of deteriorating economic conditions—only to reopen as Dollar Generals, sometimes beating Wal-Mart's prices by selling a similar inven-tory of even more inferior quality. Others struggled to find a niche Wal-Mart couldn't fill. Then, in the late 1990s, Wal-Marts across America inflated themselves from their little boxes into giant Supercenters, tripling their already yeti-sized footprint.

In Middle America, national retailers jousting with local merchants is nothing new. Not long ago, McCook's and Concordia's Main Streets not only sheltered mom-and-pop shops, they were also home to Sears and Montgomery Ward and Western Auto, and locally owned stores figured out how to compete around large corporations rather than against them. Forty years ago, you had to be in a very small town indeed to not have a local JCPenney store selling socks, dress shirts, and Scout uniforms.

Eventually, those anchor stores all faded from the scene, victims of the changing demographics of small-town America. What's replaced them is a Darwinian dream. A Wal-Mart Supercenter is not just another new chain store in town. It's retail at an evolved state, with a DNA manipulated by four decades of mutation and struggle and more mutation. If capitalism's a jungle, Wal-Mart's the king of it—and if you're a Main Street merchant going head-to-head with the beast, you're a three-legged antelope.

A forty-thousand-square-foot Wal-Mart was one thing; a Supercenter three times that size was something else. "There was more community reaction to it, I guess you could say," Graff remarked thoughtfully in the careful, qualified, understated cadences of a man who knows how loudly words can echo in a small town. "There were some people who were very concerned."

We call those people "grocers," since one of the more intrusive hallmarks of a Supercenter is a big supermarket area filled with cheap chow.

In McCook, the Supercenter was enough to almost instantly drive the community's four supermarkets out of business. As for Concordia, once a distribution point for Kroger and home to several other grocery stores, once the Supercenter opened and the IGA closed, the town was left with only a single independent full-service grocer—Rod's. The store's feisty owner, Rod Imhoff, greeted Wal-Mart's expansion with a defiant $1.2 million expansion of his own, moving into what had once been a Montgomery Ward next door. It was a gutsy move.

"Did I bite off too much?" he asked one day as we sat chatting in his little office near the busy checkout area. "Maybe. I'd be making a lot more money if I hadn't expanded, but this was a run-down store that needed attention." So far, Rod's has found a way to continue in business by doing what the local Wal-Mart can't do—kids help people tote groceries to their cars, the store delivers orders, employees run a full-line bakery and a brilliant deli counter. And the downtown location helps. In fact, simply getting to the front door of the Supercenter in Concordia is daunting for the town's aging population: The place was built on a hilltop where the Kansas wind wails whenever the Supercenter is open, which is always. "They don't like trying to push a cart through that," Imhoff tells me, with a thin smile of satisfaction. Still, it's not like the good old days before Wal-Mart showed up. "I'll never set foot in there, and neither will my family," he declared adamantly.

So, yes, if you were a grocer in either McCook or Concordia, Wal-Mart was a disaster, the last thing you needed when your problems were ready to swamp you. But for almost everybody else, the appearance of the Supercenter on the edge of town had an unexpected effect. In fact, to those most intimately involved with local economic problems, Wal-Mart has been part of the solution.

McCook's economic-development planner is an ex-farmer named Rex J. Nelson. While studying the problems faced by towns like McCook, he created a way to measure the economic vitality of a rural community by determining its ability to stem retail leakage.[2] He called this yardstick "trade pull factors." It takes into account the size of the town, how much money people have, how attractive and healthy the retail environment is, how close the town is to a major highway, and how far it is from other towns its size or larger.

These issues are not as pressing in more densely settled states, but out here, generally speaking, the smaller the community, the greater the leakage. Nelson could find only one instance where a rural county with a town smaller than 5,000—Valentine, Nebraska—enjoyed a positive trade pull factor, probably because it's many miles from there to anywhere else with stores and shops. Even so, it's an iffy thing: I once interviewed a lion-tamer in Valentine. She wore a sparkly swimsuit and worked for a circus, of course, and when the circus left, I did too because, frankly, without her, there just wasn't enough positive trade pull factor to make me want to stay.

In 2002, Nelson's study had McCook ranked at number 2. By 2005, it was down to 7. Were others doing better? Or was McCook stumbling? Nelson thought the data he used had a certain amount of inherent volatility. By and large, McCook appears to be able to supply whatever most residents might want, but, as Nelson said to me, "The expectations of shoppers change. They don't mind traveling."

And, of course, a Supercenter is a logical destination for many rural residents. Tom Lambing, the manager of McCook's Supercenter, said his research showed that his market reach extended one hundred miles or more.

What was true in McCook was also true in Concordia. "We've seen Wal-Mart studies that show people coming to Concordia from all over the area," Concordia's city manager, Larry Paine, told me. "In fact, people even come here from Salina"—a growing city of 40,000 an hour south, with its own Supercenter—"because the Salina store is too crowded." The Concordia Supercenter's market area is slightly smaller than Mc-Cook's—fifty to seventy-five miles—but it draws from a slightly more densely populated part of the state.

I admit I hadn't found what I'd expected to find when I turned over the Wal-Mart rock. I too remember halcyon shopping days on quaint midwestern Main Streets, just me, Mom, and a penny for a gumball. But while there are many problems that face places like Concordia, Wal-Mart just doesn't seem to be one of them. When I mentioned to one community leader that, aside from Rod the grocer, I couldn't find any Main Street merchants willing to tag Wal-Mart as a liability, he told me to talk to Verletta Moon, who operated a uniform store in Concordia for fifteen years—until Wal-Mart did her in. "She'll tell you what Wal-Mart did to her," he said.

So I called Verletta Moon and asked her what Wal-Mart had done to put her out of business.

"Actually," she said, correcting me, "it was my suppliers. They were undercutting me and selling to Wal-Mart. [Wal-Mart] could sell uniforms for less than I was paying for them. They weren't as good as mine, but they were less expensive." Though her own business may have suffered at the hands of Wal-Mart, she told me she didn't want that to color my view of the Supercenter's overall role in the town. "I was chair of the retail committee of the chamber of commerce for five years," she said, "and I'd have to say that Wal-Mart has been good for the community, not bad. It's attracted a lot of business."

I remembered something Kirk Lowell had told me when I'd first started looking into the effect Wal-Mart was having on Concordia. "I'd say they've made a big difference here," he had said. "I know some people complain, but my cow, the only thing worse than having a Wal-Mart in your town is having a Wal-Mart in a town twenty miles away."

So I called twenty miles up the road, to Belleville, and got Melinda Pierson, the director of the Belleville Chamber of Commerce, on the phone. She agreed. "It *is* hard on us," she said. "Having a Wal-Mart brings people to your community—and you reap the tax rewards."

Those rewards aren't insignificant, either. In 2004 alone, the Concordia Supercenter put $750,000 of revenue into the city's tax receipts, by local estimates an amount equal to a tax increase of thirty-five mills. City manager Paine ticked off a long list of infrastructure projects—including everything from new streets in an economic-development area that just saw the completion of a $4 million Holiday Inn Express nearby to the demolition of some derelict buildings to make way for a new four-screen movie theater on Sixth Street, next to Rod's grocery—that he said were largely the result of revenue generated by Wal-Mart's taxes.

However, to make it all possible, and to keep Wal-Mart from exploring its other local option of locating that Supercenter near Belleville, where U.S. 81 and U.S. 36 meet, the company had asked for concessions—Brad Lowell, the editor of Concordia's local paper, avoided technical language and called it "blackmail"—and to make those concessions possible, Concordia wanted concessions from the rest of the county. The Supercenter would be built just south of the city limits; its taxes would be used to create the infrastructure the store needed, and a tax district was established to funnel the rest of the revenue derived from Wal-Mart into infrastructure and support for a narrow district with a commercial focus—largely along the highway and along Sixth Street. Supporters of Wal-Mart said the result had been satisfying. Others weren't so sure.

I sat in Lowell's office and discussed the trials and tribulations of Sixth Street. Wal-Mart, he explained, had cost him thousands of dollars in lost advertising; the Supercenter rarely buys space, and it forced out of business the grocers who did. And he wasn't hopeful about Sixth Street's future, either. "I'm not somebody who particularly believes we can save Main Street," Lowell told me. He thought a business coming to Concordia would do better out on the highway ("closer to Wal-Mart") than in the downtown area.

Moving next door is one way to take advantage of Wal-Mart. Another is to stroll through the place and make a list of all the stuff they don't sell, because if they don't sell it, they probably can't—either the margin's wrong or the volume isn't there or some combination of the two. That's what a number of business owners on Concordia's shopping street have done. For instance, Coppoc's, a sports apparel store, sells K-State Wildcat stuff you won't find at Wal-Mart, and the store has had to expand. Sixth Street Fashions, owned by Rod Imhoff's daughter, stocks women's clothing way upmarket from Wal-Mart's stuff, along with interesting jewelry and a nice selection of quality shoes. "She's got good taste," my wife told me one day as she opened the overflow valve on our bank account and poured money all over the store's counter. Meanwhile, Marsha Doyenne, a composer who grew up in Concordia, lived in Australia and Europe, and then returned to be with her parents as they grew older, runs Essentials, a trio of connected storefronts, each a niche business. Together they offer everything from fabrics to health food to formaldehyde-free bath soaps and shampoos.

My favorite Main Street success story involves a family of Mexican entrepreneurs who stopped at the Concordia Supercenter on their way to Nebraska to investigate potential sites for a restaurant. They took a ride down Sixth Street and said, approximately, *¡Ay caramba! No Mexican restaurant!*, then parked the car and opened one. The food's fantastic and authentic and nicely priced. The place so successfully drew patrons from nearby towns that other communities began sending deputations to convince the owners to open restaurants in their towns. So now the family owns restaurants in Beloit, to the west, and Clay Center, farther downriver to the east.

Not all the businesses on Concordia's Sixth Street are new, nor is Wal-Mart their biggest worry. Art Slaughter has run the Daylight Clothing Company in Concordia for fifty years—about two complete tie-width cycles. To him Wal-Mart is just the latest headache.

Of course, Daylight is a rarity for any community—Slaughter called it "a full-service men's shop" and added, correctly, that "you don't see many of those anymore." For Slaughter, competing around Wal-Mart isn't difficult; while some Supercenters sell fifty-dollar jackets in their George line (and twenty-five-dollar trousers that match), the Concordia Wal-Mart sticks with sweats, flannel shirts, jeans, and work clothes. "I've got four hundred suits, one hundred sport coats, seventy-five blazers, and hundreds of shirts in stock," said Slaughter. His biggest problem isn't Wal-Mart; it's the culture. "Casual dress, dress-down Fridays. People just don't dress up anymore."

"The fact that a Wal-Mart exists in your town does not mean diminished competition," Carl Parker, the chairman of the economics and finance department at Kansas's Fort Hays State University, told me. "It could mean increased competition." Parker pointed to the presence of the big-retail steel-cage tag team, Wal-Mart and Home Depot, in Hays, Kansas. "They draw people from all over the area. In small communities, yes, some stores may not be able to continue, but they may have closed anyway." However, other merchants, Parker said, can compete "for years and years" with Wal-Mart. He pointed to his own experience owning an archery shop near a large Supercenter that also sold archery supplies. "I could compete with them on service and on knowledgeability—and I found I could even compete with them on price."

The bigger concern for small-town merchants, he noted, was from competitors using new technology to bring a World Wide Web full of choices to people who live in Tinytowns everywhere. The new competition for Main Street, Parker said, is going to come from the predators in a different corner of the retail jungle: "It's going to come from the Amazon.coms."

If you're a journalist, you can't just call up the local Wal-Mart and ask to chat with the manager. You have to work your way up the ladder, explaining yourself and stating what you want to know and why. Tom Lambing, the manager of the McCook Supercenter, and Roy Reif, Concordia's manager, both refused interview requests until I jumped through the corporate hoop. I don't know what Wal-Mart's worried about, but it ought not to be these guys.

They're friends. They met when they were both working at the Great Bend, Kansas, Wal-Mart. Reif was a newcomer to the business, and Lambing served as his mentor. Today, the two men still maintain a connection that extends far beyond Supercenterdom, and unlike other Wal-Mart managers people in both towns described to me, they both seem to have taken leadership roles in their communities. Lambing, bank president Graff told me, has been a very busy booster for McCook, once arranging for the Kentucky Headhunters to play in the parking lot—and attracting five thousand customers to town in the process.

In Concordia, previous store managers were "not particularly community-oriented," said Roberta Lowery of the Concordia Chamber of Commerce. People might grouse about Wal-Mart, but finding a critic of Reif, now that's work. Lowery ticked off the things that Reif—who is sixty and recently went through bypass surgery—is involved with in the town: "He's in the chamber here; he's on the fireworks committee; he's on the Christmas-lights committee; he's on the hospital board—he's invested his own money in the town, in the movie theater and things like that, and I'm forgetting a few things. I know I am."

Marsha Doyenne, the entrepreneurial composer, added more. "It's not completely the way you normally think of things when you think of a Supercenter manager," she explained. "I've gotten to know him as a result of sitting with him in chamber meetings where we both get frustrated by the pessimists in town." Reif, she said, has been instrumental in helping downtown merchants organize late-opening nights and helping to distribute merchants guides telling Wal-Mart shoppers where to go in Concordia to find the stuff they won't find at Wal-Mart. "They can't sell *everything*," she added, laughing. "I know they've sent customers to me, because they've called. And I've done the same for them."

During the summer of 2006, Reif got a call from Steve Womack, Concordia's Ford dealer. Art Slaughter had a customer in his store who'd just told him that John Wray, an eighty-five-year-old music aficionado and the organizer of the annual Clifton-Vining Music Festival, had decided at the last minute to hang it up. The festival had grown from a small folk gathering fifteen years ago to an event that routinely drew thousands of fans to hear country and folk music performed in the tiny town of Clifton, down Highway 9 from Concordia, on the far side of Clyde. "I don't think we should let this die," Slaughter said. Womack agreed and called Reif, who suggested they take it up with the Concordia Chamber of Commerce.

"We thought it was important to keep it going, to honor John Wray's commitment, and to not miss a year, if we could possibly help it," Lowery recalled. "Trouble is, we only had eight weeks to get it together." Lowery organized a committee with Reif, Womack, Paul Rimovsky, the owner of Tom's Music House, and a dozen others, and they all set to work.

"Roy made a big difference," said Womack. "He showed up and put money [from the Wal-Mart Community Foundation] on the table and provided manpower. He went to all the meetings, sold tickets, and manned a booth at the festival."

"We pulled it off," Lowery said.[3] "Amazing what you can do if you get the right people."

It wasn't the first time Reif had directed funds from Wal-Mart toward the town; the company's community foundation had been tapped to help the Concordia Police Department install an Internet tracking program to help keep tabs on sex offenders and identity thieves. A separate grant had been used by the local community college to seek government help in creating a $1.3 million wind-turbine lab at the campus, adjacent to Wal-Mart. The combination of the wind-turbine project, when it's fully developed, and the local ethanol plant will bring $400 million in investments to Cloud County.

"If Roy Reif retires or Wal-Mart reassigns him, I don't know what we'll do," said Womack.

When I called Reif to talk about all of this, I was given a polite shrug. "I really like this community," Reif said. "This is where I live."

Still, some are certain that Wal-Mart has sins for which it will be held accountable. Muschi Mues, the McCook artist who helps run a co-op gallery on Norris Avenue, had heard all about the benefits of a Supercenter. But she wasn't having it. When it came to doing their part for the community, she said, "They haven't helped at all."

"So where did all this traffic come from?" I asked, gesturing toward the window. Outside, life on the bricks was busily hurrying by.

"The people here work very hard," Mues said. "But Wal-Mart—Wal-Mart is very difficult."

That's living with them. Living without them, that's something else.

Old-Timers and Newcomers

Economically, Concordia is still far from getting over the slump of the mid-1980s. In this beautiful and charming place, situated within striking distance of Kansas City, Wichita, and Omaha, the citizens maintain a lovely park and public pool and have restored their elegant opera house, the magnificent Brown Grand Theatre, opened by Colonel Napoleon Bonaparte Brown in 1907. It was Concordia's second opera house (pieces of the first are still there, on Sixth Street, above a thrift shop) and a regular stop on the vaudeville circuit that ran from Kansas City through Concordia and on to Denver. After the Brown Grand spent a half century as a movie theater, the community restored it to its original condition.[1] That project stimulated support for others. Lately, Concordians have devoted themselves to the creation of a National Orphan Train Museum and a project to restore parts of Camp Concordia, a World War II installation that once housed thousands of German POWs.

That's a lot of civic activity for a little town. As is the case in most small towns, where one person can make a huge difference, that means a lot of work for a small cohort of energetic optimists who immediately become the targets of sometimes volatile bystanders. In Concordia, the same names appear on project after project: Susan Sutton (theater, orphan train museum, community college), Everett Miller (community college, POW camp, theater), Eric Johnson (architectural preservation and community development stuff), and Kirk Lowell, the farmer who has

turned from the uncertainties of agriculture to the even greater uncertainties of midwestern economic boosterism. Sometimes they get it right,
sometimes they don't. At least they give it a try—and either way, they are
carefully watched by others in the community who, I think, would call
themselves realists. These people, in good faith and sometimes for good
reason, think there are reasonable limits to what you can do with a small
farming community and still keep taxes at a reasonable level. The realists
in a community like Concordia (and the hundreds of other places where
pipe dreams often proliferate) play a valuable role, not only in keeping
things simple but in keeping them sensible. Any time you have a small
cadre of dreamers and the easy availability of old buildings, the value of
people willing to work as ballast to keep the whole thing from floating
away can't be overstated. When the realists feel they have been heard by
the optimists, they sometimes turn into supporters. If they don't, they become pessimists and begin to nurture the one fatal cancer to which many
small towns are vulnerable.

Experts like Milan Wall and Genna Hurd point to civic pessimism as a
kind of death sentence for most plains communities. "You can see it when
you pull into a town," my cousin Richard, a community economic-
development manager for the USDA, told me. "It's the worst thing of all."
What's it look like? Chuck Danskin, who gave up his Bay Area corporate
life to join forces with his brother, a chef, and look for opportunity in a
small town in the Midwest, tried to describe what civic failure looked like:
"We would arrive in a town for a meeting or just to look around, and you'd
see weeds growing through the sidewalks, messy vacant lots, run-down
buildings. The people running the community obviously didn't care much
either way if we started a business there or not. Sometimes, they'd just look
at us like we were crazy. We couldn't wait to leave towns like that."

Distinguishing realism from pessimism and then accepting the realism
and fighting the pessimism are critical to a community's survival. As every
small-town resident knows, the polarization of the nation is a genteel debate compared to the viciousness of local politics because so much that is
so close and so personal—your old neighborhood, your old school, your old

life—is at stake. In Concordia, relatively few citizens are registered Democrats. But almost all of them are on one side or another of an economic divide almost as old as the town itself, one that stems from the days when North Siders were working-class stiffs, and South Siders were the snobs who employed them. To this day, the wealthier citizens of Concordia feel much more comfortable spending money on the community than do the rest, who feel local taxes are supremely important. Imagine a *Huffington Post* where every angry maniac skips the blog part and just screams across the street at a person they hate, despise, wish dead because of their opinions on flower boxes or cats. On the spectrum of political passion, compared to this, the red-state/blue-state liberal/conservative conflict is at the sweet end. In Concordia, your location in the north, south, east, or west quadrant often defines your political views far more than the debate about Iraq does. A political reorganization years ago brought an end to ward representation and replaced the familiar city-council-and-mayor arrangement with a council elected citywide and a city manager hired to keep everything running, putting Concordia on the long list of midwestern towns that have adopted the city-manager model of government, adding a tinge of blue to the red model that keeps government in check precisely because you can't hire somebody else to do it for you.

Predictably, this has caused lots of problems in Concordia. Some of the neighborhoods that were part of the old wards lost their council seats, while others gained one or two. Even in a town of fifty-four hundred people, the idea that a person from the other side of the street could possibly represent people on *both* sides of the street was anathema. During my residency in Concordia, one local man, Melvin "Bud" Kennedy, kept finding anonymous accusatory documents mysteriously left on the seat of his pickup. His letters to the editor of the local paper, often based on the stuff left in his truck when he wasn't around, became a kind of alternative chronicle of recent civic events. People who had donated time and effort to various citywide efforts were linked to misdemeanors. Motives were impugned. Crimes were implied. One cynic suggested that maybe a lot of the city's problems would go away if Bud would just keep the door of his truck locked.

I mentioned that idea to him one afternoon, but there was no humor in this for him. He was angry. "I don't like what this town has become," he told me, his face hard. He recited a kind of mental graph, showing declining population and rising taxes. He spoke with the melancholy passion of a guy who prefers his sorrow wrapped in fury; he didn't know why he'd stayed in Concordia as long as he had. He didn't know how things could have gotten so far out of hand. He told me how his wife had died right here in this room, the one in which we stood chatting.

He had been a cabinetmaker for most of his life. His furniture and other objects were prized possessions in half the houses in town, and I couldn't find a soul to say anything bad to me about him; every query was met with a look of concern, not anger. Some of his civic adversaries told me how proud they were to have a piece of Bud Kennedy's work in their homes. When I told him this, he softened for a second—but only for a second. His anger was all one-way, fed by a group of disappointed fellow citizens, altogether numbering maybe four hundred or so. His blood pressure was high; he was often red with anger; people worried about him. I worried about him. One day he got sunstroke. I heard about it on the other side of the world from one of his civic "enemies" who was greatly distressed that Bud was in the hospital.

Oddly, the arrival of Wal-Mart's Supercenter had eased some of the anger he and some of his fellow citizens felt. "I think most people wanted it," he said, adding that he and others felt that making concessions to Wal-Mart should have been something opened to wider community discussion—although he also noted that "it probably wouldn't have made much difference."

Kirk Lowell was one of those whose task in making Concordia attractive for business drew him into conflict with his more dubious neighbors. As head of the economic-development organization, he was charged with bringing business to Concordia and the rest of Cloud County. Therefore, no matter how hard he worked, it was impossible for him to work hard enough. His office downtown was shared with the town's chamber of commerce, so optimism was in the ductwork and in the walls. And it was always busy—especially on Thursday mornings, when the local movers and shakers met for coffee and looked for good news. Lowell was good at finding it, even if he had to go out and wrestle it to the ground.

I stood one afternoon in the lobby of the Majestic, a four-screen cinema that had opened the day before amid much fanfare in a pretty, new build-ing on Sixth Street. Lowell had gone to Topeka and hired one of the big, 800-million-candlepower World War II–era civil defense searchlights from Boyles Joyland. Ty Boyles drove it out and parked it in the middle of the street where Lowell and others had gathered to admire it. "They tell me you can see that beam of light from fifty miles away," Lowell said. "Fifty miles! My cow!"

The cinema was a pure-Lowell piece of work. When the Brown Grand had reverted to being the opera house it was meant to be, a small two-screen moviehouse had opened across the street in a dilapidated set of storefronts. That lasted about twenty years. When it closed, it meant that Concordia's moviegoers had to drive to Beloit, where the community had built a two-screen cinema that was unfailing in its ability to get the best first-run family films, or down to Salina, where there was not only an eight-screen multiplex but a genuine art cinema where every day of the week you could go see obscure films unsuitable for children. That meant Concordians were taking their money to other towns, something Lowell's inner economic-development guy couldn't abide.

So he contacted the region's biggest operator of small-town movie-houses, B&B Theatres, a Lexington, Missouri–based family business that not only runs movie theaters in small towns throughout Kansas, Missouri, and Oklahoma but also provides film distribution and logistical support to tiny community-owned moviehouses, like the one in Beloit. When I was young, in Kansas and Nebraska you'd see movies that had played in New York or Los Angeles months earlier. Now even small moviehouses get first-run films. Lowell tried to convince B&B to give Concordia a look. "At first, we just said no," recalled Bob Bagby, B&B's president. "But Kirk, he just doesn't understand that word."

"Well, I was sort of persistent with them," Lowell had told me earlier when I'd first asked about the new cinema. "My cow, we didn't want everybody leaving town to go to the movies, did we?" Several months before the opening, I had been dubious that the new building would fill the hole on the main drag that the old storefront moviehouse had occupied. I thought of a thousand strip-mall cinemas I had seen and tried to imagine one sitting on Concordia's main street. But Lowell had shown me the architect's sketches that featured a brick-front facade not at all out of place surrounded by small-town architecture, and had explained that local businessmen were putting up half the $1.4 million investment required to launch the new theater and that he had been successful in getting B&B to put up the rest. "Isn't it neat?" he'd asked.

Now, months later, a line of local citizens from Concordia and surrounding towns waited patiently to see *RV* and other cinematic gems. "This is the smallest town we've ever opened in," Bagby told me. "Normally, our smallest town is around twenty thousand—and, well, you know this is a long way from that." He looked across the crowded lobby. "Still, this is a very good opening."

I asked how Lowell had persuaded B&B to make the commitment. "It was the bus," Bagby said. I didn't know what he meant. "Well, we're all sitting there at work when somebody comes in and says, 'There's a bus outside. They want to see you.' It was Kirk and a bus full of businesspeople from Concordia. They had chartered a bus and come out to convince us to put a theater in Concordia."

But across the street and down the block, a number of important buildings on Sixth Street sit empty. One big department store–sized building now houses a community church. Several smaller buildings—including one that had once housed the *Kansan,* a legendary paper from the days when Concordia had three or more papers fighting every day for readers—have been left to deteriorate. A lot of what the dust and the

Depression and ag policies from Washington didn't destroy was done in by the architecture of the 1970s and '80s. Once-beautiful buildings are now sheathed in garish metal grilles to create a pretend modernity that was both ridiculous and unbecoming the moment it went up. The astonishing, ornate Barons House hotel, whose bar is said to have been the inspiration for Garth Brooks's country hit "Friends in Low Places," was demolished not long ago, and so was the town's elegant Victorian county courthouse— replaced by a bland, modern block that screams its architectural statement: "Easy to heat!" Several times the city has suggested demolishing the Victorian bank at the corner of Broadway and Sixth, where a local man, Delmar Harris, used to make playground equipment in the basement, in favor of a parking lot, perhaps as a quick fix to address a claim made by one potential retailer's study that said there weren't enough parking places in downtown Concordia. Some people even worry that the grandest, most extraordinary building of all, the big, brick Victorian motherhouse of the Sisters of St. Joseph—whose nuns are disappearing fast but whose magnificent stained-glass window has enabled Concordia to cling somewhat dubiously to its sobriquet "the Stained Glass Capital of Kansas"—might one day follow suit.

The most common explanation for why so many once-grand minimetros would shrug off their most precious possessions—the old school, the old courthouse, the old everything—is as simple as it is trite: "She was just too far gone." It's probably more accurate to say that, in the end, towns in the Midwest die for the same reason marriages fail and Rome fell: It's just too much trouble and too much money to keep it all together. "This town is gone," Bud Kennedy had told me. "Those people [who invested in the theater], they might as well have thrown their money away." He echoed the sentiments of others who, years before, had dismissed the restoration of the Brown Grand Opera House. "We had people tell us they would never walk through the doors of the place," Everett Miller said.

That's dog stereo, a sound simply inaudible to people like Kirk Lowell or Concordia's city manager, Larry Paine, or the small squadron of civic boosters. In a town like Concordia, it's the city man and the economic-development guy who are paid to ignore pessimism, since to give in to it is to walk into your office and say to yourself, "You're fired!"

I remember once going to New York's Washington Heights to visit the aunt of a college roommate of mine. She lived quietly in an old apartment block. In the hallways, you could smell a million burned dinners, listen to invisible dogs yapping from floor to floor, and hear a dozen TV sets at once. Sitting in her apartment, we were interrupted by a shout and a loud thump on the wall.

"Those people!" she said, irritated but resigned.

"What are they like?" I asked.

"I should know? I've never met them."

You want to know about the culture of small midwestern towns? Start with this: they're the *opposite* of that. The minute a car door closes and a stranger's shoe hits the gravel, the news echoes up and down Main Street, stirring conversation in the local café and down at the grocery.

When I was younger, I used to think the reason for small-towners' attitudes about strangers was nosiness, maybe laced with boredom. But that's not it. In a metropolis, even the most ambitious and dynamic newcomer has close to zero impact on the social and economic ecology of the place. In a small town, where that midwestern sense of scale operates with some precision, the right newcomer—or the wrong one—can change everything.

In tiny Alma, Nebraska, which is a lakefront village sans lake since the Midwest's persistent drought has shrunk the reservoir down to a muddy minimum, a young couple, Joseph and Dusti Torrey, went back to his nearly comatose hometown after college and opened Joe's Camera, a coffeehouse and photo lab with a folk music venue out back. It's a tiny main street in Alma, but the moment you arrive in town you can see that one vibrant business with Republicans selling lattes to other Republicans is all it took to reinvigorate the town's sense of itself. Some towns, of course, may need a little more optimism than others. That $400 million newly invested in Cloud County? None of it was attracted by local pessimists.

Which brings us to Lindsborg, Kansas, an uncommonly pretty town several miles off U.S. 81, south of Salina and an hour north of Wichita. Lindsborg is as far north as Francisco Vásquez de Coronado got in his search for the seven cities of gold in 1542 before giving up and turning around.[2] Three hundred years later, in 1869, a handful of hardworking, stubborn immigrants from Sweden, all of whom had names that started with "Lind," decided to build a town on the spot. Once the streets were laid out, they went into debt to build an "academy"—now called Bethany College.

Home to some three thousand people, Lindsborg calls itself "Little Sweden USA" and not in an ironic sense at all. In fact, it touts its Swedishness aggressively, loudly, and persistently, with lots of crafts and folk dancing and Swedish signs and symbols everywhere. The Swedish pavilion designed by Ferdinand Boberg for the 1904 World's Fair in St. Louis was moved to Lindsborg in bits and pieces for use as an art classroom at the college. In 1976, the king of Sweden, Carl XVI Gustaf, came to Lindsborg to rededicate the building after a renovation. It now sits next to an old flour mill in "Heritage Square." A herd of colorful wooden Swedish Dala horses are scattered on Lindsborg's porches and lawns, while the shops sell clogs and herring. Throughout the year, several Scandinavian festivals with unpronounceable names are held. But the biggest is a biannual Swede-do called Svensk Hyllningsfest held, wisely, in October of every odd year, because if they held it every year, they'd have to spell it every year.

Lindsborg has mostly been lucky in its newcomers. Back in 1894, not long after the college opened, a twenty-three-year-old Swedish artist named Sven Birger Sandzén came across a book written by Bethany's founder, Carl Aaron Swensson, and wrote him asking for a job. Sandzén stayed on in Lindsborg, painting and teaching, for the next sixty years, until his death in 1954, helping create a distinctive local style, heavily influenced by his heavy brushwork and bright palette. Along the way he attracted other artists to the town, including such relative luminaries as Lester Raymer, Robert Walker, and Louis Hafermehl, which lent Lindsborg a creative identity unique to this part of the plains.[3]

With all the Swedish stuff, the college, the town's artistic heritage, and the healthy flow of curious tourists, Lindsborg fared better than many other towns during the most recent economic downturn. Still, times being what they were, it was more than ready for an economic and cultural booster shot. Local factions had formed around the usual small-town issues, like development of the main street, and Lindsborg's civic equanimity was increasingly found under a sullen, passive-aggressive cloud.

Enter quiet and unassuming Irwin "Wes" Fisk, a dapper chap with a white goatee. Fisk had left his hometown of Byers—an even smaller village some ninety miles southwest of Lindsborg—the day after graduating from the local high school in 1956. In 1997, after a forty-year career as a private eye in Los Angeles, he returned to Kansas, settling in Lindsborg with his wife, Susie. "We didn't really have a connection here," he told me. "It just seemed like a nice town." They moved into an old house once used by the president of the college and started fixing it up. Their arrival would eventually have at least as much of an effect on Lindsborg as a dozen Swedish painters.

As it happened, Fisk enjoyed two things in his retirement: chess and writing about chess, usually for *Chess Life* magazine. So, perhaps as much to give himself something to write about as anything else, Fisk organized the Lindsborg Chess Club. "I enjoy the game, and I thought it might be good for the kids in town, too," he said. Over the next year or so, Fisk attracted a few dozen members and even staged a few local tournaments. By 1999, the club had sought and been granted U.S. Chess Federation recognition, unusual for a club so small and so remote.

Enter a second newcomer: a Russian émigré from Voronezh named Mikhail Korenman, hired by the college to teach chemistry. As it happened, Korenman had once had ambitions to become a great chess master, so inevitably he wandered into Fisk's club and said hello in that fune-real way Russians have. The two men became fast friends; the *Kansas City Star* would later term the meeting a "harmonic convergence."[4]

"I liked him from the very start," Fisk recalled. "He wanted to make [the club] grow and he wanted to promote chess, and I thought that was fine because I just wanted to play chess." So while Fisk happily stayed in Lindsborg and ran the club, Korenman started traveling around the United States and, while playing in tournaments, drumming up a little in-terest in Lindsborg and its tiny chess club. Eventually, Korenman met a young Belorussian grandmaster named Yury Shulman and convinced him to help organize a summer chess camp for kids in Lindsborg. Twenty kids showed up. Fisk was flabbergasted but happy to have them.

"Lindsborg is a small town," Shulman told me, "so I was surprised there could be a camp. That was the first step. I didn't think there would be a second step. But Wes Fisk, he's brilliant. He's the one who started everything."

Fisk and Korenman decided that the second step should be a grandmaster-level tournament in Lindsborg—a scheme roughly equiva-lent to holding the U.S. Open at the local pitch and putt. Bringing a bunch of chess masters to a small farming community in the heartland is an expensive proposition, and the Lindsborg Chess Club wasn't exactly rolling in dough. So Fisk and Korenman started going around Lindsborg door to door, asking people to contribute—ten dollars, twenty, whatever they could afford.

Fisk is a charming, slightly debonair character, so I could imagine him knocking on the doors of depressed Swedes and asking for support for the local chess club. But Korenman? For starters, Korenman wears his melancholy like body art. I tried to put together an image of a big, sad Russian guy on the front porch saying, "You give money to me for chess" in that cheerful way of his. I couldn't do it. Yet here he was. There must be an explanation. "Is the town a big chess-playing commu-nity?" I asked.

He looked at me as if I were mad, then looked over his shoulder, apparently at the floor. "No, *no*. No. They know *nothing* about chess."

Still, every good idea deserves a go, so the local businesses and the college chipped right in. So did a group of town boosters called the Dala Wranglers, along with the local Rotary. When things looked like they might grind to a halt, Kathy Malm, at the time the chamber of commerce director, took to the phone and started cold-calling for donations. A chess tournament. Why not?

"Not that I know much about chess," Malm told me. "I just thought, Oh, it'll be like a little basketball tournament."

But it kept getting bigger, the plans more ambitious. With Fisk's support, the Russian chess master and the chamber of commerce lady soon found themselves trying to one-up each other. "[Korenman] would walk in and say, 'Get me a thousand dollars,' and I'd try to do it," Malm recalled. "Then I would say to him, 'Misha, get me the best chess player in Sweden'—and he would do it." In the middle of all of this, 9/11 happened. They pressed on.

By the time the first Lindsborg Rotary Open kicked off, on December 22, 2001, some three months after the terror attacks on New York and Washington, seventy-five of the world's top players had descended on the town, including a number of mercurial, temperamental chess grandmasters.

To most people, that little basketball tournament would have made a lot more sense, but the town was nothing if not game. So the chamber kept the books and helped with press relations and registration. When it turned out there wasn't enough restaurant capacity to feed the participants, the townspeople made casseroles and salads and delivered the food to the players. Of course, international chess masters tend to be a finicky lot; they insisted on lots of fresh fruit and dark chocolate—never mind that this was Kansas and it was late December. "It couldn't be milk chocolate, which is what we had," said Scott Achenbach, who runs Scott's Thriftway, the town's grocery. "It had to be *dark* chocolate. They seemed to think it had some mental enriching—well, I don't know, it was new to me. So okay, I got hold of some Hershey's dark chocolate."

The thing proved a big success. The Associated Press, trying in vain to convey a sense of scale and perspective, called it "the Super Bowl of Kansas chess." The wire service was so excited it forgot to report who won.[5]

But, as the AP and Lindsborg would soon discover, the Super Bowl of Kansas chess was nothing. As Malm put it, "Really, we didn't know how big it could be until the *next* year."

Far from Lindsborg, Anatoly Karpov, seven-time world champ and one of the game's most enterprising grandmasters, was casting about for a place to stay while warming up for a match against his arch-nemesis, Garry Kasparov, a man he hadn't beaten for twelve years. Korenman thought Lindsborg would be an ideal spot, so he called one of the grandmasters who had enjoyed his stay in Lindsborg, Ukraine's Alexander Onischuk. Korenman: "I told [Onischuk], 'Remember, Lindsborg was a good town for chess and maybe Karpov would like to come to see it.' He said, 'We'll see. I will call him.' And he did and Karpov said, 'Sure. Why not?' "

Korenman clearly enjoyed telling the story; he nearly smiled. He seemed to relish the fact that Karpov was willing to come to Lindsborg, sight unseen—probably something most New Yorkers, for example, would never consider doing. Karpov, Onischuk, and a Chilean grandmaster named Iván Morović-Fernández spent ten days preparing for the match. As the *Kansas City Star* reported, when Karpov finally defeated Kasparov in New York and journalists asked him "how he had prepared, Karpov told them he'd gone to Kansas. . . . The media roared with laughter. They thought the Russian champion was joking. But the joke was on them."[6]

As Malm told me, "When we got Karpov, that's when we thought, Hey, this could be big."

And how. Karpov, who runs thirty chess schools in fifteen countries in Europe and the Middle East, so loved the place that he decided to launch his first American chess school in an old storefront on Lindsborg's Main Street. Korenman promptly asked the Kansas Department of Commerce and Housing for $261,000 "to develop chess"—and, as he says, "They gave it to me."

In 2004, the U.S. Chess Federation made Lindsborg its "Chess City of the Year," putting the town on a list with places like New York and Seattle. That year, Korenman organized a six-game "Clash of the Titans" in Lindsborg between Karpov and four-time women's world champion Susan Polgar, a Hungarian and the first woman to ever win a men's grandmaster rating. Lindsborg was on the global chess map. Where once Lindsborg had been all about wheat and Lutherans, it was now about wheat, Lutherans, and fianchettoed bishops.

Just a few weeks before his next big chess event, Korenman and I sat face-to-face next to a chess set in a converted storefront in Lindsborg, the one with the big sign out front reading, "World Champion Anatoly Karpov International School of Chess." Surrounded by oversized chess pieces used for displays, Korenman, in a T-shirt, trousers, and flip-flops, looked exhausted. He summarily dealt with two women who were in charge of tickets for the upcoming event, then joined me with a huge sigh of resignation.

I thought maybe I could stir Korenman by giving him a little flag to wave, so I asked him if this was an American success story. I had been struck by the easy opportunity Korenman had found in a Kansas farming town, the townspeople's unquestioned support and all that, and I thought he would be struck by it, too. I tried to get the "Kansas has been berry berry good to me" line, but it was tough. I asked my question, but he just stared. So I tried again: "I mean, what if an American kid went to some small Siberian village and set up a baseball camp. Could you imagine—"

"Oh yeah. Russia is no problem because *everybody* there likes chess."

No, but . . . okay, so what about a bigger American city like, say, Chicago? Word around town was that Korenman would soon decamp to Chicago to join his wife, who had found a teaching job at a university there. "How would you have done if you tried to set up something like this there?"

"Well, now I can do anything because of my portfolio," he answered, referring to his success arranging tournaments in Lindsborg. "So they will listen to me." He smiled, sort of, for the first time in our interview.

But what about Lindsborg? He sighed, then reached down deep for a drop of charity: "It's a very nice town." As for the school after he leaves, "Wes Fisk or somebody will take care of it," he said.

Korenman kept stifling yawns; he's done this interview so many times, he could do it in his sleep, and he nearly did. In his mind, he was already in Chicago, maybe doing lots of TV. He certainly wasn't in Lindsborg talking to me. He was bored, and it was highly contagious. But at least he was talking about himself. I was talking about *him and chess*. I asked him if he ever played checkers. He didn't answer, so I said so long and left. He didn't appear to notice.

Later, I asked Fisk if I'd seen Korenman in full flower, as it were. "He's just exhausted now, after all of this," Fisk said. "He's just got his wife settled in Chicago. And this other thing—it's *horrendous*."

A few weeks later, I was standing next to Jim Richardson, the *National Geographic* photographer who shares a gallery on Lindsborg's Main Street with his jewelry-designing wife, Kathy. We were watching a parade the town was holding to celebrate yet another Frisk-Korenman chess event, this one the biggest yet, with Karpov and Polgar and others. The theme was "Chess for Peace." That seemed like a great trade. I was all for that, and so was everybody else: The chess titans and Jay Emler, the local state senator, passed by in old cars, waving, followed by a few informal, chess-related floats; there were large contingents of kids from local chess clubs in team T-shirts. The middle school band, its members dressed like turn-of-the-century Swedish farmworkers, preceded the Smoky Valley High School marching band, dressed like the Blues Brothers in black suits and shades. Lots of people were strolling on the sidewalk parallel to the parade, doing what *all* red-staters do: smiling, nodding, and saying hello to everyone they passed.

Suddenly I realized that one of the passersby, heading right for me and surrounded by a small cluster of guys who were dressed exactly like the members of the high school band, was Mikhail Gorbachev.

"Hello," said Gorbachev, nodding pleasantly, smiling.

"Hi there," I replied, nodding back, staring at the famous birthmark on his forehead. Richardson's smile widened. Gorbachev kept on walking, saying hello, hello, hello, as people, startled, smiled back and returned the greeting.

I followed along to the town's big main intersection. I had been there before to watch Kansans dressed in Swedish costumes do Scandinavian folk dances. Today, a spindly reviewing stand had been set up. On it: Gorbachev in the center, his ubiquitous translator—the prissy-looking fellow with the bald head and little mustache—next to him. Just behind him and off to either side were Korenman, Gorbachev's daughter, some other Slavs, and Polgar.

If you're over the age of, say, thirty-five, and you see Mikhail Gorbachev and a bunch of serious sidekicks on a reviewing stand, the rest of the mental image has to include missiles on trucks, lots of tanks, and the Red Army goose-stepping through Red Square. Not this time. Gorbachev stood there passively surveying the massed forces of Lindsborg's middle school and high school bands, tons of kids from Kansas chess clubs, and a float that was originally a wheat-wrapped *julbok,* a traditional Swedish Christmas goat, but, having often fallen victim to pyromaniacal kids, now looked like a wad of mesh fencing. It was regularly a part of local celebrations. "It's kind of a joke—something about being burned out," Fisk said. Those crazy Swedes.

Gorbachev, through his translator, explained how he'd ended the Cold War. A few spectators exchanged that who's-he-kidding look, but most just smiled, applauded, and took pictures with their cell phones. It did seem like the wrong time and place to quibble about the last century's details. The kids in the chess clubs—from towns across Kansas and some from faraway Nebraska—all waved happily.

At a speech that evening in Bethany College's auditorium, Gorbachev delivered a mildly leftish rebuke to Bush and retold the story of the attempted coup in 1991. Someplace along the line, his appearance had fallen under the patronage of former Kansas senator Nancy Kassebaum. Kassebaum, in turn, had invited her friend Alan Murray, from the *Wall Street Journal,* to emcee the speech, something he did gratis. The conceit was that Murray would move a chess piece while asking Gorbachev a penetrating question. Murray instantly admitted he knew nothing about chess. Gorbachev agreed with that, then answered a few mild questions about Reagan, whom he seemed to admire; about the conflict in Iraq, of which he did not approve; and about America's national debt: The country, he said, was not only in debt to other nations but also "to the future." Then he told the story of the failed Russian coup for what must have been the millionth time. At the end, Murray thanked Gorbachev and the president of Bethany College, along with some other dignitaries, including some of the chess masters who had shown up.[7]

Finally, as we all began to file out, I spied Fisk and his wife, Susie, about halfway back in the auditorium. They stood, smiled at each other, and walked out hand in hand and into the night, unnoticed by almost everyone else.

Later that night, when the streets were finally quiet and empty, Gorbachev slipped into the town's bar with his daughter, translator, and security detail, sans journalists. The barroom regulars gave him a cheer and a table. The next day, the owner, Mark Lysell, told a local journalist how he'd exchanged vodka jokes with the security guys while Gorbachev sat around signing autographs and drinking Absolut and cranberry juice, just another new guy in town.

Transcript 4:
Superior People

Stan: I think the depiction of the red and blue states is a newspeople thing. It's a shorthand way for them to tell a story, and it doesn't do justice to anyone on either side. We're just as varied here as they are on the East Coast or the West Coast.

Pat: But, frankly, I don't think we pay all that much attention to how the national media looks at us. Around here, in the great American desert, what's going on elsewhere tends not to impact on us all that greatly—or we on it. What we do focus on is what's in front of us for the day. I'd say we listen a lot more closely to our local radio station.

Rich: That's true. When you're raised on a farm, the biggest thing that happens is the weather. You hear that and you hear the biggest news of the day.

Pat: And for us, the commodity report is the stock market news. Because if the farmers aren't happy, no one is. As a grocery store owner, my feast or famine goes right along with those reports.

Stan: Still, as far as the outside world is concerned, I'd say probably ninety percent of us out here get our information from the evening news. I don't read the newspaper from cover to cover, like my dad did, or even our local paper—forgive me, Bill.

Rich *(laughing)*: You're the only one that doesn't, Stan.

Stan: But, at the same time, I have a terrible time trying to get accurate news out of the TV set. The news media is more slanted today than

ever. Fox gets way out one way, and the rest of 'em get way out the
other way, and you really can't believe anything. . . . Edward R.
Murrow would never broadcast the way they do now.

Bill: He didn't embellish it.

Stan: Or talk down on one part of our country and up on another. You see
reports on the Midwest, and it's the typical eastern attitude. That this
is a hotbed of ignorance and backwardness. A lot of people come out
here from the East and are surprised to find it's a pretty nice place.
The people are friendly, and they're not so dumb, after all.

Bill: One time Dan Rather's newspeople came to Superior to interview
me about a newsletter we produce for rural single people. Of
course I'm wearing a nice blue shirt and necktie for the interview.
But they find a dirty pair of coveralls, covered with ink, and they
tell me to dress in those. I say, "Those are there to wash the press
with; I certainly wouldn't wear them to meet someone." But I did
what they wanted, and they interviewed me in those filthy
coveralls. Not that I'm complaining—they made us lots of money.
You couldn't buy that kind of advertising.

But then they go out to Lakeside, Nebraska, to talk to a rancher
for the story, and like a lot of ranchers he's got a dog that rides in
the pickup with him. Well, he has an old, greasy coat on the floor
of the pickup for the dog, and they make *him* put the old coat on.
No clue—they just had these preconceived ideas of how we were
going to look, because [they] came to the Midwest to interview
these farm folks.

Stan: It's true, there's really just not all that much interest in getting to
know about people out here.

Rich: No—they've got all the wisdom back there. In the winter, when
they go to Colorado to ski, they like to fly to avoid snowstorms on
the interstate, and in the summertime the roads are clear, but it's
four hundred and ninety miles across, which is the equivalent of
three or four eastern states, and it's hot and boring. And that's
pretty much what they think about Nebraska.

The News from Brahmasthan

The ingredients label on a can of worms:

IMPORTANT NOTICE 911 CALLS

Statements by Jack Krier concerning dispatching, supported by Alan Shelton's comments, and printed in the March 16th edition of the *Smith County Pioneer* are ABSOLUTELY FALSE!

The sheriff's department will continue to dispatch all emergency 911 calls. Jack Krier's statement that we will not, is a total fabrication. Furthermore, I would advise all readers of the *Smith County Pioneer* that they should not believe any statements by Jack Krier regarding the Smith County Sheriff's Department.

Anything important about this department, which is printed in the *Smith County Pioneer,* should be checked out by calling us . . . and talking to Sheriff Murphy or Under Sheriff Tonya White.

I cannot control unethical and irresponsible reporters like Jack Krier, therefore, I ask you to please call us for the TRUTH.

Sheriff E. L. Murphy
Smith County Sheriff's Department

That ad ran in a Kansas auction tabloid, and it worked at least once. I called Sheriff E. L. Murphy for the TRUTH; unfortunately, he wasn't there, and my call was never RETURNED. But I eventually did get to talk to Tonya White, the undersheriff, who discussed in broad and careful terms the local paper and Sheriff Ellsworth L. Murphy's feeling that it had been inattentive to the facts.

After a few more calls and a couple of trips to Smith Center, I got the rest of the can open, and what a mess it was:

- You had your rumors of a misbehaving family. I wondered if the rumors involved, say, drugs. I asked *Pioneer* reporter Linda Baetz. "I wouldn't want to say *that*," she told me. "There was never an arrest or anything. Let's just say they were a pretty wild bunch."

- You had a police chief some claimed was far too sympathetic to the aforementioned family, maybe because they were her brothers.

- Kansas has all those pointless layers of government, so not only is there a Smith Center police department, there's also the Smith County Sheriff's Department, run, at the time, by a very crusty county sheriff—that would be Ellsworth L. Murphy, who had been elected to the post in 1989. He was suspicious of the police chief—not because of her family problems, apparently, but because he thought she might be plotting against him. So he did a little unofficial electronic surveillance, got caught, and in 1991 he got the boot.

- As his eventual successor, you had a twenty-three-year-old hometown boy, a high school football hero, mentored by his fifty-year-old deputy, both of whom alleged death threats because of the presence of an overwhelming drug problem. They both resigned after a few months in office and fled the area.

- That brought Ellsworth L. Murphy back to power after fourteen years, irritating the attorney shared by Smith County and

Smith Center, who said he just couldn't work with the sheriff, and who also said, approximately, "Drug problem? What drug problem?"

- Opponents claimed Murphy wouldn't answer 911 calls. The sheriff denied the claim, and the attorney denied saying that he just can't work with the sheriff.
- The county split into two factions. When I started poking around, people told me they were afraid to leave their houses. One frightened man said he thought he was being poisoned.
- A recall effort was mounted.
- The recall was successful. On May 23, 2006, Murphy lost 1027 to 272. So he sued the county for withheld wages and emotional damages. "The judge gave him the back wages," Baetz said. "But that was it."

Most of it's right here in black and white in the *Smith County Pioneer,* along with many other equally rich stories, both local and regional, of scandal, intrigue, property tax hikes, and interesting settlers.[1] There are eighteen hundred stories in this not-so-naked city, and that's more than enough for the pages of the Smith Center *Pioneer.*

The odd assortment of local residents and the dark peculiarities of Smith Center's headaches aside, the local press plays a different role out here than it does back there. In places like New York and Boston, nobody actually needs a newspaper to get the news of the day. Imagine not knowing about 9/11 until the morning of 9/12. In fact, there's so much news so much of the time that in big cities, the role of a newspaper has changed. Where once newspapers actually served up a daily menu of events from next door and around the world, now, because TV and the Internet make that news available instantly, blue-state newspapers exist largely to create what marketing types might call a "community of shared assumptions"—not only an attractive cohort for advertisers but also, and especially, a tool for helping people find reassurance for their (often liberal) hopes, dreams, and instincts.

The mainstream media is one thing. Main Street Media is another, and its owner is walking down the sidewalk in Smith Center, straight toward me, just back from taking snaps at the local track meet. Jack Krier is the extremely plainspoken sixty-five-year-old owner of the *Pioneer* and fifteen other small-town weekly papers in Nebraska and Kansas, all part of his Main Street Media, Inc., empire. Krier is a fairly familiar face in all of those towns, where local residents working as reporters, stringers, and editors turn out the weekly chronicle of church suppers, Scout troop fund-raisers, fairs and farm auctions, obituaries and marriages, all the business of the local cops and kooks. If you want to see a paper of record, forget the *New York Times*. For most of the planet, Google is the record keeper anyway. But if you're local to out here, you need the *Belleville Tele-scope* or the *Red Cloud Chief* or one of the dozens of other small, weekly papers serving a deeply interested readership. The *Times* may exist to val-idate the worldview of its readers, but the only assumption a small-town weekly must validate is that the world needs a cheaper can of peaches, which is why they're on sale at the local IGA.

Many newspaper editors out here are keenly aware of their proper limitations. "I was once at a [newspaper industry] meeting and a man said, 'Our job is to lead so change can occur,'" *Southwest Times* owner Earl Watt told me. "That is completely wrong. Our job is to reflect our community. We do that. We keep opinion off the front page, but our edi-torials tend to be conservative, just like our community"—which, ironi-cally, in his case is a town called Liberal, Kansas. "We don't think people like being preached to by their paper." The rule of thumb, according to Watt: Big-city papers try to create change by attempting to lead opinion. Smaller newspapers simply offer the facts and by so doing create a possi-bility for change "when people feel it's necessary."

For an outsider used to seeing every issue through the conservative-liberal prism, it's hard to make the adjustment. For example, in Smith Center, a local party official told me he blamed some of the town's prob-lems on his political opposites, but when I asked Krier if the usual liberal-conservative split played a role in the sheriff controversy, he just looked at me pitifully, shrugged, and said, "Probably not."

Weekly newspaper editors here have almost no professional interest in the big national debates. They know that if people want to know what Teddy Kennedy or John McCain is up to, they'll turn on a radio or computer and find out; virtually the entire Midwest has access to broadband.

When two rural school districts were debating a consolidation of their schools, I found myself the recipient of a very intelligent, perceptive commentary by a local newspaper editor whose views on the downside of the merger were, I felt, more than apt.

"So will you run this in the paper?" I asked.

"No," he said. And then explained why: The *New York Times* can alienate half the nation if the guy who runs it wants to. That's a huge company, he said. "But if I do something like that, it's *serious*. I'm out of business tomorrow."

So the editor of a newspaper with a circulation of less than five thousand in a shrinking market is in the same boat as the owner of the *Times*, but it's a much smaller boat in a much rougher sea. As a result, weekly newspaper editors are usually very careful practitioners of old-fashioned, nonpartisan journalism. They know that it's hard enough to keep people happy by just reporting facts and events; picking sides in a local dustup is practically suicidal. Krier told me he never shies away from local controversies. Maybe so, but the *Smith County Pioneer* got away with it in the Murphy case simply because Murphy's unpopularity was obviously widespread. When I asked Krier if Sheriff Murphy's ad had hurt him, Krier said, "No. It helps me. In some other towns [in which that auction tabloid also circulates], people may say, 'What's he up to?' But here, no. I think it helps us."

Tonya White told me I was the only caller she knew of who had responded to the ad. Besides, the things that get people riled up at Krier have more to do with his style than his substance. "He'll just about say anything," noted my cousin Gloria, who edits the *Jewell County Record*, published in the county just to the right of Smith Center. "Did you know he actually made a *blonde joke* in that paper of his?" She shook her blond head in disbelief.

Krier is a conservative—"the other side of Attila the Hun," is how Linda Mowery-Denning, the liberal editor of the Ellsworth, Kansas, *Independent/Reporter,* describes him—as are most of his readers, and his entire career has been spent in small-town newspapers. Small towns are mostly conservative places with a big appetite for local news, and in towns with populations barely numbering in the thousands, local news is so personal it often reads like blind-sourced gossip, except you know all the sources.

Every now and then, somebody will move into a small town and either start or take over a local weekly and run it with the lights on, clearly illuminating his own ideological obsession. If you're a conservative Republican, nobody notices. If you're something else, as some weekly newspaper editors certainly are, it's better if you keep it to yourself. A left-wing firebrand married to an abortion doctor, for example, didn't, and apparently ran the venerable *Frankfort Index* out of business before moving on to tiny Nortonville to do a pamphlet-and-blog publication called *Fightin' Cock Flyer,*[2] in which he does battle with the town's mayor, railing about "Career War Whores" and so on.

The Frankfort example is a rare one. Certainly there are liberals in Kansas and Nebraska running small community newspapers. Either through professional diligence or because local issues don't really conform to those broad classifications, the national politics of a weekly newspaper editor just don't matter. As conservative as other editors think he is, Krier gladly gives state senator Janis Lee, a liberal Democrat, a half page in his paper to explain, unedited, whatever she needs to explain to convince her constituents that she's (a) not a Democrat and (b) not liberal. For Krier, it's free copy; just paste and go. For Lee, it's a never-ending stream of kindly press clips. Win-win, unless you count readers.

Newspaper editors out here will expound at length on the difference between a daily paper, with the mayfly-like life span of each issue, and a weekly paper, which has a much longer life cycle. "Weekly papers get read more carefully," the *Superior Express*'s Bill Blauvelt told me. "You don't feel like you have to throw them out the next day the way you do when you get a new paper every day." Advertisers are drawn to the flexibility a daily offers, but they like the exposure they get from a weekly.

From an editor's point of view, it's hard to separate sensibility from sense: Although the amount of local news carried in the *Concordia Blade-Empire* would just about fill a typical weekly, the paper's a daily and that's not likely to change anytime soon. "I've never really given any serious thought to going weekly," second-generation editor-owner Brad Lowell told me. "Oh, there have been tough days, but I never really seriously thought about it." His main motivation for remaining a daily, even as larger regional dailies close in on him? "I think it gives a town a kind of importance to have a daily paper."

But as Kansas and Nebraska papers get larger, they tend to become more like big-city papers elsewhere in blue-state America. This has interesting consequences. For example, the front page of many small dailies is heavily reliant on AP content that reflects what the AP always reflects—blue-state values with a tin ear for the interests of red-state readers. It's news readers can get anywhere.

The bigger these papers grow, say critics, the less adept they become at understanding the point of view of most of their small-town readers. In Kansas, for example, the Harris newspaper chain operates regional dailies in Hays, Salina, Garden City, Hutchinson, and some of the state's other market centers. Like the *Wichita Eagle,* the *Lawrence Journal-World,* and the *Kansas City Star,* the state's larger papers, the Harris papers reflect the sort of view that would be very comfortable to voters in Manhattan or San Francisco, where the stereotypes of midwesterners are deeply embedded in the journalistic culture.

Understandably, some editors at regional dailies dispute this. As the *Wichita Eagle*'s opinion page editor, Phillip Brownlee, told me in an e-mail, "I get more complaints from liberals about the *Eagle* being biased against them than I do from conservatives."

Maybe it's the state's political acoustics. In Topeka, one statehouse reporter told me not to be fooled by the conservatives into thinking they are a majority. "They're just very loud," he said.

Brownlee maintained that while "Kansas has many social conservatives who are politically active and vocal—particularly about abortion—
polls and election results show that most Kansans are more or less in the
middle." Echoing that commendatory *New York Times* editorial, Brownlee
added, "That's why conservatives lost all the statewide races in Kansas
last election and why the officeholders with the highest public approval
ratings are moderates, whether Republican or Democrat."

If conservatives are angry at the media, the feeling's mutual. When I
attended a special session of the Kansas state legislature in 2005, I often
heard journalists join Democrats in routinely calling conservatives ob-
scene names. (I sadly must report that the conservative legislators were
far less imaginative in their language—probably all that right-wing Christian miasma.) One statehouse journalist did the whole elitist riff for me,
telling me that the conservatives in the Kansas house were pitchfork-
toting, overalls-wearing, clod-busting, sh*t-kicking hicks. He even did a
little dance. "F——ing assholes" seemed to be a common sobriquet.

Even so, there are some very good reporters working in Kansas and
Nebraska. Those with the predictable media limp do their best, and their
biases are usually unconscious ones. Their editors, however, sometimes
add credence to conservatives' accusations by awkwardly trying to spin
even their own news.

For example, a story to which we'll return in a subsequent chapter or
two: When a few students in Salina and Dodge City sued the state in an
effort to squeeze hundreds of millions of dollars more from taxpayers—
despite the fact that education was already the biggest-ticket item on the
state budget, and despite the fact that Kansas kids already routinely
scored in the top ten in the nation—the *Salina Journal* dispatched Duane
Schrag, a very accomplished journalist, to see how badly the children in
whose name the lawsuit was filed were actually doing. "When the *Salina
Journal* contacted several parents and students who were named as plaintiffs," Schrag wrote, "virtually all conceded their own children did well in
school." He found they were doing great, playing sports, going off to col-

lege, getting scholarships, all that. He quoted parents saying that the only reason they were involved in the lawsuit was because the local school administrators had asked them to play the victim's role.[3] He also discovered that the amount of money the state was being told by the court to pay was millions of dollars more than what the study said was required. Schrag had been an editor of one of the Harris chain's papers and he knew his stuff—but the paper's editor, a staunch advocate of more spending, also ran an editorial suggesting that readers should be careful not to be misled by what they read in the paper. "On the surface," he wrote, "it appears the findings [in Schrag's reporting] undermine the basis of the lawsuit. But look a bit deeper and the facts start to show themselves."[4]

Of course the only place to "look a bit deeper" was in the newspaper itself. And the deeper you looked, the crazier it all got. Hundreds of millions of dollars were at stake, and Shrag's reporting seemed to reveal little in the way of plausibility for the argument that kids in Kansas were being cheated by the state's taxpayers.

"Alan Rupe, one of the lawyers representing the plaintiffs in the case, said the fact that some of the plaintiffs had good grades isn't the issue," Schrag reported. "In fact, efforts were made to keep academic information private. 'We made sure these kids, who are representative of the kids in Kansas, weren't held up to any kind of public scrutiny,' Rupe said." Wrote Schrag:

Indeed, when Attorney General Phill Kline's office released a statement noting that some of the plaintiffs were good students, Rupe sent him a copy of the court order making school records in the case confidential and reminded him the subject was off-limits.

The plaintiffs in the case are not supposed to represent just the districts' failures, Rupe said, but rather represent all their students.

"The fact is, you do have kids who are doing well," Rupe said.

But he maintains that isn't proof those students are getting a suitable education.

The growing suspicion—seen only dimly on the eve of a 2005 special session convened to resolve the education funding issue—was that there had to be something other than a concern for reading and writing afoot. To state senator Jim Barnett and others, increasing the size of government may have been a part of it, but "gambling was the imperative," as he told me later. It wouldn't take long to see how right he was, not that you'd have discovered it by reading the *Salina Journal*.

There seems to be very little centrist about the *Salina Journal's* editorial pages. They usually feature a cartoon by Toles—the *Washington Post* caricaturist who favors hospital-bed metaphors using amputee soldiers as fodder for Bush bashing—along with a daily dose of Doonesbury. Until recently, fiery conservative Ann Coulter made a weekly appearance. But the Coulter column was dropped. Why? Her "cruelty" to "Cindy Shahan" [*sic*]. Coulter "crossed the line," the paper said, with her "vicious personal attacks." The paper's editor wrote that he had been an eyewitness to the crime himself. It happened when he saw, with his own eyes, Matt Lauer read a couple of paragraphs from Coulter's book aloud on the *Today* show.

On the front page of the *Journal* are huge editorializing headlines, like the one reading "Solidarity" above a bunch of flag-waving Mexican demonstrators demanding rights for illegal immigrants. Some of these "journalistic" techniques mystify many readers, while others, like the headline concerning a scandal above a photo of Sam Brownback—who wasn't mentioned in the article and had nothing to do with the story—are just bizarre. The paper's editor, like his colleagues on other Harris papers, writes with the shrill artlessness of those who fear that they are not being read at all. In fact, the paper's numbers are slowly sinking, even while Salina's population is growing.

To boost its circulation figures, the *Journal* is now doing what the *Wichita Eagle* and the *Kansas City Star* have tried to do before: widen its readership area to take in small towns like Mankato, a hundred miles from Salina. The result: well-designed newspapers that might as well be from Mars—or Los Angeles—delivering ads to readers too far away to care. "I avoid it," my laconic cousin Marvin told me.

Joe Capolino, an editor-reporter for the tiny *Erie Record*, in Neosho County, can't avoid it. His town of around twelve hundred is sandwiched between two Harris papers, those in Chanute and Parsons. "Our competition is friendly but real. We cover local people, local stories, local stuff better. They aren't really able to compete on that." While Salina's population slowly inches up, Erie's keeps getting itself buried. "Our main problem is attrition by death."

Krier agreed that the big regionals in Kansas and Nebraska are producing a different product than the local weeklies. The Harris papers "really can't compete with us," he told me. "We're not like the big dailies around here, like the one in Hays [the *Hays Daily News*]. People look to us for one thing: good coverage of local news, which they can't get anyplace else."

Krier is right. Local news is the one commodity a small-town newspaper still has locked up; during the last few years, a great deal of effort and money has been spent wiring Kansas and Nebraska for Internet access and even the smallest town has a cable system. As a result, state, regional, national, and international news is ubiquitous. Buying a day-old version of news you already know in a paper published in a town fifty or a hundred miles away makes no sense for many people, apparently, or the daily newspaper business would be doing better than it is. Papers like the *Salina Journal*, Krier said, are "dropping in circulation, dropping in advertising." In fact, for a growing number of people, it makes no sense to buy the local daily if you live in a town big enough to have alternative news sources, like a TV station, that provide more immediate reporting.

So even the editors of small-town dailies, like Allen County's *Iola Register*, have to remind themselves to keep their eye on the local ball games. "For so many readers, we are their only paper," Susan Lynn, the *Register*'s editor, told me. "I subscribe to the *L.A. Times* and *Washington Post* wire service, and I can hardly use it. My readers want to know what's happening in Allen County, so even though I personally like reading those, I'll probably drop them as soon as the contract is up. I never use them."

Everywhere I went, whether it was to small towns like Smith Center or to larger communities like Concordia, the phrase "doesn't connect with readers" was the one local editors applied to the big regional dailies. The *Salina Journal* "will do a story here and then nothing for ten days or two weeks," said Lowell, referring to the paper's coverage of Concordia. "It's just to show they've been here. That doesn't have much effect on us." The irrelevance of the big regional dailies is a judgment not limited to small-town editors, either.

"There *is* no statewide paper," said Dale Goter, a former Harris paper editor and reporter but now the public affairs editor at KPTS, Wichita's PBS outlet. "The *Star* and the *Eagle* both competed for that, then withdrew." And, Goter added, despite the fears of some conservatives—and the hopes of many liberals—"there isn't an issue here where the press has changed *anybody's* mind. Look at the immigration issue. The people know how they feel about this."

But that doesn't stop some editors from trying—or even from persuading themselves that what they write makes a difference. Take the Ellsworth *Independent/Reporter's* Linda Mowery-Denning. Like many editors of larger newspapers in Kansas, she opposed the Kansas Marriage Amendment forbidding same-sex marriages; in 2004 she ran a determined editorial campaign against the measure and, predictably, was quoted as describing its supporters, who included not a few Democrats, as "hatemongers." After the measure passed, with 69.9 percent of the vote, and became law, Mowery-Denning proudly told me, "We made a difference. It carried, but by not quite as much as it did in other counties." The difference was less than 1 percent.

David Awbrey, a former editor at the *Wichita Eagle*, thinks it is such shrill defensiveness that is largely responsible for the massive irrelevancy of the regional press. Although they may still see themselves as civic boosters, Awbrey claims that the larger daily newspaper editors have become fringe partisans whose largely liberal fulminations are unimportant in the lives of their readers. That seemed to be borne out in the conversations I had. Most people told me they sometimes bought the dailies from the bigger cities, but only if there was a front-page story about their smaller town. "The *Salina Journal* doesn't have much to say to me," said Brenda Losh, a Concordia real estate agent. "It's not really for people like us in small towns."

"They're completely disconnected from their readers," said Krier of the Harris papers, repeating the critical mantra. "There they are in Hays and Salina, sitting on a big conservative base. Salina's paper is bad, and the one in Hays is worse. No wonder they only circulate twelve thousand copies over all these counties. And they slant their news coverage—and that's one thing we can't do."

Is it harder to torque the news if the news is local and personal? Probably—but it's doubtful that it feels that way to those who feel slighted. If you're as angry at the paper as Sheriff Murphy, for example, the last thing you care about is market penetration. An afternoon in a small town, in fact, will convince you that the only people who really care what the papers say out here are journalists. "Their editorial pages just don't matter," said Alan Cobb, a political activist and head of the state chapter of Americans for Prosperity, a taxpayers' watchdog group. Cobb said he thought political donors might be influenced by an editorial or two. "But they don't change many minds otherwise."

If the disconnect between the majority of midwestern people and the media class can be traced to a single event, one that changed a number of institutional, political, and cultural relationships, it must be to the Summer of Mercy, which stretched over forty-five days in 1991, when thousands of pro-life demonstrators converged on Wichita, where Dr. George Tiller has his clinic.

Until that summer, the Sedgwick County political landscape was decidedly left of center. Dan Glickman, a local resident whose family had been involved in the Wichita-area business community for a couple of generations (scrap metal), was in his seventh term as the Democratic representative to Congress. First elected in 1976, he had become the Congress's go-to guy on issues involving general aviation—a big deal in a growing city of more than 300,000 that has at one time or another served as the home of Cessna, Beech (Raytheon), Stearman, Lear, Mooney, and other aircraft manufacturers. Cessna, along with Boeing, is still a big local employer. The statehouse delegation was comfortably mid-left, reflecting the interests of Wichita's old-line elite, with a mixture of Democrats and liberal Republicans representing the state's largest city. By the time the summer of 1991 was over, nearly three thousand protesters had been arrested, conservative sentiment had been galvanized, and the credibility of the press in red-state America had been severely undermined.

The pro-life protest against Tiller's operation and others led by Operation Rescue had targeted Wichita early. In fact, months before the first demonstrator showed up, the *Eagle* was running warnings on its front page, such as this one from May 1991: "A national anti-abortion group whose blockades of abortion facilities has led to thousands of arrests around the country plans a week of protests at a Wichita clinic in July." The *Eagle* may not have realized how ready many locals were to join forces with that "national anti-abortion group," blockades and all.

"It was a solid grassroots effort," recalled Goter. "It came right from the churches," where abortion had already been a topic of conversation for nearly two decades, thanks to the Roe decision. "Those people had really organized and were very serious about it. It was a religious belief."

"We knew it was coming," said Awbrey, at the time an assistant editorial-page editor at the *Eagle*. "But as far as the newsroom was concerned, it was just not on the radar at all. I would go to meetings and realize that journalists knew nothing about religion and even less about people with religious beliefs." The prevailing mood, Awbrey said, was one of "mildly irritated indifference." Awbrey told me that he'd tried to explain what was being said on Sunday mornings, but his colleagues had shrugged it off. "I just gave up. The *Eagle* marginalized itself. They just didn't get it."

The storm broke on a Saturday in July. The city was filled with thousands of protesters, demonstrating, picketing, singing, and going belly-to-belly with the Wichita police, who were trying to contain them in some areas and move them out of others—including away from the entrance to an abortion clinic. When that failed, fifty were arrested—a big deal in Wichita.

The *Eagle*'s reporter was Susan Rife, at the time a young general-features writer assigned to cover the demonstrations by an apparently uninterested weekend editor. "We all did weekends," she recalled later. "If you were on the rotation you went. Because it wasn't what I usually covered, I didn't give it much thought. I certainly don't remember anything like a mobilization of the newsroom or anything. In fact, I think the only time we mobilized the newsroom was for the River Festival—well, that and the state fair."

The paper ran her two-paragraph report in a local roundup buried deep in the next day's paper.

At least initially, the decision by the *Eagle*—and by most papers in Kansas—to ignore the story wasn't the product of animosity toward antiabortion protesters. It was simply a result of indifference toward the issue and those peculiar people who were so inexplicably worked up about it— a pattern some conservatives still see in the coverage of state news. However inadvertently, the *Eagle* set the tone for much that would follow. Some regional dailies didn't even mention the massive demonstrations— certainly among the biggest in the state's history—in their July coverage that year. "They missed it," said David Gittrich, at the time the executive director of Kansas for Life. To him and to others, the lack of coverage was deliberate. "They missed it on purpose. And people saw that. Not just some people, but thousands and thousands."

By the time all the shouting was over, abortion had gone from being a topic nobody wanted to discuss to the topic everybody felt compelled to discuss—at least everybody outside a newsroom. "Suddenly it became an issue mentioned in *every* political discussion," said Goter. "And it really became an overwhelming litmus test." For reporters and editors, however, it remained an adventure in uncharted territory. "Abortion was an issue no reporter wanted to cover," Goter said. "It meant you were talking to people who were different from the people you covered in government."

"Newsrooms everywhere are insulated secular places," explained Awbrey. "I remember Susan Rife telling me she had never met a pro-life person. Yet here were all these religious people. Nobody really understood
them at all."

But Awbrey, it turned out, had studied religion when he was a student at the University of Kansas. "Word got out that there was a guy in
the building who had read the Bible. I was doing Bible study with reporters!" Awbrey joked. "I could have sold a lot of copies of *Mere Christianity,* that's for sure. Reporters don't know this stuff at all. Try asking a
journalist the difference between an evangelical Christian and a Pente-
costal Christian. Think they know?"

The polarizing effects of the abortion controversy are now familiar,
but at the time, they caught many by surprise. People were forced by
events to think about something most of them didn't like thinking about,
and the strong consensus appeared to be that abortion—or at least the
gruesome abortions that made Tiller rich and made Wichita the fly-in,
anything-goes abortion capital of the nation—wasn't something most people wanted to support if they didn't have to. This pitted them against a
smaller but equally determined group who wanted the opposite and began organizing for a future battle. "I kept waiting for a moderate response
to galvanize," said Goter dryly, "but none ever did."

Eventually, the *Eagle*'s editorial page started to catch up with public
sentiment and began moderating its stance. Awbrey took over as editorial-
page editor on September 15, 1991. "It was just at the end of the Summer of Mercy, and we decided to try to be a little more open about things.
We definitely got the message much sooner than the newsroom did."

Awbrey started inviting different leaders from the community into
the paper's editorial meetings. "We tried to make it a real community discussion. People started talking with each other. Once I saw a Catholic
monk having a quiet discussion with a hard-line feminist. I thought,
'They do have something to say to each other.' You could start seeing respect, and that really helped."

Nevertheless, one of the more indelible effects of the Summer of Mercy

coverage—or lack thereof—was that it simultaneously animated both conservative political sensibilities and conservative skepticism about the role of
the regional press and linked the two together. Conservatives and liberals
live in parallel worlds now, and what happens in one is often shocking to
those in the other. In 1994, for example, Dan Glickman was defeated by a
political unknown, Todd Tiahrt, whose campaign had been organized in
church basements and on sidewalks, not on TV or in the newspapers. The
press was completely mystified by the result, and it still is.

What has caused the midwestern press and its big-city-style daily regionals to fade in importance in the public life of the region and its communities? Awbrey, whose father, Stuart, was an editor with the Harris
chain for forty-six years, thinks it's a combination of the growing public
fatigue with the lunacy of the leadership class in both parties and across
the political spectrum and the almost hysterical defensiveness of a huge,
arrogant, largely unaccountable cultural institution—the media—that is
no longer taken seriously by most people. Out here, the pervasive influence of the media ends the moment you leave the newspaper's office.

The declining significance of the national press, so faithful in mirror-
ing the views and concerns of blue-state voters, is everywhere in the Midwest. Awbrey ticked off a roster of names of editors from across the state,
from Winfield to Iola to Marion to Marysville to Emporia—all of them no
doubt self-described as "moderates" but seen in their own communities
as marginal if sometimes eccentric liberals. Their most common shared
characteristic, according to their critics? One they have in common with
many big eastern dailies: condescension.

"It all descends from that progressive Republican tradition that has
been so strong in Kansas, from White to Alf Landon to Dwight Eisenhower," Awbrey said. "Then those guys died off—and the legacy is something you can see in the Harris chain, that moderate, Main Street,
banker-type Republicanism, the small-town community boosters, movers,
and shakers.

"I grew up with Harris papers, and it's sad because they are all so disconnected from their communities. Jim Bloom"—the then-editor of the *Hutchinson News*—"in Hutchinson is just a joke. He's so far left—and that community is just not that at all." Awbrey claimed that although local editors may still see themselves as small-town advocates, to their readers they've become partisans and are therefore viewed more warily.

"They've really broken faith with their communities," Awbrey said. "It's just sad. In my father's generation, the community leaders would just get together at the country club—you and the banker and five or six other guys—and you'd all make decisions for the town. You don't do that anymore. But these guys still think you do. They have no understanding of their own communities or the people in them." What they do understand is their own point of view—but that, said Awbrey, blinds them to what matters a great deal to others. "They don't understand religion, for example," he said.

Awbrey, when we spoke, had returned to the Midwest from New England, where he had been editing a Vermont newspaper, to be near his wife's family. He had reluctantly and temporarily accepted a job advising Bob L. Corkins, at the time the Kansas commissioner of education, a man greatly despised by the state's dailies, on matters concerning the media. As a new father and a man liberated from the newsroom, Awbrey said that for him, community issues had taken on a new importance and that he had a new perspective.

The editors of regional dailies "don't understand what's going on right outside their door," he told me. "For example, the state board of education recommended teaching abstinence before marriage. Well, now I've got a six-year-old daughter—so to me that's pretty good! I'd *like* that to be taught in the schools. But Jim Bloom at the *Hutchinson News* took on the people who favor that and called them 'prairie ayatollahs' for 'imposing their religious beliefs' on the community. Well, I know a lot of secular fathers who dearly don't want their daughters to come home pregnant—but I guess that's a conservative religious value.

"That's the kind of reaction that these guys create. The Harris people, the *Wichita Eagle* [are] the same way—the *Kansas City Star* is *hopeless*.

None of these people have made any effort to get to know their own communities. Instead, they read the AP and they all bought the Tom Frank line, that conservatives are so stupid they don't know their own interests, that those people are so ignorant, so fundamentally moronic that we don't have to pay any attention to them, except to beat them up.

"Except the media keep losing. They're on the losing side of history and they don't understand why. So they just keep lashing out, calling people 'prairie ayatollahs' and things like that. Then they wonder why nobody pays attention to them. They're used to having the only soapbox in town. But now, with the Internet and the democratization of information, people see [that newspaper editors] aren't exactly oracular. Suddenly, the walls have come tumbling down and they've all been exposed."

So is the heyday of Kansas journalism, once so vaunted and important, now finished? "Kansas is divided," Awbrey said, "but those editors do have a constituency. And besides, newspapers—they're mostly there for advertising. The editors can be as crazy as they want, and people can ignore them, but if you live in a small town and want to sell your tractor or you want people to come to your store to buy appliances, where else can you go? Some of the things, like Craigslist and the Internet, the things that are killing big-city papers like the *Star* and the *Eagle,* haven't yet come to smaller communities to steal away advertisers—but they will. Then I guess we'll see."

As Awbrey suggested, there's a sense in which class plays a role in how the media in the Midwest see their readers, listeners, and viewers. For decades the "moderate" Republican establishment—the Kassebaums and their kith—have been far more comfortable with Democrats than with conservative Republicans, whom they detest, personally, viscerally. Most journalists seem to feel a class affinity with liberals and respond instinctively to their knee-jerk hatred of conservatives. Not since the days of populist class warfare, in the 1890s, has there been such revulsion felt by the moneyed establishment toward those they see as underclass usurpers.

Since most moderate Republicans in Kansas and Nebraska, after all, would be comfortable Democrats anyplace else, it may not be surprising that they no longer have an exclusive claim on the hearts and minds of Republican voters. But they do have their redoubts in places where conservatives can't readily disturb them: the courts, the bureaucracy, the media. They also have what many people elsewhere see as the bland, clear-channel symbol of cultural elitism, National Public Radio. But out here, even some of those broadcasters are a little bit different.

Kansas has not one but *two* NPR faucets: Radio Kansas and Kansas Public Radio, the result of the efforts of two educational institutions seeking licenses more or less simultaneously. Kansas Public Radio is affiliated with the University of Kansas and covers Lawrence and Kansas City. Radio Kansas, affiliated with Hutchinson Community College, in the middle of the state, gets what's left.

Of the two, Radio Kansas seems to make more of an effort to be something that most Kansans wouldn't tune out with a smirk. Their announcer has a Tom Burdett flat twang; you kind of expect him to say, "We'll leave the light opera on for ya." Kansas Public Radio, meanwhile, uses a woman with a British accent, caricaturing some of their listeners' fondness for cultural chintz. Even a KPR staffer admitted to me that the woman sounded "incredibly phony" for Kansas.

"I find [the two local stations] are remarkably similar," Radio Kansas's Ken Baker told me. "Great minds think alike, I guess. But I do find there to be a great deal more dissimilarity between these two Kansas stations and stations in other states." Radio Kansas says it attracts about seventy-five thousand listeners each week; Kansas Public Radio claims it draws about five thousand more than that.

They sure aren't very similar to Nebraska's NPR outlet, Nebraska Public Radio, which is, in part, funded directly by the state and where condescension is delivered undiluted. The targets are invariably the stupid hicks who are expected to foot the bill for the insults heaped on them. Example: The night before Easter 2006, Nebraska's public broadcaster offered "music for Easter eve," including songs like "Chocolate Jesus" and other juvenile ditties. Easter morning, while Radio Kansas was playing a little Bach and at least trying not to offend, Nebraska went with NPR's *Morning Edition,* where the only mention of religion was a segment inspired, apparently, by *The Da Vinci Code* that made the largely baseless claim that in the early Christian church, women "were apostles, priests, deacons, and bishops"—then added ominously, "but the Vatican's official view of church history presents women in a different light." Papists. Next thing you know, the Vatican will be claiming Christ rose from the dead.

In blue states, news is why NPR exists, of course. Local outlets argue that left-center information is just so hard to find in places like Boston, New York, and Washington that taxpayers should pay for more of it. But out here, even leaving aside the absurdity of spending millions of dollars to deliver a little Rachmaninoff to the fruited plain when a good CD player costs less than twenty dollars, the sensibility of NPR's news operation, at both the state and the national levels, is just more Hawaiian noise to those who not only know a scherzo from a largo but also know when they're being fed blue news. By broadcasting news from elsewhere, the nominally local stations risk the same disconnect experienced by the bigger dailies, a risk they seem to understand.

"We are aware of that," said Baker. "It seems to be evident. But our guess is we have less crossover between our news and classical than, say, a Massachusetts station. So we make sure our promotional messages are aired in both [news and classical] to make sure we get the word out. We can accept the assertion that only the two percent of the most educated people listen to public radio, but that's not our choice." Baker also felt that this didn't really speak to political affiliation, "especially out here. It's probably fifty-fifty."

Not that it matters. Despite 2006, the conservative movement is slowly converting the state's establishment Republicans—who represent the Kassebaum class of politicians—into former incumbents. If the liberal Democrat running unopposed in the Ellsworth-Salina area is the darling of the liberal papers in Ellsworth and Salina, his darlingness with voters will last only as long as he keeps his politics in harmony with the Republicans he represents, not the editors who represent him. In fact, former senator Nancy Kassebaum's son was ousted from his state legislature seat in 2004 by Shari Weber, a savvy, solid conservative who ran against his liberal record—and against his mom, who campaigned actively for him. Jack Krier explained it this way: "The influence of a newspaper in a big city or a small town is completely overblown. No matter what I say, fifteen percent of the people will agree with me, and another fifteen percent will disagree. The rest will just do whatever they want."

But what the regional dailies in Kansas and Nebraska find they can do is exert a great deal of influence two ways: first, in creating a very clear storyline along which a complex issue, like state funding for education, can be told. That's why, when that particular issue dominated the media in the summer of 2005, the media narrative was "conservatives want to close schools," a snapshot that fits comfortably with most journalists' view of right-wing heartlessness. The suspenseful part of the story was whether or not conservatives would succeed in their mean-spirited ploy.

The other way the press can use its influence out here even more sharply is by simply not reporting news clearly, or, in some cases, by not reporting some stories at all. This classic strategy of the mainstream media is resorted to often in rural states; it gives cover to many politicians by simply obscuring their political leanings and dissembling when it comes to reporting their votes in the faraway state capitals.

This is possible for a number of reasons, but there are two that are most characteristic of rural red states. First, small-town papers and county weeklies don't have a state capital bureau that reports on the individual votes of individual legislators. With almost no reporting resources available, weekly editors, like Jack Krier, take whatever is given to them by local politicians and generally ignore state issues unless they have a direct bearing on their towns.

Second, and perhaps more important, state government—where so much governmental misery is hatched, usually in the guise of education

"reform"—*is just not very interesting to people.* It's the flyover part of political life. When it comes to politics, people are passionately engaged at the
local level, where they see their opponents every day and unclench their
jaws long enough to mutter a begrudging "Hello." And they're deeply entrenched on one side or the other of the great national divide between
right and left. On both levels, politics lends itself well to simplistic views.

State politics is more complicated, usually involves discussions of
economics and education and studies and experts, and is therefore simply
less interesting to most people. State-level politicians are virtual un-
knowns. Almost every state senator or representative in Topeka I talked to
had a story about constituents upbraiding them because of some crazy
thing going on in Washington, D.C. Regional daily newspapers, NPR,
and local TV stations are often the only source of information about what
happens at the statehouse. That leaves isolated "moderates" and Democrats from conservative districts relatively untouched: The weekly paper
will be happy to run their photographs at the local elementary school (if it
hasn't already been closed because of consolidation) or, as in Smith Center, run whatever press release a local politician cares to donate, but doing real coverage and analysis of statehouse politics is beyond the reach of
many weeklies. As a result, "moderate" Republicans from conservative areas are able to vote for legislation that carries hefty price tags and significant social implications without having to worry about how their votes
will be received by their constituents.

And providing that kind of information is really not what weekly papers are in business to do anyway. People in small towns want their paper
to cover what happens in front of them, on Main Street, or in the towns
nearby, and with a shoestring staff and an army of volunteer community
stringers, the county weekly obliges. Every small-town paper relies solely
on its embeds for its stories, which chronicle and celebrate the triumph
of life in a hard place. A local weekly is about the only place you can get
your picture in the paper without having to rob a convenience store first.

Most regional dailies help "moderates" in this charade, of course. But
even more balanced papers, like the *Southwest Times,* are guilty of letting

legislators operate under cloak of darkness. When I asked owner Earl Watt about this, he said that the voters in *his* area were represented by Tim Huelskamp, a conservative state senator backed by the paper. That's quite true. But his paper is also the dominant daily in smaller nearby towns, such as Hugoton, home to Steve Morris, the liberal Republican senate president, who often prefers working with Democrats and the governor to Republican conservatives, and Rolla, the home of Bill Light, the Democrat-turned-Republican who routinely votes with Democrats and "moderates" on key issues.

"We could have done a better job" explaining the votes of Light and Morris to local voters, Watt admitted when I talked to him in early 2005. "We'll start trying to explain to people [in Hugoton and Rolla] what's been going on in Topeka." Light ran unopposed in 2006.

Meanwhile, the rest of the area's regional dailies paint conservatives in broad, often brazen strokes and clichés—the "prairie ayatollah" motif Awbrey mentioned is mild compared to some editorial screeds. Other than conservative e-mail-list types, nobody monitors the press out here, so playing with stereotypes is common, and not just along the Republican River, either. It's a tried-and-true journalistic practice: For years, Jews were driven crazy by the way TV news producers would reflexively reach for a clip of Brooklyn Hasidim every time a story about Jews aired. On Fox News recently it was reported that a young man had murdered some people in southeastern Pennsylvania. Although none of the victims were Amish, the instant Fox News tag was "Murder in Amish Country"—and viewers were treated to factoids about the Amish and their quaint folkways even as they watched police take away the bling-laden African-American kid who was arrested for the murders.

Stereotypes make journalism easy. To large blue-state newspaper editors, the default position of midwestern red states is one of empty dereliction, where cartoon-like preconceptions are propped up in front of a flat and unfamiliar horizon.

Superior's a light on that distant line. As Nebraska market towns go, there's not very much strange about the place, except maybe that annual Lady Vestey Festival and the unusual tenacity of the place. But when *New York Times* editors wanted to do a story about small towns in America, they sent their reporter to Superior, apparently because for the Midwest, they figured, Superior must be about average, red-state-wise—"old, white and relatively poor," as the paper put it.

As we know by now, the *Times* loves this kind of exotic locale. It is very reassuring to the *Times'* readers to know that heartland types, all conservatives no doubt, live in dusty squalor, so the paper often runs pieces like this, as if it were annotating the famous *New Yorker* cover that shows a map of the United States from a Manhattanite's perspective: the Hudson River, then . . . well, really nothing. Remember the screenwriter who reported to the *Times* that he had discovered by driving across Nebraska that there were acres and miles of unpaved earth between the houses? That was nothing. In 2005, the paper found a county in Texas that had sixty-six people in it! It was as if the *Times* had found a new planet; it was front-page news. When the *Times* reporter and his photographer showed up in the county seat, the population immediately grew by more than 10 percent, and added two new smirks. The paper's Great Plains travel pieces are kinder. But when it comes to midwestern news, it's mostly bad.

In editing its story about Superior, for example, the *Times* reverted to its familiar red-state tune as the paper's editors broke into a dirge:

> In many ways, Nuckolls County is not unlike any other rectangle of open space in the American midsection. Over the last half-century, when the United States added 130 million people and the population grew by 86 percent, rural counties in 11 Great Plains states—those counties without a city of at least 2,500 people—lost more than a third of their people. The farm-based counties, and those away from interstate highways, lost the most. . . .
>
> When Sylvia Crilly moved to Superior, she said she was surprised by the open secret of rural America.

"As an urban person who lived within blocks of the East Oakland ghettos, I have been just shocked by some of the poverty I have seen here," Ms. Crilly said. "Some of these people are just drowning."

She noted that 26 percent of children younger than 5 lived in poverty in her community. During the greatest economic boom in modern American history, the late 1990's, the income gap between city and rural workers opened wider than ever. People in rural counties of the Great Plains make 48 percent of what their metro-area counterparts make. That compares with 58 percent in 1990, according to one study. . . .

For these communities to survive, they will have to loosen their dependence on farming, many economists say.

If not farms, then what? Factories? The state has been helping with grants for small-town industrial parks. But companies sniff and go elsewhere, to counties with mountain views or even better tax incentives.

"You can go to any county in Nebraska and you'll see the same thing—these empty industrial parks," said [an official] of the rural affairs center.[5]

I asked Sylvia Crilly if the *Times* had gotten the story right. "[The *Times* editors] had a certain slant," she said. "They always do. I asked [the reporter] about it and he sent me an e-mail that said he had put it all in, all the positive things, but the editors cut it. Some of the things I said didn't make it into the article."

Crilly said she was surprised at the reaction to the story from the paper's East Coast readers. "I got calls from all over back there, including somebody who wanted to send care packages to Superior! I think people on the coasts—well, I think New Yorkers are nice, but they are so uninformed."

Although it is an "open secret" in the Midwest that people wish they had more money than they do, Crilly said, she had emphasized in her interview that poverty was experienced differently in places like Superior. "Out here, everybody goes to the same doctor, the same stores, the kids go to the same school—it has a leveling effect, it equalizes it. We're all mixed together. In urban areas, poverty is more isolated and segregated.

"Out here, if somebody's sick, there'll be a soup benefit, and everybody will show up. It might not raise a lot, but people will show up and contribute what they can. If a farmer gets sick, the neighbors step in to help bring in the harvest. There's a sense that if somebody needs help, they'll get it, it'll happen."

"I was a little surprised" at the quotes chosen by the *Times,* Bill Blauvelt told me. "Sylvia's one of our biggest boosters."

Not much of that showed up in the *Times,* however. The *Times* article "left out all the positive things," she said. "Someplace along the food chain, they got dropped."

It's the turtle-crossing-the-road story, the unpopulated-plains story. Even in the hands of a good reporter, Nebraska looks to the editors at the *Times* the way the newspaper industry looks to the rest of the country. Want to see decline? In 2006, the Project for Excellence in Journalism began its annual report this way: "Scan the headlines of 2005 and one question seems inevitable: Will we recall this as the year when journalism in print began to die?" In 1900, there were 2,726 newspapers in America; one hundred years later, there were 1,480—and the biggest ones are all slowly going broke, too. In fact, as it bleeds readers and advertisers at a rate that would alarm Superior's blindest booster, the *Times* itself may dry up and blow away, at least as a newspaper. Talk about a vanishing point: The publisher of the *Times* recently told an interviewer that the paper may not be printed at all in five years. The whole thing might become just another Web site. It might be the only way to save the *Times;* such is the power of the eternal archives of the Internet that in Superior months after the *Times* article appeared, the phone was still ringing with new businesses looking for a home.

"Nobody knew about us until the *Times* printed our obituary," Blauvelt told me. We were eating lunch in a crowded restaurant after a walk up Central Avenue. Superior didn't look like much of a goner. In fact, when I'd set about finding a place to live and write while working on this book, I had looked for a house in Superior big enough for me and my family. It was impossible. Everything had already been rented. Where was depopulation when I needed it?

The real story of Superior won't appear in the *New York Times,* because it's not all bad news. For example, the Leslie Hotel, which I once painted, has been done up as a fancy elder-care residence. Meanwhile, newer, more modern places to stay have been built nearby. The town has tremendous stability because the median age is 45.7 years, some eight years older than the national average. And it's a farming town, which means that while in terms of buying power Superior's less affluent than, say, a neighborhood in the Bay Area, the cost of living is *much* lower—you can purchase a two-bedroom house in Superior for much less than what a *Times* reporter spends on her new Lexus GS hybrid. Plus, as Crilly noted, the crime rate is microscopic, there's a great hospital in town, and the schools are good. The people who live there know they could move up to Grand Island or even all the way to Omaha and make more, but maybe they feel that in all the things that matter, you just can't get better than Superior, so what's the point?

To a certain extent, big eastern news organizations know they won't have to account to locals for their odd reporting about places like Kansas and Nebraska. Their interest is in showing the rural Midwest to people who know as much about it as they do. For example, NBC News sent a crew to Concordia in 2005 to do a story about the irrational support of Bush in the heartland: Exactly how endangered a species were Kansas Democrats? A producer went to the local newspaper to get some help ferreting out a local Democrat or two—surely a newspaper would know where to find one, yes? Yes! Sure enough, a pleasant young Democrat working at the paper duly directed the network to some local blue voters, who made jokes about meeting in dimly lit basements and exchanging secret handshakes. *They* knew it was a joke; NBC's correspondent didn't seem so sure. In 2004, Bush carried Concordia by 50 percentage points, 75 to 25 percent. That still left more than several hundred Democrats—and enough "moderate" Republicans—to safely deliver the county to Sebelius in 2006. Of the apparently random townsfolk NBC interviewed, other than the Democrats the correspondent sought out, another was a Democrat—"but I register Republican," he told me. "Doesn't make sense not to around here." Another was a Republican moderate—pro-choice but also pro-Bush. "I'm a moderate but I would *never* have voted for Kerry," she said, laughing. NBC was unable to find a single conservative Republican in Concordia, Kansas. They missed the wheat, too.

The day after the broadcast, I called Kirk Lowell, the town's economic-development director, to get his view on what national exposure on network news might mean to tiny Concordia, but he didn't know what I was talking about. Same thing at the local supermarket. Perplexed, I sent my daughters on a polling expedition up and down Concordia's business district, asking if anyone had seen their town's star turn on NBC's *Nightly News*. Not a soul—except for a teenager they found at Creations, a local hair salon. "Remember, Mom?" she said to her mother. "I told you it was on." The mother just shrugged. Nobody else the children talked to saw NBC's reporter, John Quiñones, remark acidly that "even the river's Republican." Another stereotypical view of the Midwest on TV.

The news never stops, as they say. Even in Smith Center. Just outside town a week after Ellsworth L. Murphy's ad ran, a group of followers of Maharishi Mahesh Yogi broke ground on a $14 million, 480-acre commune, organic farm, and "coherence creating center," where a little "Unified-Field based political science [*sic*]" would be taught.

At a press conference, Maharishi's people announced to a bunch of reporters and a few alarmed residents that they had decided that Smith Center would become the "US Peace Government's capital of the Global Country of World Peace," lending a little much-needed Vedic aura to the spacious plains.[6] The president of the US Peace Government, sometime

Natural Law Party presidential candidate John Hagelin, "the meditating physicist" who, perhaps not incidentally, favors decriminalizing drugs, showed up for the groundbreaking, and so did the Global Country of World Peace's governmental relations guy.

Maharishi's followers—who have included the Beatles, Mike Love, Donovan, and Mia Farrow but who are perhaps most famous for offering courses in levitation at the small college in Fairfield, Iowa, they took over—said they were just looking forward to living in the middle of the United States—they call it the "Brahmasthan"—in quiet, rural splendor.

At first, the local Brahmasthanis were . . . um, kind of unclear about how they felt about all this. But the mayor of Smith Center, Randy Archer, told a reporter that he had finally overcome his earlier prejudices.[7] "Rumors are it's a cult and they are going to make underground bunkers and build nuclear weapons," he said. "That's not what they are about." He also offered some consoling words to the *Pioneer*'s readers: "Their ceremonial garb is unusual to us, but it is their 'dress-up' clothes. . . . Just give them a chance. They are like you and me."

It didn't take long before more townspeople came around to the mayor's sanguine view. "They're just regular people," the clerk in the convenience store at the junction of Highways 36 and 281 told me. "They come in around eight, eight-thirty in the morning and sit right there." He pointed to a little cluster of plastic tables. "Some get up and go, and then others come in. They're very nice, quiet people. *Never* a problem. They say they're going to send their kids to the school, so that will mean more kids and money. Maybe we'll get a boost up to 4A! That would be good." When I asked if he thought they would take over the small community, he echoed the comforting words of Mayor Archer. "They're really very normal," he said. "We really get along. I always let them park their limo out there by the pumps."[8]

Compassionate Conservatism
(the Early Years)

There's a certain irony in the ubiquity of museums in little towns with a history barely longer than a life span. Practically every small town has a museum, including towns that barely existed to begin with and continue now only because there's a museum of some sort in the old buildings.

In fact, sometimes the museum grows precisely because the town is shrinking. When the last grandkid sells—or simply abandons—the house that once sheltered his mom and dad, he'll donate several generations of army uniforms and wedding dresses to the local museum, along with an assortment of other household odds and ends, on the assumption that the museum will look after it. Lacking antiquity and an abundance of fine art, the effect is less Louvre and more eBay. Most small-town museums contain an astonishing assortment of items: household goods, typewriters, ancient tractors and farm implements, antique baseball gloves and uniforms, musical instruments, artifacts of war.

In larger towns, the museum grows because the trustees think it can become what the marketing people call a "destination." That's what happened in Hastings, Nebraska, for example—much to my surprise, since I always figured the museum was already a destination. This was especially true in July or August, when, on a hundred-degree day, the museum was totally cool. My city cousins and I used to ride our bikes across Hastings, get good and lathered, then go into the museum and catch a cold while we looked at the dinosaur bones and arrowheads—the stuff that consti-

tuted two of the three dots on what we imagined to be the timeline of
midwestern history:

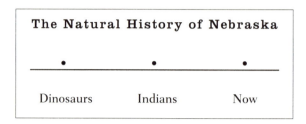

Roy Chapman Andrews, a famous dinosaur hunter, became my hero
for a summer or two, and when I'd get back to Granddad's farm near Burr
Oak, I'd walk everywhere watching my shoes to make sure I didn't accidentally disturb the stegosaurus jawbones that I was sure must be there,
if I could only see them. Andrews found huge monsters in nondescript
pastures just like these. If he could do it, I thought, maybe I could, too.
The closest I came were seashells from the days when Kansas and Nebraska were an ocean floor—hardly museum pieces, although they did
decorate a shelf for me.

In its own way, the museum in Concordia is a destination itself.
Housed in a mammoth neoclassical structure that was once the local
Carnegie Library, the museum—officially called the Cloud County Historical Society—attracted the attention of a visiting friend from the East
who pronounced it reminiscent of the New-York Historical Society. Its
contents, he said, arrest the unsuspecting visitor at every turn.

The place certainly detained my family: My wife and children volun-
teered to help organize the museum's costume collection, which must be
as massive as that once found on MGM's back lot, and which, in sum,
gives a complete picture of the sartorial tastes and habits of an America
now recalled only in sepia photos. The little museum itself provides a
kind of pocket tour of days not long gone: Here's a turn-of-the-last-cen-
tury dentist's office, over there a dry grocery; to the left, a portable jail cell
(complete with bunk bed and ball and chain); to the right, a delivery
truck; and above, an old airplane.

Then there are the pair of fascinating displays doubtless unlike any found in any other museum anywhere. In different ways, both speak to a quality common to rural midwesterners and one little appreciated in other parts of the country—particularly, of late, by urban Americans. In an age increasingly given to ostentatious, celebrity-driven displays of concern for the less fortunate—think Oprah, or any of several dozen rock-star pop empathizers, or the innumerable grandstanding politicians—people out here tend to be notable for their reserve; given how they usually vote in presidential elections, those who view the world through blue-tinted glasses readily take this as callous disregard for others. In fact, as the historical record shows, midwesterners have always been among the most generous-spirited of all Americans.

The first display is devoted to Camp Concordia, a POW camp, opened during the final two years of World War II about two miles northeast of town. With a capacity of more than five thousand (which is nearly the town's population now), it contained more than three hundred buildings—including a bakery, a library, a performance area for the camp's symphony orchestra, and a 177-bed hospital, all neatly organized up and down streets named after Davy Crockett, Sam Houston, and other American heroes. There were more than a dozen of these POW camps in Nebraska, Kansas, and Oklahoma, and dozens more "satellite" camps where smaller contingents of Italian and German prisoners were housed. Indianola, Nebraska, farther west on the Republican, had a POW camp, for example, while Alma had a satellite camp. There were thousands of prisoners scattered across the Midwest (and even more in the South and Southwest).

My grandfather agreed with other locals who said that the choice of such midwestern sites was due, at least in part, to an intimidation factor: Heading west on slow-moving trains, overawed Jerries would come to see that escape from, let alone victory over, such a vast and powerful country was impossible. "Very impressing," as ex-prisoner Franz Kramer wrote to a Concordia man after the war.[1] But what impressed the Germans as much as anything was that after all the boxcars they'd ridden in Europe, in prosperous, generous-spirited America, even as prisoners they got to ride in comfy passenger coaches.

To be sure, Camp Concordia had its *Hogan's Heroes* moments, like the time the camp truck carrying prisoners overturned on Sixth Street, knocking out the guard and leaving him unconscious next to his rifle in the middle of the street. A prisoner quickly grabbed the rifle—and then ran through the gathering crowd thrusting it at alarmed people and shouting, "You take!" until he finally found a Concordian willing to guard him and his fellow prisoners until the American soldier came to. Meanwhile, the POW newspaper, *Neue Stacheldraht Nachrichten* (New Barbed-Wire News), had to be shut down after it was discovered to be "one of the cleverest pieces of Nazi propaganda fostered in a German prisoner of war camp in this country," according to an offended U.S. military inspector.

There were occasional escapes, useful demonstrations of the wisdom of at least learning a little menu English. For example, a German in full uniform made it as far as Belleville, where he wandered into a local café to buy breakfast but couldn't speak English very well and had trouble working out American money. The alert waitress was suspicious of a non-English-speaking man in a German military uniform trying to order sausage and eggs, and while waiting for a train out of town the escapee was arrested by the police chief. Meanwhile, fifty miles north, in York, Nebraska, a German POW was arrested in a bar, 375 miles from his camp at Fort Robinson, when it was discovered that he had problems ordering a hamburger, of all things, in English.[2]

And, of course, among the prisoners there were some unregenerate fanatics. At the Concordia camp, some anti-Nazi prisoners met mysterious deaths—always claimed by the Germans, who had obviously killed the backsliders, to be acts of suicide. Among the items seized from the barracks was a giant map of the United States, drawn by a prisoner with ambition, showing all the major American cities and the railways that connected them. You can see it right there at the museum.

But mainly what remains in memory, both for most surviving prisoners and for elderly townspeople, is a surprisingly large residue of good will. Captured in North Africa or France, and brought to an America still somewhat innocent to the full extent of Nazi horrors, the POWs found themselves in the equivalent of a dull country club, with frequent concerts, plays, and movies, as well as a casino, rathskellers, and bars and even the "University of Camp Concordia," which offered hundreds of courses taught by inmate professors. The UCC was so widely esteemed that the courses were recognized for credit by the University of Kansas and, after the war, by several German universities as well. Germans took up painting with a passion—several examples are on display in the museum—while Rommel's military band, captured en masse in North Africa and shipped to Concordia, provided musical interludes.[3]

The town's residents were proud to be playing a part in a war that was in many ways half a world away. Moreover, when the camp opened in July 1943, many suddenly found themselves mixing with people they'd heretofore known only from geography texts and newsreels. Some worked at the camp itself, and innumerable others had frequent contact with the Germans who were used as free labor on local farms—something that might appall Amnesty International today. Accompanied by armed guards, the farmworkers were technically forbidden to mix with civilians, but the rule was widely disregarded. "The first day, my mother insisted they were to come in and have lunch with the family," recalls one local man, a young boy at the time, "and they did every day after that. They were very intelligent and very cultured—one guy played the violin."

Indeed, as the letters from former prisoners and others on display at the museum reveal, the Germans found their treatment at the hands of the locals not just amazingly decent but enlightening; many saw it as representing the ideals of America itself.

"My rethinking [of Nazi ideology] started already after my first contact with the Americans at the beginning of my captivity" in Concordia, one ex-prisoner, Reinhard Mohn, recalled to the *Topeka Capital-Journal* in 1994. Returning to Germany from Camp Concordia after the war,

Mohn soon took over the family business—Bertelsmann, now one of the world's largest media companies and, as it happens, the publisher of this book.

Camp Concordia closed in 1945 and was quickly dismantled. At the museum, however, the appearance of old German ex-POWs—or their curious family members—is a common occurrence. Indeed, some former prisoners returned to the area after the war and settled along the Republican River.

But it is the other unusual exhibit at the museum that more fully conveys the quiet generosity so long common to this region: the exhibit devoted to the "orphan trains" that between 1853 and 1930 brought more than 200,000 children from the crowded, filthy alleys of New York, where at any given moment as many as 30,000 homeless children roamed the streets, to new homes in spacious places like rural Kansas and Nebraska.

As migrations go, the system of rounding up kids—some genuine orphans, some juvenile delinquents, many just abandoned—and placing them in the homes of strangers more than a thousand miles away strikes the contemporary sensibility as more than a little shocking. "It was certainly not a politically correct way to treat a social problem," noted Susan Sutton, who serves as, among other things, the president of the National Orphan Train Complex in Concordia. It certainly could never be undertaken today—not with the maze of regulations governing adoption and child welfare, not to mention the racial politics.

But here's the thing: It worked. Not always perfectly, of course, but usually, and for the most part better than anything tried since.

The trains were the result of the determined efforts of a New York clergyman, Charles Loring Brace.[4] It was Brace who organized the Children's Aid Society, on St. Marks Place, and then spent the rest of his life exporting children from Manhattan to small towns and encouraging other organizations to do the same. And they did. The result was a network of orphanages and agencies that led children into the embrace of Children's

Aid (and, for Catholic children, the similarly intentioned Foundling Hospital, created by the Sisters of Charity out of fear that Catholic infants might fall into the hands of midwestern Protestants).

The placement of Children's Aid kids was left to enterprise and chance, with the assumption that there was a boundless reservoir of decency in the middle of the country. The mechanism was quite straightforward: Ads would appear in midwestern newspapers announcing the arrival of "asylum children," who would be put on display for an afternoon at a train station or in a church hall so locals could meet and choose the children they wished to adopt. "The sight of the little company of the children of misfortune always touched the hearts of a population naturally generous," wrote Brace. After the children were tentatively placed, agents from the society would periodically visit them to check on their progress.

The results were staggering. Though occasionally a match went badly—some of the children placed were treated as indentured labor and given little affection or education—according to the society's carefully kept records, nearly nine of every ten placements were deemed successful. Written off as the dregs of society, many already in trouble with the law, the children found safe, comfortable homes far from the perilous and brief lives they would have led on the streets of New York. "Many of them grew up," wrote one popular historian, "to be pillars of their communities—farmers and farmers' wives, doctors and lawyers, preachers and teachers, a couple of governors and a couple of congressmen, mayors and judges—in short, solid citizens by the score."[5]

"I will always be grateful for what I was given," Anna Harrison told me when we chatted. As a young girl, she had ridden an orphan train west to a new life. Now, after a long, adventurous life as an entertainer, including a return engagement in New York City, she lives in retirement in Nebraska. "I can't imagine what would have happened to me," she said.

The unpleasant hypothetical is a familiar device in many of the reminiscences offered by orphans. "What I would have been if I had stayed in

New York, God only knows," wrote one grateful fifteen-year-old in a letter found in the society's files. "I had not gone far in vice when you rescued me, it is true, but I was rapidly sinking into that terrible pit of darkness."

In fact, in Concordia, as Sutton and others supervise the conversion of an old railway station into the orphan trains museum, researchers seek access to the files of photos and documents that will soon be housed there, each file detailing the experiences of children who once lined up at such stations to find new parents and new lives.

One such account, found in one of the society's annual reports, speaks eloquently to this region's long history of acceptance and tolerance. It's about a four-year-old boy named Willie, found on the streets of New York and initially adjudged to be "almost beyond hope." He was carried from the station, angry and screaming, by a German immigrant farm couple, and when a society agent returned to check on him a few months later, the farmer approached him in disgust. But it was not for the reason the agent thought, but because the farmer feared the agent wanted to take the boy back. "I haven't come to take him away," the agent explained. "But how in the world do you manage him?"

The agent recorded the response of the farmer's wife, accent and all: "Oh, dot's easy. You see, we all luff him."

"There is an abundance of love and shelter and pity out here that will never be exhausted," the agent wrote his superiors back in New York. "Send out the little ones in yet larger numbers. The work is a success."

I asked Tina Long, the communications director of the Wichita-based Kansas Children's Services League, about the orphan trains, and ventured that such a thing must now seem pretty far out to people like her in the adoption business.

"Actually," she said, "there are more similarities than differences. They"—the Children's Aid Society and the Foundling Hospital—"were going out and trying to find homes where people wanted kids, the same as we do now. It was very similar—other than the sometimes maddening bureaucratic process we have."

The bureaucratic process matters, of course. As far as many midwesterners are concerned, in other places the government has largely mucked up this vital aspect of life, as it has mucked up so much else, resulting in child-care systems that leave countless children consigned to poverty and neglect and sometimes even dead at the hands of those who escaped the notice of children's services bureaucrats. And for all the incessant talk of government acting "for the children," no one seems inclined to change any of that.

Indeed, the one politician who even dared to suggest a meaningful alternative to the current system—former House Speaker Newt Gingrich, who speculated in 1994 that high-quality orphanages might be a more humane approach for children than abortion or languishing at risk in the circumstances found in cities like New York and Los Angeles—was widely denounced at the time by "child-care advocates" as a Neanderthal. "It seems like an awful experiment to do to children," Miriam J. Cohen, a Vassar College history professor and a specialist in the history of welfare and reform, told a reporter.[6] "It's a radical experiment in something we haven't seen in a hundred years." She added dismissively, "What's new about it, is what I haven't seen."

Of course, in places like Kansas few take it for granted that the best way to attack a social ill is with a massive government program. In New York or Los Angeles, this easy midwestern disregard for ambitious government plans is regularly caricatured as indifference, just more anti-government talk, the self-justifying nonsense of hard-hearted, Republican misanthropes. But to people out here it's simply common sense, based on long historical experience and a confidence that individuals, not the government, can come up with solutions that are more humane.

"Based on our experience of working with foster care and those who need homes, you find a lot of people who are supportive," said Long, "and a lot of support for the families themselves within their communities." Most of the kids they place are African-American children from Wichita and Kansas City; most of the new parents are white folks from smaller communities, often where there are no other African-Americans. "We work with forty newspapers and TV stations across the state who donate space or airtime to show pictures of kids who need homes. We could never pay for that," she noted.

Still, the media-bred image of red-state callousness is so pervasive these days that even those who should know better can get caught short by the far more nuanced realities. I was standing in a passageway in the Kansas House of Representatives one afternoon when a cute little African-American boy scooted past, clearly making a break from his father—who, it turned out to my surprise, was Tim Huelskamp, a conservative state senator from Fowler.

In fact, Huelskamp's son is one of five adopted black children in Fowler, a town of only five hundred. Every African-American in the community—all five of them—has been adopted not just into a family but into "the entire community," said Denise Kuhns, editor of the *Meade County News*. "In fact," she added, "they're not the only African-Americans in Fowler, but in the whole county, I think." She was unaware of any incident that would make the children feel unwelcome. "You know, kids are color-blind," she said, "and we should be too."

Three of the kids—aged ten, nine, and four—are Huelskamp's. "It's really just us and another family," he told me. Huelskamp had been a primary sponsor of the Kansas Marriage Amendment, the bill that eventually led to the state's ban on same-sex marriages. He's the kind of legislator who is normally happy to talk to journalists and is used to taking the abuse that comes as a result. But he was a bit reluctant to discuss this. "We don't make a big thing of it," he explained quietly. "It's just something we do that's consistent with our religious faith and our belief in the sanctity and value of every life." Huelskamp, a Roman Catholic, admitted that some people are surprised. "But I don't know why they should be. We're just like most people. We love our kids."

In New York or Washington, D.C., placing African-American children with white families can be politically problematic. Stories about white families being denied the right to adopt African-American kids in need of homes are commonplace. The fear is that black children raised by white parents won't learn how to deal with racists. As it happens, the day I was writing that sentence, the *Philadelphia Inquirer* was reporting on just such an instance:

> Though white people might view interracial adoption as evidence of societal progress, experts say, for many black people it is a painful harkening back to a time when their ancestors were treated as property—and proof that the child-welfare system discourages African American adopters.
>
> "The race issue gets played out right through adoption," said Joseph Crumbley, a Jenkintown family therapist who studies the issue. . . .
>
> Some social workers and educators question whether white families can learn, much less teach, black children the survival skills that African American parents already know.
>
> Last month, a judge denied a white Chester County couple's bid to adopt the black foster child who had lived with them for nearly two years. U.S. District Judge James T. Giles ruled that Randall and Susan Borelly of Uwchlan Township failed to prove that county officials racially discriminated by refusing to let them adopt Kevin, almost 4.[7]

Judge Giles may be a run-of-the-mill jurist in places like Philadelphia, but "not in Kansas," said Sandra Dixon, vice president of social services at the Kansas Child Services League. "We have a multiethnic placement act that says you can't deny permanency because of race."

A good thing, too, since most kids who need families out here are nonwhite, and, as KCSL's Tina Long noted dryly, "In Kansas, most people who want to adopt are white. We just have a lot of white people here. If you're looking for a loving home [for a child] in Kansas," she added, "race just doesn't play a role."

Kansans didn't invent racial tolerance, but unlike many wealthy blue-state suburbs, at least they have a long history of real-world experience with it, starting with the determination of Free Staters in the 1850s to resist slavery, through the arrival of the black "exodusters" in the 1870s, who came to build successful all-black towns like Nicodemus after Southern Democrats began rolling back some of the postwar progress African-Americans had made, to the *Brown v. Board of Education* case in the 1950s, when Republicans took control of the Topeka school board and sent the case to the U.S. Supreme Court in order to get rid of the nonsensical "separate but equal" segregation that had been imposed on Kansas's largest towns. (There was never segregation of any kind in any of the medium- or small-sized communities in the state.)

"I'm proud to be a Republican, and I'm a Republican on principle," said Cheryl Brown Henderson, the sister of Linda Brown, the little girl at the center of the case. Brown Henderson is the president of the Brown Foundation and is the family's spokesperson. "This wasn't Alabama here," she told me. "We weren't marching through lines of National Guardsmen. We in Kansas didn't want that law at all." Kansas isn't Boston, where race riots marked integration and busing, and there are no Al Sharptons in Topeka.[8] "We were never under threat here" because of race, she said. A sometime candidate, Brown Henderson ran for the state legislature in 2004 but was defeated by a Topeka Democrat who gathered strong union backing. Is her sister a Republican? "She was the last time I ran," said Henderson. "I know, because she voted for me."

Lori Kemling, a thirty-year-old part-time physical therapist who lived across the street from me in Concordia, has the kind of family that would look familiar to young professionals in New York or Boston: She and her husband, Brian, who works in the bank a block away, are the parents of two adopted children from southern India, and they're expecting their third—a baby from China.

But her reasons for her choice might be considered unusual by some readers of newspapers like the *New York Times* or the *Boston Globe.* Describing herself as a more or less "typical Kansas conservative Republican," raised on a farm and educated at a good college, Kemling sat at her kitchen table watching her daughter play and explaining to me how she and her husband reach their decisions. "We are led by our faith," she said. "In fact, I don't know how you could explain this any other way. How would I explain all of this"—she gestured toward the street outside—"to them?" She nodded toward four-year-old Sreya, who had just discovered how to make a catapult out of a plastic spoon, a child-sized miracle if ever there was one. "That's what we tell them all the time, that God brought you to us, because, really, literally, He did."

Alien as this sounds to many contemporary ears, it is entirely in keeping with local tradition and the cultural assumptions of midwestern Christians. The Children's Aid Society, too, was fundamentally a religious mission, and its legacy continues to grow abundantly on the plains, far from the inanities of Philadelphia judges and bureaucratic racists.

Transcript 5:
Superior People

Rich: You know, personally, I hear the word "progressive," which is what some liberals call themselves, and I wonder, What do they think they're progressing toward? If we're progressing so our children have less respect for marriage or their marriage vows, is that really progress?

Pat: The way the culture is today, you've got to pack as much of your value system as you can into your children by the sixth grade. After that, it's probably too late—you've gotta throw them in to swim with the sharks, and hope they're equipped to deal with it.

Rich: So much of it has to do with mothers no longer being in the home. Until the last couple of decades, she was always there to send the kids off to school, and she was there when they got home. On the farm, she was the one instilling values and responsibilities—from gathering the eggs to feeding the bucket calf to driving the tractor. I'm talking at the age of six or seven. You talk to a kid in grade school today, and maybe he'll know about a tractor—he could explain it to you and tell you what one was—but that's as far as it goes. I'm not trying to be sexist here, but if we could turn back the clock maybe thirty years in that regard, it would do a world of good.

Bill: Well, back then, both parents felt that way, that family came first. Early on, Grandfather worked a little while as a brakeman for the

Rock Island Railroad. But then he meets Grandmother and marries her, and quits. He says the railroad is no life for a married man— he should be home with the kids.

Rich: That hits it on the head. He gave up his career for family. We have sold ourselves short lately in this country because so few people are willing to do that.

Pat: That's a bill of goods that's been sold *to* us in this country. So many people are looking to have a million dollars in their lives. In this part of the world, you still meet a lot of people looking to have a million-dollar life, sure. But they realize you can't take a U-Haul to that cemetery. It's probably against some state law, anyway. *(Laughs.)*

Stan: The trouble is, you have a concentration of liberal people on both coasts, and they have a lot of influence. They control the media, they also control the colleges—

Rich: And Hollywood. Let's face it: Sin sells, and they're very successful at glamorizing it. People with a more conservative viewpoint—the ones trying to hang on to what used to be the norm—they see that, but they don't have the means to compete. So they try to hone in on areas where they feel they can still have some control and some influence.

Val: That's very true. Even in sports we see that.

Pat: That's why you're seeing a lot of people around here turn to homeschooling—because they don't like the values kids are picking up in our public schools. I'm a teacher by profession, and even I agree with that. The parents are concerned, legitimately so, with the bad social environment—the bullying, the vocabulary, the lack of respect and honor for your elders. And, of course, the poor quality of instruction.

Rich: And what are we paying for that—eight thousand dollars per student? More? I started out in a one-room school, and by every account the education in those days was superior at a tiny fraction of the cost.

Stan: Well, I suppose when it comes to morals, people on the coasts just think we're behind the times. *(Laughs.)* Heck, our kids live together before they get married, just like they do everywhere else.

Pat: But I do think that it's different. They have a pretty good sense of reality. To a certain extent, the slower pace here is a counterbalance to all the ram-and-jam they see on MTV. The kids from here may go down to spring break—

Stan: To South Padre Island, Cancún—

Pat: But the difference is, our kids have to pay for their own tickets. *(Laughter.)*

Stan: That hits it right on the head.

Learning, the Hard Way

*The Journal knows a good joke on a Salina man. This man
ordered a book from London, England. The book was one
that cannot be procured in this country. It came all right,
but most of it is printed in Latin, and it has been 20 years
since the Salina man looked into a Latin book. He is going
to have his children read it to him at nights.*

—The Salina Journal, *October 4, 1905*

A century later, the joke's on Salina—and almost every other community in America, where "Latin" describes a dance beat, not a classical language, and where, as every attentive parent knows, public education is both in collapse and in denial. Not long ago, the *Chronicle of Higher Education* published a survey showing how well American college grads were doing.[1] The results were, of course, depressing: In history, civics, geography, and literature, results are declining. This is consistent with other studies, including the National Assessment of Educational Progress "report card" that shows that even though Kansas students edge out New York kids, about two-thirds of Kansas eighth graders consistently lack proficiency in math and reading—despite sharply escalating expenditure per student. In fact, almost all studies show no correlation at all between expenditure and outcomes.

Yet the pressure is greater than ever now to increase spending on education even further—especially since state courts in Kansas and elsewhere have insinuated themselves into the business of setting consistent funding levels for public schools, traditionally the role of the legislative branch.

For midwesterners—as for most Americans—already there is no more expensive, invasive, or powerful example of governmental overreach than its control over local schools. In just twenty years, Kansas and Nebraska schools have grown from small, efficient classroom-oriented facilities producing well-educated students from families rich and poor to hubs of big-government activity, providing a welter of social programs and services, many of which have nothing at all to do with education. There are few regional differences in schools in twenty-first-century America; a school in Alaska is similar to a school in Alabama or Arizona. They are all part of the nation's dull, homogeneous, uninspiring view of what experts and bureaucrats in places like New York and California think schools should be. Ironically, one of the most successful varieties, the small rural school, has been left in the dust, literally. These buildings stand abandoned all over the plains.

A hundred years ago, Kansas had 9,106 schools in which many rural Kansans learned to read the *Georgics* in the original. Even if a mastery of Latin isn't the best way to measure scholastic excellence, in the eyes of many sensible people, it definitely beats mastering the stuff rationed out in the diluted, politically correct, culturally torqued courses most kids are made to absorb today.

Many parents, and not just midwestern parents either, may resent this morphing of the little red schoolhouse into the big, confusing, nameless bureaucracy in charge of social engineering, but as cynical politicians know, the last thing parents want to do is get involved in education. Perhaps as a result, in Kansas today public schools, like schools everywhere, chew through two-thirds of every taxpayer dollar, leaving pocket change for everything else, from highways to troopers to courts to jails to old folks.

You can see the difficulty of trying to maintain expensive, unwieldy institutions in the ongoing consolidation of small school districts into larger ones—such as recently happened in Cuba, Kansas, population 231, down a mere 10 people in the 1990s.

Historically, the school in Cuba was typical of that in many in the rural reaches of Kansas and Nebraska. Small and locally run, housed in a modest facility, it was the single most important totem of civic life, the scene of generations of proms, football and basketball games, and homecomings. But no more. The school in Cuba has been consolidated with the school in Belleville, the seat of Republic County. So now every morning Cuba's children board buses and ride off to a cluster of buildings that belong to one of the largest employers in the area, as school districts often are in the rural parts of red states.

The decision to close the Cuba school came a couple of years ago when the school board of Cuba met with the school board of Belleville in the basement of the senior center. The discussion wasn't about whether Cuba wanted to lose its school—thanks to school administrators, that was a fait accompli; it was only about how soon it could be made to happen. Since everybody knew that without a school, you might as well just go ahead and move to Belleville, essentially Cuba was negotiating the terms of its own municipal death. It was painful to watch.

At one point in the strained discussion, a disheartened Cuba school board member turned to the guy next to him and asked, "Do we have any alternatives?"

The guy could only shrug.

The first man looked up at the school superintendent standing next to him. "Well, what about charter schools? Can we get money for that?"

"You'd be the first," said the superintendent. "I wouldn't go there." This effectively put an end to that line of inquiry, and everybody turned again to Cuba's civic demise.

Of course there are alternatives. For example, in tiny Tipton,

Kansas, a town about the size of Cuba and less than a hundred miles away, consolidation became an issue in 2003, but unlike Cuba, Tipton simply said no. Led by Fred Smith, a retired Chicago cop who had moved to the town where his grandmother had lived, Tipton's residents needed only forty-one days to build a small but perfectly sized, modern school for the community's kids—and they did it for less than $60,000. Then they sold the old public school to a private company that specializes in educating kids with special needs, and at the same time set up an endowment to help support the local Catholic high school—with thirty-odd students, the smallest high school in Kansas. The schools of Tipton meet or exceed the state's outcomes.

In Lindsborg, the imaginative administrators of Smoky Valley High School launched a virtual charter school to work with area homeschoolers and other distant students. Kids in grades seven through twelve are equipped with an Apple iBook loaded with the state curriculum and provided access to teachers or tutors whenever one is required. As a consequence, Smoky Valley has students all over Kansas and beyond.[2] Lawrence's virtual school is even bigger. For those willing to create alternatives, or revive them, alternatives exist.

The trouble is, many Kansans don't want "alternatives." Thirty-odd years after the nonstop inflation of what constitutes a public school, parents in even the smallest town now expect to get the kind of school only a big city can provide, particularly one with a big, expensive sports program, along with a menu of other stuff that has nothing to do with reading and writing. Increasingly, Kansans and Nebraskans care less about enlightenment and more about *Friday Night Lights*. As one mother in Mankato, Kansas, told me, "If there aren't sports and extras"—proms, and the like—"then they can just close the school, as far as I'm concerned. Those things are what school's about." So strongly is this felt that even some of those red-state readers who may have been nodding along in agreement for much of this book will stop in a few pages and drop the thing in disgust. The notion that schools should reflect regional realities is practically revolutionary.

After four decades of the government providing a growing list of goods and services through the schools, it's no wonder that, at this point, the consolidation of small schools is pretty much state policy, one often sold to local taxpayers as a cost-cutting measure. Smaller schools are pushed to join larger ones, which in turn join even larger ones. The same thing that Cuba went through is happening in rural areas all over America. Indeed, in Kansas there are rumors that soon there will be only one "unified" school in the biggest town in each county—and as counties merge and consolidate, those will eventually be replaced by a scattering of big regional institutions. I asked Larry Lycell, Belleville's superintendent, what the long-term prognosis was for the local school. "If Concordia"—twenty miles to the south—"builds a big school north of town, then we could eventually see our school close and consolidate with theirs," he said. There's even talk of putting up dormitories to house ten-year-olds who otherwise would have to travel for hours to get to school.

This could all be groundless speculation, but the overriding theory behind all this is, of course, the obvious one: As educational bureaucrats will tell you, economies of scale and all the rest mean that larger schools are better for kids, especially poor ones. And in the Midwest, as everywhere else in modern America, "better for kids" is a magic incantation. At a special legislative session held in Topeka in 2005 to implement a court-ordered increase in funding for schools, I clocked the phrase "for the children" seventeen times over one twenty-minute span. The argument for consolidation is pretty compelling: What could be better—you save children *and* save money.

Sadly, the facts don't support this. For example, a 2003 Louisiana report summarizing the research into consolidation pointed out what every small-town educator already knows: Small schools *always* do better than large ones; small schools are much better at narrowing the gap between rich kids and poor kids; large schools are unruly, unproductive, wasteful; large schools often end up spending more money on nonessential services and programs unrelated to education; and the myth of economy of scale is just that—a myth.[3]

Common sense (not to mention all those pesky studies) would suggest that what's "better for kids" is a system that creates more smaller schools, not fewer big ones. But, of course, there is a larger agenda at play here, one dictated by those with a view of government very different from the one that has long held sway in Kansas and Nebraska. For while the value of the educational "reforms" may be in doubt, there is no question what the new education policy *does* achieve: vastly expanded government power and influence over the most important of all relationships, that between a parent and a child. The growth of public schools not as educational institutions but as government services facilities only creates more dependency on government to save parents from having to get involved, even marginally, in the education of their children. In fact, increasingly, it helps limit parents' involvement in raising their kids at all.

Many midwesterners have learned, to the dismay of some, that as long as a reform claims to benefit children, you can grow government as high as an elephant's eye. Really, since the bureaucracy's notion of benefiting children is so elastic, it can be made to include keeping kids in school longer (and starting them in school younger); even the values rooted in generations of belief and practice can be readily undermined. Soon, the village it takes to raise a child in Kansas will be as big as the whole state.

Critics contend that if you want to find one of the wealthiest people in almost any small-to-middlin'-sized town in Kansas, just stop by the local school superintendent's office, a tiny blue island in the big red sea. Because the chances are that's where you'll find a very well-paid functionary slicing and dicing policy for the busy parents populating a school board that is usually convinced that the superintendent, as the resident expert, must know what's best for their children. Conservatives sharpen their blades when they talk about educational reform, but they save their fury for those they call "educrats." "They are the wall against reform, the six-figure-salary fat cats," said controversial former Kansas State Board of Education member Connie Morris.

The feeling's mutual. When I asked Larry Lycell, the superintendent of Belleville's schools, how many conservative superintendents he could think of, he said, "Two"—and he was not one. Overwhelmingly, midwestern school administrators enjoy the support of the state's daily press. School administrators are very adept at spending money on themselves and on the administrative layer of public schools.

In 2005–6, the administrative costs of the three hundred school districts in Kansas, according to the Kansas Association of School Boards, will gobble up more than $300 million, more than any other category of noninstructional service—and more than twice as much as is spent on libraries, technology, and testing combined; more than the state spends for "student support," including social workers, truancy police, and public health workers; more than the cost of operating, maintaining, heating, and insuring the state's school buildings; more than is spent for all the food served to Kansas students; more than Kansas spends for all the buses on which the state's kids ride to school. Some of this administrative windfall pays the salaries of school principals and other essential personnel, but almost half goes to pay the local superintendent and his small bureaucracy.

Not all administrators are overpaid for the work they do, of course, but judging by the numbers, you'd be hard-pressed to convince taxpayers. In tiny Republic County, where barely more than eight hundred students attend the public schools, more than $550,000 is paid to administrators. The hardest-working of these—the school principals—usually get the least. As for teachers, forget about it. They aren't even on that administrative list. Farther to the south, near Wichita, there's a district with three people—the superintendent, the assistant superintendent, and the "business manager"—who together pull down a quarter million a year, all for running a district with around fifteen hundred kids. The performance of that district is routinely overshadowed by a local Christian school; there, students easily outscore kids from the nearby public schools on standardized tests—and administrators make a tiny fraction of the salaries paid to the public school officials. The superintendent of Catholic schools in the diocese where Cuba is located looks after the needs of thousands of students in schools large and small where scores are always higher than those seen in public schools—and does it all for less than $70,000 a year. As is invariably the case, students' performances in many smaller towns, like Concordia and Lindsborg, where superintendents are justifiably paid on a par with other local professionals, are generally better than those in places like Salina and Wichita, where school administrators are paid much more.

Three years ago, the average salary for a Kansas super in an average town, one the size of Salina or Dodge City, was $150,000. That didn't include the average benefit package:

- $600 a month for car allowance
- $50 a month for cell phone
- $260 a month for health insurance
- $1,900 a year for disability insurance
- $5,100 a year for life insurance premiums
- $15,000 a year for the Kansas Public Employees Retirement System
- $15 a year for a medical exam required by the contract
- An undetermined amount for membership dues to professional organizations, to be approved individually by the board
- One-time moving expenses not to exceed $10,000.[4]

As it happens, my cousin Dale Boyles was for many years a school superintendent in districts in north-central Kansas, buying blackboards and hiring teachers for more than thirty years, until the early 1990s. In his day, he was an underpaid man in poor districts, working more or less the way local government workers did elsewhere in the Midwest: doing as much as possible for as little as possible because somebody had to do it.

He was recruited to teach in the one-room schools of north-central Kansas even before he had graduated from one himself. Eventually, he became a supervisor in towns like Downs and Cuba. His schools flourished, even though Dale was so tight with the taxpayers' money that when he got to Mankato, he personally drove the school bus on its daily rounds to save the cost of hiring a driver. In fact, he still does, and still for free.

I told him I was having a hard time trying to find a relationship between the amount of money paid to administrators, especially superintendents, and the amount of work they did or how well they did it. I had a page full of notes and figures with me. It seemed that in the last ten years, superintendents' salaries had ballooned unbelievably. Example: The superintendent who told that school board in Cuba there were no alternatives to consolidation was paid $103,000 a year—the same as the salary paid to the governor of the state of Kansas. His job was to look after two schools with a combined enrollment of fewer than 250 students.

"If you're looking for a correlation between pay and performance, you won't find one," Dale told me, echoing comments made by several other modestly paid superintendents. "They get paid whatever they can convince people to pay them."

One superintendent, Concordia's Beverly Mortimer, who had risen through the ranks from teaching to the principal's office to the super's desk, said, "I make twenty thousand dollars less than people with half as many students. How can that be?"

The superintendent's job description is a simple one, said Dale. Superintendents implement education regulations imposed by other educational bureaucrats, he said, and they set goals. They create procedures and processes the layman couldn't possibly understand without an advanced degree in educational process making. It sounded to me like basket-weaving without baskets. "The point is," said Dale, "it's mostly PR." The superintendents' most important job is convincing the locals that they've got a great school and traveling to Lincoln or Topeka to persuade the state to give them more and more money for proportionately less and less classroom education.[5] And when that doesn't work, their job, apparently, is to sue the taxpayers to get even more money.

That's what the school superintendent in Salina did, setting off a chain reaction of judicial excess in a case called *Montoy v. Kansas* that will burden the state's taxpayers for a generation—without doing a thing to improve the education of the state's kids.

The political implications of the *Montoy* case form the basis for the following chapter of this book, but a summary might be useful.

The lead plaintiff in the case was Ryan Montoy, the son of a Salina administrator who admitted to reporters that his problem wasn't with academics; he just wanted better athletic facilities for his school because one of his kids, Ryan, a member of his school's football team, was a good athlete. Montoy had been called by his boss, Gary Norris, then superintendent (salary at the time: $131,000, plus perks) of the Salina school district and president of something called Schools for Fair Funding, a group of fourteen cranky, midsized, litigious school districts in Kansas run by administrators who wanted more money.

Norris was looking for some plaintiffs of an ethnic persuasion, and Montoy—well, he was Hispanic. Besides, the guy worked for him. So Montoy said, Yes, boss, and so did a bunch of other people Norris rounded up, some of whom were completely befuddled by the whole thing. He and the others sued, claiming the state didn't do enough to support "at risk" students—a formulation that uses family income to determine who gets cheap meals in the school cafeteria. If you're a family of four with an income of around $36,000 a year—above the average income in the state—your kids are poor and get cheap eats. Less than that, they're victims and "at risk." Nearly a third of the state's 440,000 students eat at little or no charge. The Kansas state supreme court made *Montoy* law in June 2005.

"This is wonderful news for kids in Kansas," announced Norris, who is a former school chorus leader with a Ph.D. in "education leadership." He helped implement a local sales tax to fund Salina schools before heading for Florida. On his way out of town, he told a reporter from the Pittsburg, Kansas, *Morning Sun,* "We now get the chance to prove in court that the school finance system in Kansas is broken. The end result should be a more adequately funded system that is more fairly distributed to Kansas school districts. Eventually, kids will win."[6]

Especially once they adjust to the new artificial football turf (cost: $537,000) Salina installed after the decision.[7] Rah!

Obviously, the massive governmental failure that is public education is accompanied by a shift in how today's administrators define an "education." At the beginning of the last century, it was widely understood that the purpose of an education was to sharpen the mind and stimulate intellectual and spiritual health. Back then, for instance, the kids in Kansas's Wyandotte County were expected to achieve marks of 80 percent or better in science, arithmetic, reading, and writing by the time they left high school—along with all that Latin stuff.

Today, nearly three-quarters of the eleventh-grade students in Wyandotte County schools cannot read well enough to meet the state's minimum level of proficiency. As a rule, when this happens "reforms" are made to create a better set of test results, but even that ploy can't mask persistent failure. In fact, the most consistent result of education reform is more education reform. Eventually, when reforms of other reforms that have been given to experts to reform finally fail, then it's time to *overhaul.* Reforms are expensive, but when you start talking overhaul, you're talking real money. Like hundreds of millions. When the overhaul goes belly-up and schools are still declining, the only way to keep the fiasco in the box is to stretch the concept of education to include the distribution of social welfare services.

This is something many school systems in Kansas have sought to do with vigor. For example, yes, the Wichita schools lag behind both the Kansas average and the national average in ACT scores. There's that. But Wichita schools also conduct various outreach programs and feed children breakfast and lunch on school days. Some children leave school on Fridays having been given enough food to last them through the weekend. The Wichita schools also coordinate "psychosocial groups"—and the "social" part is crucial.

"Pardon my French," one Wichita teacher said disgustedly, summing it up for me in plain English while moonlighting in a liquor store I'd accidentally wandered into while looking for directions to the Côtes-du-Rhône, "but we can't teach them because we're too busy raising them."

Many of the social programs operate without the kinds of controls and accountability that govern conventional government services. Wichita's backpack program is an example. Lena Lank, a program director at Communities in Schools of Wichita/Sedgwick Co., Inc., explained it to me: Her program provides food to "chronically hungry kids"—identified as such not by medical staff but by teachers who are asked to help implement the plan. The program "can't really follow up" on making sure the help is getting to the right people or that the food they distribute for kids ends up feeding people. "We just can't do that," she said. So they don't. First introduced into primary schools, the program has now expanded to include middle school students, and has become part of a raft of other welfare programs administered through schools. When more money is needed for more backpacks, you don't ask for more welfare funding—or even for backpack funding. What you ask for is more "education" funding.

No one doubts that social programs like these may be very valuable services, especially when carefully administered and narrowly targeted. The question is whether this is something one can reasonably call "education"—or whether it's a faith-based initiative for those who have faith in the government. In other words, maybe it's just welfare—and not "education" at all.

But by now it's clear that no matter how many dollars the schools extract from government, sending their administrators off to Lincoln or Topeka to convince the state to give them even more money, it can never be "enough."

Using education as a way of fertilizing government isn't peculiar to Kansas, of course. In Oklahoma the push recently has been for school from the cradle onward—a result, of all things, of Governor Brad Henry's trip to France, of all places, late in 2004. Of all the cool French things Governor Henry, a Democrat, might have found to bring home to Oklahoma—an Eiffel Tower–sized oil rig for Tulsa, maybe, or a topless beach to amuse the fisherfolk of Grand Lake—what he found *most* appealing is the way the government of the Fifth Republic sees to the "education" of French toddlers. (While it's hard to imagine instruction for a two-year-old going beyond real training in the use of WCs, in France it's not unusual for even the littlest students to be in state care for ten hours a day.) Among other things, the governor saw free day care as a surefire vote-and-money getter. No wonder Kansas's Governor Sebelius is advocating something similar.

Of course, the French educational system is entirely consistent with the way the French view government: as the ultimate provider of goods and services, from free day care to free funerals—all at a cost of just under 70 percent of all their earnings in aggregate taxes.[8]

Until recently, the American—and, even more so, the midwestern—tradition has been very different, grounded in the belief that government's role is to establish laws and enforce them so we don't kill one another while trying to make a buck. Beyond that, the role of the government has been to get out of the way. Our assumption is that personal responsibility is the preferred means of ensuring our own welfare.

However, thanks to lawyers, judges, and their political enablers, education in America, even out here, is becoming more French by the minute; and so, in subtle ways, are other aspects of midwestern life. Every minute of every day, midwestern schools become bigger, more expensive, more intrusive, and less effective, less able to teach basic skills and more adapted to expanding government. Big-government advocates know that if red states are to turn blue, the die must be cast in the Midwest's school yards. It's the one area of government expansion that people will embrace uncritically, regardless of their political inclinations. No matter how low outcomes are, the solution is always going to be money. In fact, the lower the outcomes, the easier it is to get the money. And if the outcomes decline so steeply that even badly educated citizens start to catch on, then you just change the way the outcomes are measured and take it from the top again.

It must be exhausting to challenge what has become the prevailing educational orthodoxy, that money is the solution to what ails education, because when political and community leaders object to overfunding education, the press portrays them as hateful and worse. When the Kansas branch of Americans for Prosperity took a bus tour of the state in 2005 to stir interest in a tax-limiting statute, they were met at most of their stops by angry school administrators and board members—the people most responsible for bloating the state's education budget to the point where nobody's certain exactly how they can spend it all—who tried to shout down the tour's speakers. The Kansas Association of School Boards is militantly liberal, demanding ever more money for administrators and the districts they run. Of course, school administrators themselves often lead the charge for bigger checks.

Tour organizer Alan Cobb told me that at one stop in western Kansas, he recognized the superintendent from a district an hour or so away who had taken time off from his job to drive over to spend some time "screaming," Cobb said, at the top of his lungs trying to interrupt the visiting speakers. The behavior of school administrators, he said, was "just rude. They were the ones who yelled the loudest."

Someone else trying to point to the consequences of the runaway expansion of "education" is a former ice-cream exec turned seminar leader from Iowa, Jamie Vollmer, who visits some eighty districts a year to give pep talks to school administrators and who was very careful to tell me he was not by any means a conservative.

At his visits, Vollmer hands out posters with a long, long list of all the social engineering and government services that have been added to what schools are supposed to do in addition to teaching the basics. The list starts with teaching "health" in 1900 and goes on through the decades to include teaching "peace"; drug education; "character education"; women's studies; "inclusion"; and, finally, "death education." Teaching reading, writing, and arithmetic to kids is what parents like to think their school is doing, but there's no time for that kind of education. Vollmer sees a near-complete disconnect between the community's perception of "school" and what the thing actually is and does. "Parents just don't know," he said.

An enormous part of the problem is the accretive nature of the educational bureaucracy itself. Bob L. Corkins, who served briefly as state education commissioner, seemed to share some of the concerns of those who think public education in places like Kansas needs a serious rethink. When I asked him about the crazy compulsion to consolidate, for example, he told me that he felt the state "should try to help small rural communities and try to give them choices and alternatives." Corkins, like almost all Kansas parents, was an outsider to the state's education establishment. You might suspect that after decades of the same old failed approaches to solving the growing problems of children and public education, an outsider is what's needed. But when one was appointed, he was reviled by the state's governor, Democrats, "moderate" politicians, and especially by the regional press. Kansas liberals were furious because somebody from the class of people who had created the problems with education hadn't been brought in to "solve" it. So when Corkins suggested venturing off the well-trod path of banal formulas and tired platitudes and started talking about vouchers and school choice, they went into full howl, not bothering to counter the ideas with some of their own but settling instead for trivial and embarrassing ad hominem attacks. Not surprisingly, Corkins is now gone, along with a couple of the conservatives on the Kansas State Board of Education, all targets in the 2006 elections.[9]

Consolidation will continue no matter who's in office, of course, but for those who are serious about innovation in education, especially in smaller, rural districts, some Republican state legislators have seemed willing to pitch in to help. "I think there are a number of us open to finding new solutions," said former state representative Kathe Decker, who chaired the legislature's education committee in 2005. "If [rural district school boards] come to us and say we want to do something new and present some different ideas, the legislature would embrace that," she told me at the time. "You do what you can, whatever it takes, to save your school."

Decker's replacement is Clay Aurand, the former majority leader in the Kansas house and a farmer who represents Formoso, Mankato, and Burr Oak in the Kansas legislature. "I'm surprised more [parents] haven't come forward to ask for help," he told me. "With consolidation and these other problems, we have some ideas that can help. But they have to ask. I wish they would."

Ironically, these days in Kansas (as in Nebraska and elsewhere in America), there are huge obstacles to restoring common sense to public education. But the biggest may be parents themselves. Parents everywhere feel they need help. As more than one told me, it's hard not to be seduced by the array of government services there for the taking, very many of them through the schools, even if it also means the schools ultimately will shortchange the children.

Kansans watch Oprah and Katie out here as avidly as any other Americans, and taxes always go up, so who can blame them if they're increasingly open to the notion that social welfare *should* be what schools are for, along with a little reading and writing. For the Salina man a hundred years ago, this might have all seemed like a joke. But it's been at least twenty years since midwesterners thought seriously about education, and during that time it has grown in costs and declined in performance. It's the kind of cynical story a Salina man could have his children read to him at night, if only they could read.

Judging and Politics

You'd think that if a runaway judiciary could be stopped anywhere, it would be in Kansas. But the state's ruling class spent most of the last half of the twentieth century building a fortress judiciary, one designed to stand up to decades of protest, ridicule, and resentment such as it is only now beginning to attract. Small wonder Kansans have been as unsuccessful restraining their judiciary as everyone else.

And now they're going to pay for it: Like the taxpayers in forty-five of the fifty states, Kansans are being forced to pay a tax imposed on them by judges deciding exactly how much money taxpayers should spend on those expensive schools of theirs.

In Kansas, as elsewhere, these decrees are usually a consequence of a ruling in an "equity" lawsuit. There are dozens of these lawsuits going on at any given time in almost every state. Many of them involve hundreds of millions—even billions—of dollars. For bureaucrats, it's a genius way to sneak big, expensive government into communities suspicious of it. For lawyers, education is the new tobacco, and business is smoking.

As a rule, educational equity lawsuits involve relatively small cohorts of plaintiffs with specific gripes. In Kansas, for example, a small group of parents and the school administrators in those midsized school districts in Salina and Dodge complained that small, rural districts got more per pupil than they did, while big schools in affluent neighborhoods were able to augment state funds with local levies. In *Montoy v. Kansas,* they said they wanted more money for some of their Spanish-speaking, disadvantaged, and at-risk students. The basis for the complaint: A passage in the constitution that says the "legislature shall make suitable provision for finance of the educational interests of the state."

Of course, that's probably what most Kansans thought they were doing already. Not much was the matter with education in Kansas. The 2005 session of the legislature had already voted a $142 million increase in educational spending, a boost lawmakers awarded to make up for not voting increases for several years. Funding throughout Kansas was rising faster than school enrollment, and even without the increase, the state spent more than its neighbors did on schools—two-thirds of the state budget, in fact—and it already distributed that money more equitably than most other states in the Union did. Every year, nearly ten grand is spent on every student in the state—up from just under $7,000 a mere five years ago. Kansas pays its teachers fairly; they make more than most citizens in this low-cost-of-living state. The state produces graduates whose performance is in the top ten nationally, something that has been constant for the last few generations—although in 2005, as spending reached an all-time high, achievement in some areas showed a slight decline.

As the *Wall Street Journal* noted that year, "the link between school spending and educational achievement is close to nonexistent." Nonetheless, in *Montoy,* the court found that the word "suitable" translates in money-talk to exactly $143 million *more* than the $142 million increase the legislature had just approved. In 2007, that figure will begin to swell, until it reaches nearly a billion dollars and, according to some experts, starts costing the state jobs and a loss in productivity.

Where did the court find its figures? It accepted as evidence a 2001 study by Augenblick & Myers, one of a handful of education experts who are retained by state officials and unsuspecting legislatures to help them think about how much should be spent on reading, writing, arithmetic, and condom use for middle schoolers. The study called for an increase of $850 million for the schools of Kansas.

Consultants like A&M are well-known for their methodology—findings are often heavily influenced by researchers simply going to school administrators and asking, "How much money do you need?" Which is roughly akin to asking a meth-head, "How much crank do you need?" The huge sums these experts recommend are laughed off by the legislators who ask for them. When they got to the bottom line on the A&M study, for example, the Kansas legislature didn't even bother saying, "Forget it!" before tossing it aside.

But it's dangerous to leave studies like these lying around. They're loaded guns in the hands of lawyers—in Kansas, it was a sexual harassment and workers' rights litigator named Alan Rupe—who grab them and bring them to court, along with bales of even more data harvested from George W. Bush's ill-conceived No Child Left Behind education plan, with its stacks of test scores, charts, graphs, and other fodder for evidence-starved brief filers.

The judge in the *Montoy* case was Terry Bullock, a colorful judicial character, who drew on decisions by other activist judges in crafting his own and who used the A&M study as evidence because, he claimed, there was no other evidence presented. In his decision, Bullock admitted that although "ordinarily it is not the Court's role to direct the Legislature on how to levy taxes or on how to spend the funds it does collect, this case is the exception. . . . [The legislature] has no choice when it comes to funding education. Under the Constitution, it simply must do it and do it adequately." He ordered the legislature to allocate the additional $143 million or he would close the state's schools. He also took control of local funding away from the school districts so that parents in wealthier areas, where taxes are higher, wouldn't be able to augment state money. This required state levels to be increased everywhere—that was the "equity" part of the deal.

But, of course, the real nature of Bullock's interest wasn't education. It was taxation: "As a result of the significant tax cuts passed by the Kansas Legislature during the past ten years," he wrote, "the state has forfeited nearly $7 billion in funds which it would have otherwise had in the treasury. The depletion for 2005 alone is $918 million!"

Forfeited? Depletion? Exclamation point? Funding schools is one thing; writing tax policy is another. Neither of them is typically a judge's job. By making it his, Bullock worried more than just Kansans. Concerns rippled across the country. In Washington, D.C., attorney Megan Brown, commenting on *Montoy*, warned, "If more states follow this path . . . reducing deference to legislatures in administering school systems, the jurisprudential and practical effect may be to substantially erode the functional and structural separation of power between branches of state government."[1] Bullock essentially took the power of taxation away from the elected legislature and its unpleasant array of conservatives and put it safely in the hands of lawyers, "experts," and judges like himself.

Foolishly, the legislature failed to take Bullock's odd *Montoy* decision seriously, assuming the state's supreme court would do what other courts around the country had done and declare the funding of public education a political matter. The legislature treated the Bullock decision the same way it treated the Augenblick & Myers study: It ignored it and assumed the state's supreme court would throw the decision out. Of course, it didn't.

The court—and especially Justice Donald Allegrucci, whose wife had been the governor's chief of staff and whose stepson Governor Sebelius had appointed as state tourism director[2]—was not very subtle in hiding its disregard for the legislature, and especially for the conservatives who led the house. At one point, when it was noted that the legislature had just approved $143 million more for education in the 2005 regular session, Allegrucci snorted, "That's not saying much."[3]

In the end, of course, the court not only upheld *Montoy*, it went further: In addition to telling the legislature to spend the money, it also decreed how *much* to spend—another $143 million was a good start, with hundreds of millions more to come. If the legislature failed to come up with the money, the court said, the schools would be closed.

The court was now in a pitched battle with the Kansas house. The court also didn't like those tax cuts Bullock had yelled about, so either the tax cuts would be rolled back and more money spent or all the schools in Kansas would be closed—an ultimatum that the court thought might get the attention of most parents. Politicians from both parties, along with a majority of Kansans, agreed with the common-sense observation that the court had overstepped itself, and some legal experts thought the same thing. In making its decision, then-attorney general Phill Kline told me, the court "clearly demonstrated the creative evasion of constitutional principles."

Reading the polls wasn't difficult for Sebelius. She issued a statement containing a Clinton-class waffle: "While I share the displeasure of many Kansans at the court decision, especially ordering the Legislature for a specific amount of money and weakening our local control over schools, I believe that investing in our children and their education is the best way to guarantee future prosperity for our state."[4]

But thinking the court was wrong was one thing; exploiting the court's wrongness was something else. Lots of people were much more interested in milking Kansas taxpayers than in the separation of powers enshrined in *Marbury v. Madison,* so the governor, joined by liberal Republicans and Democrats, all quickly lined up behind the court, while the conservatives in the house—led by then-speaker Doug Mays of Topeka and joined, at least at first, by a small number of moderates who also thought the court was out of line—dug in for a fight they thought they might not win but at least had to wage. The press waded in with its boilerplate narrative: Mean-spirited Republican conservatives were trying to close Kansas schools! And were wasting everybody's time in order to avoid spending a little money on the children![5] To this narrative would all details conform in the weeks to come.

If the legislature, at its own peril, had ignored the Augenblick & Myers study and the Bullock decision, Sebelius was more than happy to ignore the significance of this nutty judicial power grab by what amounted to a group of the governor's friends and political allies. She moved quickly to lend support to the media narrative and to make it clear just who the bad guys were: "The Legislature's inability to fulfill its obligation to Kansas students has finally come home to roost," she said in a June 3, 2005, press release. "Still, I am relieved that the Legislature, after six years of wrangling, has been given another opportunity to find a real solution for funding our schools. We need to act in the best interests of Kansas children and their parents, above all else, and we cannot afford more legislative irresponsibility."

Releasing that statement was as close as the governor ever got to providing public leadership on the potentially volatile issue. She simply went mum, retreated behind closed doors, and began working with Democrats and liberal Republicans on a strategy to defeat the house leadership. The court had done its part, and now Kansas's ruling elite would do theirs.

The budget Sebelius had presented in 2004 had asked for an additional $310 million for education, spread over three years—but with an income tax and sales tax increase to pay for it. The legislature looked at the performance of Kansas students, saw they were among the best in the nation, and voted the tax increases down.

In January 2005, the state's supreme court had made its decision to set funding (and therefore tax) levels for education and had given the state until April to do the work. The legislature paid as much attention to this as a supreme court justice would to a parking ticket issued by a legislator. As for Sebelius, her 2005 budget asked for more money for state bureaucrats and more money for welfare—to be paid for by drawing down the state's reserves—but not a cent more for the public schools.

In January, when the court had fallen in line and backed Bullock, Sebelius had staked out her strategy: "I think it's important for the majority party who runs the House and Senate to have a plan that they think meets the Supreme Court challenge, and then we can talk about it," she told a group of statehouse reporters. "So I'm just saying to the leaders, 'Show me the meat, boys.'"[6]

Sebelius kicked back to watch the state's constitutional crisis unfold.

Her work had been done for her by the court. She was safe. After all, the legislature hadn't really been "given another opportunity to find a real solution for funding our schools," had it? It had been given an opportunity to accept judicial power grabbing or face a state full of closed schools. Sebelius's version of "legislative responsibility" was to use the courts to increase the size of government and raise taxes, since the chances were nobody would ever vote for such a thing, especially without a good reason.

So to give the legislature "another opportunity to find a real solution for funding our schools," the governor called a special session of the legislature to respond to the court's demand. She told the reporters she had only one question for the legislature: "How are you going to solve this?"[7]

When the state house and senate convened in June 2005, the real focus of the special session became instantly clear. You could see it in the smiling faces of the patient gambling lobbyists loitering in the hallways and corridors outside Sebelius's statehouse office. During her campaign for the governorship, she had received contributions from gaming interests—Kline said he had "only heard secondhand, but it's a lot"—and she liked the idea of gambling as a way of raising revenue. The consequences of gaming and the expense of its attendant social ills were ignored, as was the hunch—even felt by some statehouse journalists—that gambling was the wrong way for the state to raise more money. Poor people love to gamble; for the state to exploit that, some felt, is to put a tax on hope. While Kansas already had some limited gaming—local Native American tribes run casinos under a deal made in the great spirit of restitution with a previous Democratic governor in which the state receives no revenue at all—the new plan Sebelius wanted would be different. The casinos would be owned by the state of Kansas.

As the session got under way, house speaker Doug Mays realized he was in for what he later called "a nightmare." Everyone knew that what happened in the special session would be more important than anything that had been passed in the previous two sessions. A lot was at stake. But Mays was trying to govern a caucus, which, during the special session at least, was often filled with Byzantine intrigues and hostile suspicion. He was very reluctant to discipline his wayward liberal members, since if he threw them out of the Republican caucus, he feared the Democrats might be able to take control of the house. Mays knew he needed about ten more conservatives in the house before he could play bad cop.

I have been told that the statehouse wasn't usually as politically heated as it was during the summer of 2005. In fact, Mays was often effusive in praise of his Democratic opposite, Dennis McKinney, that quiet, intelligent farmer who is usually so reasonable he's routinely reelected without opposition in a district that is only 25 percent Democratic. The two men attend the same church in Topeka, where they sometimes share a pew. According to McKinney, "Between a third and a half of the Democratic caucus is pro-life," and many describe themselves as social conservatives.

In the middle are those "moderate" Republicans, nearly two dozen of them, making their deals and holding back the conservative tide to make sure the liberals and Democrats can block legislation—or, when necessary, even produce outright Democratic victories. It's a very complicated place, the Kansas statehouse. On one day, there might be three parties (never less) and on another, seven or eight. As longtime local TV newsman Mike Mahoney wisecracked during the house debate, "I tell people I know what it's like to cover European politics. I've been to the Kansas legislature."

The deal making began at the bell: Mays told a Republican caucus that Sebelius had already offered to make a deal to get a gambling agreement passed. "This special session is about gaming," Mays grimly informed the assembled Republicans. Indeed, the governor herself had told a press conference that gaming was the only way to pay for extra funding for schools—well, that and cutting unnecessary spending elsewhere. When I asked what unnecessary spending she had in mind, she couldn't answer.

The 2004 elections had seen an increase in the number of conservatives sent to the Kansas house. They arrived for the special session in no mood to surrender and agreed with Kline when he said the court had "obliterated" *Marbury v. Madison* in making its decision upholding Bullock. Many conservatives felt the best strategy was to do nothing at all and let the court stew in the mess it had made. The Associated Press crushed that strategy by moving a piece across the state under a rather disingenuous headline reading, "Are Conservatives Trying to Force Shutdown of Schools?" The "analysis"—with the headline intact—was picked up by most of the newspapers in the state. The heavy-handed slant outraged the conservatives.

"I really have criticism for the media coverage of the issues in this state and the use of deceptive terms," Kline said. "Most Kansans walk with their feet on the ground and have common sense about them. If they understood what was going on here and the issues that were in play, I think seventy percent of them would be with us." He singled out the AP for special criticism, but also blamed "the cynicism of the state's editorial pages."

"The media folks have no understanding of what the separation of powers means or even if it has value," Kline told me. "To them it's all about how can they get the *policy* they think is important. They don't care if it's mandated by a court or if it's passed in a bill. It doesn't make any difference to them. 'Just get me what I want when I want it, and that's now.'"

But other, more moderate conservatives, led by veteran lawmaker Mike O'Neal, arrived with a different plan in mind. They argued that the function of the special session should be to amend the constitution to keep the courts in check and out of the budgeting business. So a freshman legislator, Lance Kinzer, an attorney, tried to introduce an amendment prohibiting loopy judicial power grabs like Bullock's and cited a 1962 precedent by the court itself in which the court sensibly admitted that it lacked the power of the purse. The amendment would have had to pass voter scrutiny, of course. But although it was minor—a couple of clarifying sentences—and, in the perhaps misspoken words of the governor, "wouldn't really change the . . . constitution," the Democrats and liberal Republicans blocked it. When conservatives tried for another constitutional amendment, this one designed simply to tell the courts that they can't close schools as a means of enforcing a decision, the Democrats and their liberal Republican allies blocked that one, too.

The argument made by those who successfully blocked the amendments was that the issue was "too complicated" for voters to understand, Democratic leader Dennis McKinney told me. Although he had earlier allowed that a constitutional amendment prohibiting the courts from closing schools to force funding might be acceptable, he changed his mind as it became clear the Democrats wouldn't have to give up anything to get what they wanted. After a week of the special session, the amendment idea was going nowhere in the Democratic caucus. "There just isn't time to think through this clearly," McKinney said.

As the special session ground on, Mays was put under increasing pressure—and not just from conservatives, some of whom were still quite militant in not wanting to give the court a cent, on the principle that doing so would be tantamount to agreeing with the court's seizure of legislative authority. He knew that wouldn't hold for long. Joann Freeborn, at the time the moderately conservative Concordia representative, thought at first the house might get away with awarding $4 million. Within hours, she had revised that to $40 million. A day later, her guess was over $100 million.

The Republican caucus meetings took on an increasingly somber tone. Mays looked especially shaken after one private meeting with the governor. When I asked him about it later, he said a furious Sebelius had berated him at length and in personal terms in front of a room full of other legislators. "It was the worst meeting I have ever attended, the worst experience I have had [in Topeka]," he said.

That says a lot, since Mays had had many rotten experiences just during that special session. It was clear that the conservatives were going to fail in their bid to restrain the court; the media, against them from the beginning, were now fully engaged in portraying the conservatives as school-closing, penny-pinching monsters. And Mays himself was coming to be seen under an increasingly harsh light.

At the same time, the state senate, which had at first been noisily denouncing the court with meaningless speeches and bills, suddenly went silent; when I asked Phil Journey, the wry and clever senator from Haysville, what was going on, he just shrugged and joked, "I was going to ask you." Dennis Pyle, Karin Brownlee, and other conservative senators were in the dark, too. Moderate Republican Derek Schmidt, the ambitious and ambiguous majority leader of the senate, kept a profile so low he was shadowless. He apparently didn't want to return my call looking for a comment.

Finally, as the battle raged on inconclusively, Clay Aurand, the house majority leader, called the Republicans into caucus to refine the GOP strategy and get a reading on the mood of the caucus. Mays listened distractedly as a conservative delivered a not-a-nickel-unless-they-pry-it-from-my-cold-dead-hand rant, but looked a little taken aback when somebody idly asked him what senate president Steve Morris was up to. Mays shrugged and turned to Aurand and asked him if he'd heard anything. Aurand shook his head. Finally, Mays said, "I don't really know." The senate leadership, he said, wasn't telling him anything.

That's when Ward Loyd, a liberal Republican from Garden City, stood up and told Mays and the assembled Republicans *exactly* what was going on—that he and the other moderate Republicans had been working with Morris, the Democrats, and the governor and that a deal had been done. Aurand's jaw tightened. Mays sat in stunned silence.

The Republican legislative hierarchy is schismatic, to say the least. Moderate Republicans and their Democratic allies hold the ultimate power, and the 2006 election gave them a little more of that.

Steve Morris is the gentlemanly, soft-spoken leader of the state senate, nominally controlled by its vast Republican majority, but safely onside with the Democrats and "moderates" when it really matters. He is also widely, although perhaps unfairly, suspected by some statehouse in-siders of being a pawn of John Vratil, an influential attorney and senate vice president.

Morris and Vratil often avoid contact with the speaker of the house altogether—as was the case during the most pivotal moments of that special session. Morris admitted to me in an interview that he and others had "a number of meetings" with the governor and decided to block the conservatives when he and his coalition of moderates and Democrats felt they "needed to go ahead and do something else." When I asked why he hadn't alerted Mays to the plan Loyd had sprung on the house Republican caucus, he explained it simply for me: "For me to pick up the phone and say, 'Well, Doug, we're just going to roll over you with this coalition'— we just didn't want to do that."

Morris used the terminology of the media in describing the problems he faced as a "moderate" senate president trying to work with a conservative house. "Ideology is a problem," he said. "We have a number of house members who are ultraconservatives—and we have some in the senate, too—and they just don't want to do anything."

This sort of thing, of course, only infuriates those "ultraconservative" state senators. Morris is aware of the animosity conservatives feel toward him and returns it. "They make life miserable, to put it bluntly," he told me.

Not everyone, however, was prepared to accept that the cause was completely lost. Representatives Mike O'Neal and Kathe Decker, correctly seen on the spectrum of the legislature's Italian-style political factions as "moderate conservatives," determined to at least get the senate to fall in line with a plan that would clarify the constitutional issues.

O'Neal, a genial attorney from Hutchinson, was seen as perhaps too moderate by some conservative lawmakers, but most viewed him as a thoughtful man who commanded respect. Decker was a no-nonsense woman used to the political infighting of a sometimes fractious district. Backed by the increasingly desperate house, the pair worked hard to fashion an agreement with the senate's moderate leadership, represented by the leaders of the senate education committee, Jean Schodorf, an employee of the Wichita school district and a former Wichita school board member, and the senate vice president, Vratil.[8] The effort ultimately led to what I thought was the defining moment of the session.

In the wee hours of Saturday morning, after an extended Friday night session had produced an agreement that Vratil and Schodorf had promised would be taken to a waiting senate, O'Neal and Decker, the two house negotiators, were left sitting at a conference table in a silent, nearly empty room, waiting for the slow wheel of legislative process to come around to their position.

The promise of senate support was the house's one last hope, and after a lengthy negotiation, Vratil and Schodorf had taken an agreement out of the room. "We were told the senate was there, that they were in session, waiting to hear" from Vratil and Schodorf, O'Neal told me later. "We were definitely told the senate had not gone, that we should wait and we'd see what would happen next." The house might have to throw a big pile of money at "education," but at least its representatives would leave the state with some constitutional clarity. It would be yet another example of Kansas's default to common sense.

I watched from the nearly vacant visitors' area. Two o'clock passed. It seemed that the room grew dimmer and dimmer. Suddenly, quietly, Vratil entered. O'Neal looked at him expectantly. The senator picked up a pen he had forgotten, then, without a word, shrugged, turned, and walked out the door. Schodorf had already gone home; I was told later that she'd left feeling personally slighted by some aspect of the process. There was no waiting senate. The whole thing had been a sham. O'Neal quietly said to a shocked Decker, "They're gone." They stood and left, and by sunrise, the deal was dead.

What had happened? More than a year later, I asked O'Neal what he thought Morris and Vratil's strategy had been that night. "It was obviously a play for time," he said, still troubled by the episode. "But why, I don't think I'll ever know."

The crucial battle of the special session had been lost and, with it, the house's hope of restraining the state's courts. Isolated and outmaneuvered by the governor, the state senate leadership, the Democrats and liberal Republicans in the house, and the state's judiciary, after twelve days Mays and the conservatives were finally done. "I'm amazed we held out this long," Mays said.

In a prepared statement given to the press after the session ended, Sebelius said, "This is exactly the outcome I was hoping for when I first brought legislators together back in January to start working on a school plan."

The legislature ended up voting to spend even more than the court mandated—an additional $148.4 million to add to the money they had given schools in the regular session, and increasing school spending by almost $300 million in less than a year. As the session ended, Sebelius and the liberal GOP–Democratic alliance in the statehouse seemed set to pass additional legislation that, over time, would pipe another billion or so into Kansas's educational bureaucracy. The collapse of Republican unity is a preview of how Democrats hope to turn Kansas deep blue. When the house finally adjourned, the state's media was jubilant. The AP's accurate, if acidic, end-of-session headline: "Conservatives Get Rolled in Special Session; Sebelius Big Winner."

In the aftermath of the special session, the cozy relationship between Kansas's ruling cliques tumbled into the spotlight. Two very good Topeka reporters, Tim Carpenter and Chris Moon of the *Capital-Journal,* made inquiries following a report that Morris and another moderate senator, Pete Brungardt, had met over lunch with supreme court justice Lawton Nuss. As an attorney, Nuss had previously represented the Salina school district before going on to the court and awarding millions to his former clients. Morris first claimed that running into Nuss had been a happy coincidence—a coincidence made even more joyful by the fact that Nuss had brought along a spreadsheet showing school funding projections. Nuss recused himself as demands for an inquiry grew.[9] At the same time, Morris began bragging to others about his ability to "back-channel" his communication with the court. Mays launched an investigation of all this with a house committee headed by Mike O'Neal. Representing Morris: his attorney, John Vratil. The investigation went nowhere.

The funding issue will drag on for years—for as long, one suspects, as the lawyers can submit their bills. Rupe told local reporters he didn't want to disclose his fees, but even by mid-2005, as the *Capital-Journal's* Moon reported, the bill was getting pretty steep: "As the Kansas Supreme Court continues closed-door deliberations over the constitutionality of the state's school funding system, the tab for the six-year legal battle is approaching $3 million. All of it is funded by taxpayers."[10]

This exasperates some of Kansas's older political veterans. Ross O. Doyen, who spent thirty-four years in the statehouse, including a stint as president of the Kansas senate, was critical of the behavior of the "moderates" during the special session. He told me he thought it was time to rethink education completely. "We need to get back to basics and start from there," he said. "I hate to see money just being poured on this problem. That's not going to help."

It'll help somebody. Gambling lobbyists are especially hopeful. They swarm around the cool statehouse, waiting out the Kansas weather. On nice days, they lounge in the park surrounding the beautiful building. On cold nights, they frequent the local bars, where they greet the occasional legislator stepping out for a drink.[11] They know that eventually a huge debt for funding education will be generated by the courts and the legislature, and their moment will come. In fact, on my way out of the statehouse after the special session finally ended, I found myself in an elevator with three cheerful Democrats—two representatives and a staffer.

"Come back next year," one of them told me. "We'll be passing gaming!"[12]

Descent of the Straw Man

As I was working on this book, a friend of mine called from New York to ask me what in the world was going on in midwestern classrooms. He'd just read that Kansas—or maybe Nebraska? anyway, one of those states out there—had passed a law saying science teachers had to tell kids the world had been created in six days and that they couldn't mention Darwin. "No Darwin? Are they crazy? Or just stupid?"

That again. The answer was still neither, of course—although I couldn't blame my friend, since the press's coverage of the suggested revisions in the Kansas state science standards itself had been less than scientific. Schools are often a battleground in the culture wars, covered with the smoke of hocus-pocus and superstition. In this case, the myth was that Kansas conservatives wanted the Bible to be used as a science text. That wasn't quite the case, however.

So what had happened? Well, not much. On November 7, 2005, the state board of education had changed a passage in the state's science guidelines, from this:

> Science is the human activity of seeking natural explanations for what we observe in the world around us.

to this:

Science is a systematic method of continuing investigation that uses observations, hypothesis testing, measurement, experimentation, logical argument and theory building to lead to more adequate explanations of natural phenomena.

The board also suggested that students should be required to "understand the major concepts of the theory of biological evolution," and they allowed that some teachers might want to inform their students, without going into detail, that there might be some controversy surrounding the theory of evolution.

It seemed minor to me, but since a million words or so had been written damning Kansans for being religious primitives, I felt I should look into this sudden eruption of medievalism. So I went to the state's education department and asked somebody to explain to me exactly what effect this revision would have in classrooms. One woman, who asked not to be named, told me she had felt pressure "to say it would have a big effect. But really," she added conspiratorially, "it won't change a thing. There are three hundred school districts in Kansas, and each of them decides what will and won't be taught in their classrooms, and nothing we say will affect that."

Maybe, but that message wasn't getting through to those who were concerned most—including many smart but, given what they were being told, justifiably worried parents. For example, a longtime former state representative who now serves on his local education board explained to me that while the state board of education "has almost no real power," like many Kansans he was concerned that the board's influence could be significant. And his wife, a teacher, was deeply troubled by the possibility that she might be asked to teach something scientifically indefensible in a science class. Like many parents, they were worried that the school system was going to be used to do the job given to churches.

The state board members, realizing how volatile the issue had become, tried to make the science-standards question into a nonissue. "We don't want religion taught in the schools," Kathy Martin, a conservative state board member from Clay Center, told me when I called to ask about it. "We don't want intelligent design taught in schools. We want science taught in schools." Martin said that for her and for the other members of the state board of education, that meant that when it came time to discuss the emergence of life on earth, the theory of evolution would do nicely, thanks, controversy or not.

Nevertheless, the very notion that there could be *anything* controversial about Darwinian evolution ratcheted up the already deafening level of the controversy until eventually it evolved into full hysteria.

Whatever its intentions may have been, the Kansas State Board of Education produced a fabulously effective set piece of political theater, complete with a special effect in which a dead but eminent British naturalist—Charles Darwin—evolved first into a straw man and then into a baby seal, while earnest, middle-class conservative board members morphed into huge, club-swinging Canadians.

The history of this kind of controversy is as old as Scopes's monkey. In fact, the famous courtroom battle between Clarence Darrow and William Jennings Bryan was an event staged by the ACLU, eager to beat up on biblical literalists. All they needed was a little casting and a good location. In 1925, they found a town dumb enough to volunteer for pitiless self-parody in Dayton, Tennessee, and a willing "victim" in John Scopes, a part-time biology teacher. The rest is bad history.

Eighty years later, the revival was playing in Kansas. The board's mouse-sized alteration in a set of practically meaningless "standards" liberated the inner thespian in every pundit and politician. Everybody wanted to be Clarence Darrow—especially as played by Spencer Tracy—even if only for a thousand words.

For Ted Koppel, perhaps unaware of what's been happening in education for the last two generations, the Kansas standards "really could lead ultimately to the undermining of the public school system." Charles Krauthammer accused the board of ed of causing "a national embarrass-

ment" and "forcing intelligent design into the statewide biology curriculum." George Will found the board members "the kind of conservatives
who make conservatism repulsive to temperate people" and seemed to
agree with a *New York Times* reporter who claimed that the standards revision would "require that challenges to Darwin's theories be taught in
the state's classrooms [and] change the definition of science itself." For
more nuanced pundits, like Salman Rushdie, "in dumping Darwin,
Kansas becomes a kind of Oz."

To find out how this had happened, I went to visit the state board of education's most controversial member at the time, Connie Morris.

Morris is the wife of a plumbing and heating contractor and lives in the
northwest corner of the state, at the opposite end of the Republican River
from Clay Center, near the quiet, dusty town of St. Francis—which was
named not after the critter-loving monk from Assisi but for the *wife* of a
poor man named Captain A. L. Emerson, in 1885. The town's on U.S. 36
near where the Republican crosses beneath the highway the first time, out
by the Colorado border, but there aren't many good reasons for blue-staters
to be on this stretch of 36, unless it's to write about how empty it is for
the *New York Times.* Interstate 70, not far to the south, siphons off most of
the Denver-bound traffic through Goodland, where there's a thirty-two-by-
twenty-four-foot reproduction of one of van Gogh's sunflower paintings sitting on an eighty-foot easel sold to the town by a Canadian artist for a mere
$150,000. You can see it from the highway. It looks tiny.

It seems like everything's supersized out here, from the sky on down
to the end of the road that connects Goodland to 36 and St. Francis. This
end of Kansas is the wide, high, dry, flat part people from someplace else
think about when they think about nothing in particular. It contrasts in
obvious ways with the eastern side of the state, which, in comparison, is a
lush, green paradise.

Even for folks in Holcomb, St. Francis is out there; by the time you
arrive, you certainly can't help having the feeling that you're a long way

from everyplace else—and you are. As the sign on the highway reminds you, St. Francis is "As Good as It Gets"—unless you're willing to turn around and drive all the way back to Goodland.

Self-sufficiency is the civic subtext. St. Francis is prepared for the rest of the world to go away. The town is even county-fair sustainable: St. Francis owns its own midway rides and parks them in the fairgrounds, so there's no need to import those nasty carnies with their colorful tats and habits just for a once-a-year shindig. For fifty-one weeks, the Ferris wheel, the hammer, the Tilt-A-Whirl, and the rest just sit there. During the first week in August, workers cut down all the weeds, plug everything in, turn the switch, rev up the cotton candy machine, and everybody in St. Francis goes to the fair. The complete artifice of metropolitan life is evident everywhere in northwestern Kansas, where all the streets are extra-wide because *everything* is extra-wide.

Morris's new home is surrounded by miles and miles of scrub, sage, and some of the nastiest briars and thornbushes this side of a Tibetan hell. When I arrived, one of the first things she told me was where she wanted to locate her alligator farm—and she was serious. "Shoes, bags, that kind of thing," she said. Then she took me inside her temporary shelter—a mobile home parked in a barn while work on the new house nearby wrapped up—and told me about the two boys who had come out to make a video documentary about her to show at Sundance. I looked around, wondering—but she caught me. "No, I trust them," she said. "I think they'll be fair." To the alligators, maybe.

Morris is young, pretty, and fits the description I personally think is meant by the word "pert." She's got short brown hair and dresses tomboy-style, and was remarkably frank in answering my questions.

- Did she call Darwinism a "fairy tale"? "Yes."
- Does she personally believe in evolution? "No."
- Does she personally believe in good and evil? "Yes, I do. I believe in the traditional Judeo-Christian teachings."

- Does she personally think the Book of Genesis should be used to teach science in Kansas? "Goodness no!"
- How about evolution? Even if she didn't believe in it, did she believe that it should be taught? "Of course. It's the dominant theory we have, and it would be ridiculous not to teach it. I personally believe there are holes in the theory, and I don't know if it should be spoon-fed as *fact* when it's a theory, but I'm okay with that. I mean, it's science and it's what we have and I think we should teach what we know."
- Had she been prepared for what had happened to her in the press? "No, I've been around—I've been hurt, abused, molested, and raped twice. I've been around, but I wasn't prepared for *this*."

"This" is a relentless barrage by the press not only in Kansas but across the country. By the time I met with her, it had become intensely personal, going far beyond the usual "conservatives are mean" and "conservatives are stupid" pieces that are the staples of op-ed pages everywhere. When a Kansas City tabloid ran a hatchet job under the headline "The Strange Redemption of Connie Morris, High School Slut Turned Kansas State Board of Education Anti-Evolutionist,"[1] a journalist sent an e-mailed message to his colleagues touting the piece as a good read. It certainly got around. A year and a half later, if you Googled "Connie Morris" and "slut" you got nearly two thousand citations.

When I asked her about the media in general, and that piece specifically, she was visibly upset. For the first time, her voiced cracked, as she accused the writer of having just regurgitated the "ugliest" parts of a tell-all memoir she had written years earlier.[2] It was true that the piece contained nothing that hadn't already seen ink. "But [the tabloid writer] hit a new low. He called my *parents,* who are nearly eighty, and my father . . ." Her voice broke off for a moment. "Well, that hurt me. I hate to admit it, but it did. To see them smear your name—for what? A political issue? One they don't even understand?"

The board of education in Kansas is divided into two permanently warring camps, with control going back and forth, depending on who's paying attention. In 1999, conservatives were in. In 2001, they were out. By 2005, they were in again. Darwin dogged them everywhere. Liberals on the board are in a state of perpetual anger and vote as a bloc.

Conservatives are less cohesive; they recently split on some sex-ed policies, for example. But in the back-and-forth of things, Morris had become a favored target of some of the liberal members of the board, no doubt because of her blunt style.

When it came to explaining the revised standards she and other conservatives had put in place, Morris at least had been clear in her explanations of what the standards do and don't do. "Intelligent design doesn't have anything to do with what we're debating," she told CNN. "I know that lots of people want to make it true that we're trying to insert intelligent design or, heaven forbid, creationism in the standards, but that's not what we're doing. Nowhere near that. We're not trying to insert religion whatsoever."

She described to me how she had finally challenged one of the board's liberals, Sue Gamble, to shine a little light on the debate during a showdown at one board of education meeting. "I asked if somebody, anybody, would show me where there is religion or 'creationism' in any form, because I'd like to take it out. She hemmed and hawed and finally said, 'I don't have to.' She's a very unhappy woman."

Morris wasn't very joyful either. She thought the whole issue was being blown out of proportion for reasons she didn't quite understand but, she suspected, might be an effort to make a liberal-friendly issue where there wasn't one in order to beat up on conservatives.

"Even the president fell for it!" she wailed. When a reporter asked Bush if kids should be exposed to intelligent design, he had said he thought kids should be exposed to all kinds of different views. "That really infuriated me," Morris said. "The headlines said, 'Kansas Seeks to Insert Religion into Science' and somebody took it in to the president and he comes out in favor of intelligent design! It was infuriating! We weren't trying to put intelligent design into the schools at all."

The state board conservatives had only themselves to blame, of course—if not for their tinkering with standards, then for the hearings they organized to support them. Morris admitted she thought they were hurt by, as she put it, "allowing" the intelligent design people to help organize the discussions, since that meant that pro-evolution scientists would refuse to attend, although she claimed that there were plenty of people at the board of education hearing who disagreed with intelligent design. "John Calvert"—a Kansas City–based leader in the intelligent design movement—"organized the hearings, and maybe that was a mistake, but really, it was not an ID event. You can read it for yourself in the transcript," she said.[3] "But nobody bothered to do that."

Morris told me she believed "the government is taking over" family life in America and that "they're doing it in our public schools. We are doing some dreadful things to our children in public schools. I'm trying to hold that back some. If the people who elected me don't want that, they'll vote me out, and that will be fine." By the time she was telling me this, she had already been the target of recall efforts, and there was a crowded field of candidates ready to run against her in 2006. Even people in St. Francis who would normally be sympathetic were fed up. "I think she's making too much trouble," said a woman I met at the town museum, "but on the other hand, my son is a teacher and I don't see what's wrong with mentioning religion. They can't pray or anything, but just mentioning it shouldn't be a problem. But she's made too much trouble."

In her bid for reelection in 2006, she lost, of course. If she hadn't, it would have been one of those miracles scientists hate. "I may not last long" in public office, she told me before that became the truth. "But you know what? That's a plus for me."

Months after the election, the *Kansas City Star* was still running "I hate Connie" pieces.

If their intention had been to turn science over to the preachers, the state board of education conservatives hadn't accomplished much. What was more interesting to me was how they'd come to be elected in the first place.

Morris's views on the disconnect between families and values sounds extreme in her mouth, but it's a thought that many parents have had from time to time. Whether it's justified or not, many quite reasonable parents feel they no longer trust schools to teach the sort of stuff that reinforces what they hope their children will believe about the world and how to behave in it. Dismissing all of them as cranks is arrogant and unhelpful. Even a Topeka journalist not known for his sympathy to the rabble-rousing religious right told me he didn't have a problem with telling kids about the creation story from Genesis—so long as it wasn't presented as science.

As one education "controversy" after another demonstrates, the frustration of mothers and fathers is often brought to a boil when schools force a set of secularized assumptions on children—when they forbid mentions of Christmas, for example, or ban the Easter bunny, or prohibit moments of silence before a sporting event, or force little kids to attend gay-pride consciousness-raising sessions. Nobody in the Midwest this side of a tongue-talking snake juggler wants schools that teach religion instead of science. But many do object to fostering a knee-jerk *disrespect* for religion; suggesting to schoolchildren that religious belief is the refuge of morons offends most of the people who pay for schools.

Yet when parents protest these politically correct violations of common sense, they're slapped down by those who cry that they aren't condescending—editors, educators, and judges, for example—but who certainly act it. Attempting to influence the state's curriculum through the governing bodies that rule schools is really about all that most parents feel they can do—and so that is exactly what they do from time to time in Kansas and in many other states and localities around the nation.

Of course, as political debates go, the skirmish over evolution seems like it was made in heaven for atheists and agnostics on the political left. It casts the advocates of evolution as thoughtful and open-minded thinkers and makes conservatives look like zealots or simpletons or sluts. It doesn't matter that, according to a USA Today/CNN/Gallup poll, 88 percent of Americans of all political persuasions believe that God had at least *some* role in the creation of life, or how many times you remind worried people, as writer Jonah Goldberg once memorably did, "Your Darwin fish are safe," the elite on both sides of the political spectrum will still seize on the caricatures of that debate to pillory dissent, drowning out the rest of the conversation with a shrieking that approaches hysteria.

The issue, of course, is not science. Most of the pundits, journalists, and politicians who were arguing for or against evolution or intelligent design or creationism are as clueless as all those guys in college in the 1960s and '70s who took "Rocks for Jocks" as their science elective. (I confess to being one of those guys, even though I was no jock.)

Meanwhile, those who do actually have a claim to know something about science have been hopelessly polarized by this crazy "debate." Most fall on the Darwinian side of the argument, of course, but that argument is mostly about biological sciences. Cosmology, the dwelling place of theoretical physicists, seems to be different; its ways of claiming evolution as a way of looking at "creation" might seem a little tortured to normal, reasonable people who find they get frustrated when they try applying "evolution" to light or gravity or a glass of water.

In fact, the closer you get to the proto-nugget of creation, the goofier *all* theories become. For example, here's a useful chart comparing two competing views of creation at the cosmological level. You decide.

Creation Theory A

There are many universes, co-existing like bubbles of foam, in a "multiverse".... The laws and constants of any one universe, such as our observable universe, are by-laws. The multiverse as a whole has a plethora of alternative sets of by-laws.... We happen to be in one of those universes (presumably in a minority) whose by-laws happened to be propitious to our eventual evolution....

The standard model of our universe says that time itself began in the big bang, along with space, some 13 billion years ago. The serial big crunch model would amend that statement: our time and space did indeed begin in our big bang, but this was just the last in a long series of big bangs, each one initiated by the big crunch that terminated the previous universe in the series.

... [Another] theoretical physicist, Lee Smolin, has developed a tantalizingly Darwinian variant on the multiverse theory, including both serial and parallel elements. Smolin's idea, expounded in *The Life of the Cosmos,* hinges on the theory that daughter universes are born of parent universes, not in a fully fledged big crunch but more locally in black holes.... The fundamental constants of a daughter universe are slightly "mutated" versions of the constants of its parent.

Source: Richard Dawkins, *The God Delusion,* pp. 146–47.

Creation Theory B

We're just God's idea.

Source: My daughter Maggie at age three.[4]

Most Christians don't subscribe to a literal reading of the six-day creation described in Genesis. In fact, many thoughtful believers feel that interpreting biblical "science" too literally diminishes God and insults man. I agree with them. Dogmatic Darwinists and King James literalists both share an ambition to reduce the essential argument about creation to something more reasonable, something about the size of a man—or at least something the size of a man's ability to comprehend.

Theological issues aside, many may find it difficult to wonder what difference it makes *what* people believe, even in a Kansas science class. An eighth grader who doesn't properly understand how to read and write because of screwed-up schools is probably going to have *On the Origin of Species by Means of Natural Selection, or the Preservation of Favoured Races in the Struggle for Life* wasted on him, including the fact that there's little in the book that requires readers to sign up for a godless scenario. Darwin was an agnostic, but not an intolerant one. As he admitted in his *Autobiography,* "The mystery of the beginning of all things is insoluble to us."

Besides, there are plenty of college graduates out there who believe all kinds of really stupid things, and the things they believe have real consequences: Left-wing ideologues believe George W. Bush can make hurricanes. Dick Durbin, the senior U.S. senator from Illinois, believes that U.S. soldiers guarding terrorist prisoners have a lot in common with Nazi storm troopers. My wife believes I'm good-looking, and my children think I'm smart. Most Americans think that believing God had something to do with creation isn't all that crazy in comparison. And no doubt a vast majority think a descent into name-calling and bitterness over something like this is swamplike behavior.

Yet there is virtually no public person who has not yet called critics of evolution—or even those who think evolution doesn't explain *everything*—dangerous lunatics, religious primitives out to wreck America's excellent education system, a system that now performs at such a miserable level of incompetence that most high school graduates can read only at a basic level, if that, as they attempt to suss out the implications of evolutionary science.[5] The chances that offering the information that some people have criticisms of Darwinian science[6] in a tenth-grade science class is going to make an iota of difference to the evolution and development of scientific thought is much, *much* more far-fetched than claiming, as Genesis does, that you and I are descendents of a handful of dust—which, if you add water and stir, is pretty much what Darwin said, too. Whoever cures cancer will do so even if somebody along the line mentions the fact that some people think evolutionary theories are controversial.

The posturing is impressive because the mantle of scientific reason is in style in blue neighborhoods no matter who's posing in it: Charles Krauthammer, George Will, and other intellectuals on the right and almost every commentator on the left has called the critics of evolution names and played loose with the facts in order to justify their calumnies. Bret Stephens, an otherwise reliably earth-bound conservative essayist at the *Wall Street Journal,* looked into a Fox News camera on February 18, 2006, nearly a *decade* after the latest round of the evolution debate started, and said, "I think the losers in this debate would tell you that all they want to do is teach the controversy but, in fact, it was just an effort to introduce intelligent design discussions through the back door. . . . It should not be taught in science classrooms. And I think it's time somebody said that." What the valiant Stephens meant was, "It's time *I* had *my* chance to say that on TV," since literally thousands of other writers, policy makers, and commentators, even including people like Connie Morris, had already said exactly that, some of them many, many times, at length and occasionally at great volume.

Of course, it would be cynical to suggest that the "controversy" in play here may exist solely to introduce "intelligent design discussions" into Fox News' talk shows. New York conservatives are as happy as New York liberals to take a cheap shot at those red-state creationist hicks in Kansas.

In fact, virtually the entire establishment intelligentsia, left and right, has thrown its support in this "controversy" behind the people who run the country's public schools and don't seem to do it very well. For people on the left, this debate works to their obvious advantage: Not only do they get to dismiss their enemies as trailer-park conservatives, they know it's hard to argue the virtues of complex issues, such as school choice, while all the shouting is about what a lousy science book the Bible is. For those on the right, worried about defending their claim to cultural credibility, it provides a golden opportunity to distance themselves from the funda-mentalist right and those others whom they find slightly unwashed, intel-lectually speaking.

Nonetheless, the synthetic furor gave a genuine boost to Kansas's moderate Republicans and Democrats on a wide range of issues, none of which have any more to do with creationism than the Kansas state sci-ence standards. The left believes that no other issue, with the possible ex-ceptions of partial-birth abortion and embryonic stem cell research, has the potential to turn this red state blue, which is why it still rages on in the state's dailies. The phony debate has allowed secularists to demean all religious belief with impunity and has brought to the surface some very angry, anti-religious zealots—just more proof that the evolution debate makes anyone who touches it look terrible.

To find out how terrible, just go to Lawrence, home of the University of Kansas. Wading into the evolution controversy, the university announced "courses"—really, 1960s-style teach-ins—designed not to teach but to ridicule religion, each taught by a prof with an agenda.

Personally, I think it's a sign of improvement that universities are finally being used for satire rather than self-parody, and on this point I ap-pear to agree with the former chairman of KU's religious studies depart-ment, Paul Mirecki, and the campus group he mentored, the 120-member Society of Open-Minded Atheists and Agnostics, or SOMA.

In the fall of 2005, Mirecki announced plans to teach "the fundies"—as he referred to his personal demons—a lesson by offering a course called Intelligent Design, Creationism, and Other Religious

Mythologies. The course announcement was instantly picked up by the AP, CNN, the state's press, and a bunch of daily papers and TV stations across the country.

"The KU faculty has had enough," Mirecki told reporters with revolutionary gusto. Conservatives were irritated, of course, but universities—well, what can you do? The class would have passed into the archive of silly courses all colleges offer for whatever reason, if Mirecki had just gone about his business. However, he had made the strategic error of using SOMA's Yahoo! user group—open to any who cared to click and join it—to post to the list his admission that the purpose of the course was not education at all. It was agitprop.

"To my fellow damned," he wrote. "Its [*sic*] true, the fundies have been wanting to get I.D. and creationism into the Kansas public schools, so I thought 'why don't I do it?' I will teach the class with several other left KU professors. . . . The fundies want it all taught in a science class, but this will be a nice slap in their big fat face [*sic*]. . . . I expect it will draw much media attention. The university public relations office will have a press release on it in a few weeks. I also have contacts at several regional newspapers." No doubt.

The forum post was forwarded to an ad hoc group of conservative Kansas bloggers and writers led by John Altevogt, a former *Kansas City Star* columnist, a political activist, and perhaps the only man in Kansas as angry as Mirecki. Altevogt blew the whistle, and the embarrassing post caused KU chancellor Bob Hemenway—a fervent backer of the course—to blink. Calling many Christian Protestant voters "fundies" wasn't helpful to a public university.

After nearly a week of backpedaling, Mirecki issued an apology. "I have always practiced my belief that there is no place for impertinence and name calling in a serious academic class," he wrote. "My words in the e-mail do not represent my teaching philosophy or the style I use in class." The word "Mythologies" was dropped from the course title. The chancellor said he would conduct a "review" of Mirecki's e-mail. The university insisted the show would go on.

But the cat was out of the bag. Even as Hemenway was telling reporters that the course was "serious," Mirecki was telling readers of his SOMA list, "This thing will be a hoot." At the same time, conservatives had set about conducting a review of their own, sorting through and circulating the rest of Mirecki's SOMA posts on the Internet. They came away more concerned than ever.

"These aren't just lighthearted messages," said Altevogt.

From the posts he wrote, Mirecki appears to have enjoyed adolescent outrageousness as much as his students. In one note, for example, a SOMA member suggests creating anti-Gideon pamphlets: "While the Gideons are distributing their propaganda, we would distribute a single folded page of the same height and width of a Gideon bible. The cover would contain wording on the order of 'For complete assurance that your soul will be safe from the Fires of Hell . . .' The inside would continue 'quit believing that [obscenity] God and Jesus [obscenity].—Join us, the Society of Open Minded Atheist and Agnostics [sic]. Our Bible is a quicker read.' "

Mirecki's post in response: "I think the language is a bit strong in what you suggest, but I still like the general idea." Then he went on to offer his own version. In another post, Mirecki explained to his students that German Christians saw "Nazism as compatible (the fulfillment of?) Christianity [sic], with Hitler as final messiah."

Mirecki offered an explanation of his point of view in a post he published to the list in May 2005: "I had my first Catholic 'holy communion' when I was a kid in Chicago and when I took the bread-wafer the first time, it stuck to the roof of my mouth, and as I was secretly trying to pry it off with my tongue as I was walking back to my pew with white clothes and with my hands folded, all I could think was that it was Jesus' skin, and I started to puke, but I sucked it in and drank my own puke. That's a big part of the Catholic experience. I don't think most Catholics really know what they are supposed to believe, they just go home and use condoms and some of them beat their wives and husbands." Mirecki went on to explain that he was going to meet with Monsignor Vince Krische, then at the university's Catholic Center.

What did Monsignor Krische remember about the meeting? Not much, he told me. Although Mirecki claimed in his posts that the two were "very good friends," Monsignor Krische said he had met Mirecki only twice, once at the Catholic Center and once at dinner. The priest could offer no explanation for the comments. "I just don't know why he would say such a thing. I think this is a very offensive and irresponsible thing for him to say. What is it based on? Why would he say this?" Mirecki did not return a call from me—or from most other journalists—asking for comment and clarification.

That left room for many others to make comments of their own, and to many, the controversy was no laughing matter. "Our concerns," Altevogt told me, "are simple and not related to one particular course, but to more general issues. First, we're worried about the academic decline of the university under [Chancellor] Hemenway: KU has slipped seven places during his tenure and things like this may be one reason why. Second, we are concerned when an entire category of people—including the very students he is most likely to run into in his current assignment as an instructor teaching classes about religion—is maligned by the faculty sponsor of a university-sanctioned organization." Third, Altevogt said, is the concern many Kansans have for the religious studies department itself. It had, he told me, become "a hotbed of religious bigotry and intolerance."

For Mirecki, the reaction must have seemed like a kind of religious epiphany, since it so closely resembled the wrath of God. State senator Karin Brownlee told me she felt that Mirecki's SOMA comments were "consistent with the tone and attitude of his other remarks" concerning the course he wants to teach. "I think students look up to a professor, whether he's an adviser or in a classroom . . . but as the head of a religion department he clearly has a disdain for those who have a Christian belief." Brownlee's complaint was echoed by many others as the story passed online from blog to blog.

Eventually, Mirecki had to give up the class and resign his chairman-ship.[7] Another prof—this one a fervent devotee of Burning Man Solstice ceremonies—said he would stand in the gap and take a bash at those goofy Christians with a course of his own.

Of course, Mirecki is very much in the mainstream of academics whose views on religion—no matter how bizarre—are accepted with an enthusi-asm that can cause thoughtful parents to wince. There seems to be a strain of nutty irreligiosity in midwestern religious studies departments. For ex-ample, just north of Lawrence, at Omaha's Creighton University—a Catholic institution, no less—the religious studies department published a paper called "Cross-National Correlations of Quantifiable Societal Health with Popular Religiosity and Secularism in the Prosperous Democracies: A First Look," by a man named Gregory Paul, in its peer-reviewed *Journal of Religion and Society.* The article was picked up by the London *Times's* cred-ulous "religion correspondent," Ruth Gledhill, who apparently borrowed from the study's summary and reported it this way:

> Religious belief can cause damage to a society, contributing to-wards high murder rates, abortion, sexual promiscuity and sui-cide according to research published today.
>
> According to the study, belief in and worship of God are not only unnecessary for a healthy society but may actually con-tribute to social problems.
>
> The study counters the view of believers that religion is nec-essary to provide the moral and ethical foundations of a healthy society.
>
> It compares the social performance of relatively secular countries, such as Britain, with the US, where the majority be-lieves in a creator rather than the theory of evolution. Many con-servative evangelicals in the US consider Darwinism to be a social evil, believing that it inspires atheism and amorality.
>
> Many liberal Christians and believers of other faiths hold

that religious belief is socially beneficial, believing that it helps to lower rates of violent crime, murder, suicide, sexual promiscuity and abortion. . . . But the study claims that the devotion of many in the US may actually contribute to its ills.

The paper, published in the *Journal of Religion and Society,* a US academic journal, reports:

• Many Americans agree that their churchgoing nation is an exceptional, God-blessed, shining city on the hill that stands as an impressive example for an increasingly sceptical world.

• In general, higher rates of belief in and worship of a creator correlate with higher rates of homicide, juvenile and early adult mortality, STD infection rates, teen pregnancy and abortion in the prosperous democracies.

• The United States is almost always the most dysfunctional of the developing democracies, sometimes spectacularly so.

Gregory Paul, the author of the study and a social scientist, used data from the International Social Survey Programme, Gallup and other research bodies to reach his conclusions.[8]

That was all Gledhill had to offer. The story traveled around the world in a heartbeat, thanks to gullible editors who would believe this stuff long before they'd believe there's any controversy over theories of creation, perhaps because it conforms to one of the emerging media narratives of the twenty-first century: Religion is bad, dumb, promotes violence, and so on.

Apparently, neither Gledhill's editor nor anyone else bothered to look at the credentials of Gregory Paul, social scientist, before giving the article credibility. Even George Gallup objected to the use of his stats by Paul. There seems to be little that would suggest Paul is a "social scientist" in the academic sense at all; a Wikipedia entry identifies him as a "freelance paleontologist" best known for painting pictures of dinosaurs.

It appears he had no professional credentials in either social science or religion and that his obsession about religion before this had caused him to link it causally to Nazism.[9] Perhaps his best-known published work, other than the paper the *Times*'s reporter celebrates, is a so-called transhumanist book he coauthored called *Beyond Humanity: Cyberevolution and Future Minds*. If I understand it properly, the book asserts that evolution won't be complete until humans and computers get it together sufficiently to crossbreed.

This is the sort of thing that animates reasonable concern by reasonable people, since Paul is perhaps more familiar to education lawyers as an avid anti-creationist, appearing as a witness whenever an "expert" is needed to testify on behalf of Darwin et al. against a school district's outlandish wish to suggest that there may be something controversial about theories of creation.[10]

Faced with eccentrics like Paul and Mirecki—or, for that matter, Richard Dawkins—who are given serious consideration despite what seems to be their pathological hatred of people who order their lives around matters of faith, it's not surprising that people in Kansas and elsewhere are worried about the schools in their communities and want, however slight, some dignity allowed for the values they hold. Surely, against men like these, having a teacher devote less than a minute to simply stating the obvious—that there is some controversy about the scientific theories of creation—before going on to study Darwinism isn't the end of reason in the twenty-first century.

Some members of the legislature—the source of the university's funding, after all—were concerned that even in red-state Kansas the educational establishment, and especially the state's university, was so disconnected from the people who pay for it that somebody so apparently "lacking in respect" for religion, as Karin Brownlee put it, was given charge of KU's department of religious studies.

For most people out here, religion isn't actually a very contentious issue at all. While Wichita has its huge megachurches, there are thousands of country churches scattered across the midwestern prairie, often the last living remnant of what must have been at one time a bustling little village. Some, like the church in St. Joseph, are huge buildings; that particular Catholic parish is all there is to St. Joseph, Kansas, practically. Completed in 1908, it used to serve two masses every Sunday, for eight hundred people. Now the vast building is used only for occasional weddings and funerals and the last parish priest left years ago. Farther west is the Cathedral of the Plains, St. Fidelis Church (completed in 1911), whose twin limestone steeples soar 141 feet over tiny Victoria, Kansas. The sanctuary, still used for regular masses, is 220 feet long and seats eleven hundred—about the population of the town itself. The dramatic size of the building, its elegant architectural exclamation, more than doubles the population of the town every month by drawing gawkers. Sometimes, the landscape itself takes on an ecclesial coloration; once, driving a small road someplace north of Clay Center, I passed a sign surrounded by miles of open prairie and absolutely nothing else. The sign read, "This Changes Everything." I had to agree.

But most churches are like the tiny church most of my family members have attended at one time or another, Olive Hill Church. It's not near anything, really—just a crossroads out in the country, its quiet presence indicated only by a sign pointing down a dirt road off Highway 14 south of Superior on the Kansas side of the river.

It's a nondenominational church, and when I was little, it was a very hot one. I remember coloring in pictures of Jesus while the perspiration dropped off my nose and the sweat bees swarmed. It seems like a snapshot now, but I can remember my uncles—Neal, Gerald, and Delmar—singing in the church while their sister, Goldine, or my grandmother played the piano and my grandfather sat and smiled. I'd try to sit next to my aunt Twyla when I could, because she didn't make me sing along. My uncle Gerald is a great guitar player and singer—in the tenor tradition of Ralph Stanley, you might say—and his renditions of great white gospel hymns, especially in duets with his daughter Gloria, are some of the grandest musical memories of my life. If you're in the vicinity on a Sunday morning, stop in, see my aunt Jacqueline, my cousins Pat and Gloria, or Bill and Rita Blauvelt and Bill's parents, or the Winslows, Zelda Schuster, and a bunch of others. They're all there, singing "How Great Thou Art."

The Olive Hill Church, like the little church in Ada, the one in Norway, and those in a pile of other towns you'd have to look up to find, had a way of extending its message far beyond the dirt crossroads where it was located. Once, I had to call an editor at HarperCollins to tell her I would be away during the preparation of a manuscript for publication. When I got through to her office, it turned out the company was going through one of the many shuffles that characterized the 1980s on East Fifty-third Street. I finally reached a temp, some poor guy who'd been parked in front of a phone to tell everybody who called that nobody was home. I asked if I could leave a message saying I'd be away.

"Where you going?" the guy asked.

"Someplace you've never heard of," I said, with what I thought was midwestern smugness.

"Try me."

"Okay. Burr Oak, Kansas."

"Doesn't Lester Snider give the best sermons you've *ever* heard?" Amazing. Tom Zoellner had just arrived in Manhattan from his trip across the country, one that had involved taking his first newspapering job with Bill Blauvelt in Superior. As a way of unwinding after a stint as a straight shepherd in Montana, he'd worked his way across U.S. 36 until he eventually walked into Bill's office at the *Express* and got a job and a ride out to the Olive Hill Church.

The preacher in those days—not so long ago, really—was a lean, silver-haired, hawk-faced man in cowboy boots. Lester resembled John Brown in those statehouse murals—all forward-leaning intensity. He had a past in the Society of Friends and the oratorical style of a country preacher, with cadences that sang, punctuated by long, dramatic silences; Lester had so many pregnant pauses that you thought he could give birth to a full year once a week. Plus, he had mastered the art of—well, not of the rhetorical question, exactly, but of the rhetorical grill: *"Do you like fun?"* he would say, leaning forward and frightening the children behind their funeral-home fans. *"I like fun."* A relief. Then the trap: "Heaven's fun—*but if you want to have fun in heaven, you better be good here on earth!"*

When my grandmother finally died, at the age of ninety-eight, leaving the Olive Hill Church behind at last, the church was packed with people who turned out to say good-bye. For most of her life, she had been the most intimidating woman I had ever known. I'd spend summer after summer with her and my grandfather, passing the days swatting sweat bees in a grain truck and the evenings reading *True Detective* and closely examining the lingerie inventory in the Sears catalog.

When diabetes finally took her leg, I was tempted to send her a peg, an eye-patch, and a clip-on parrot. But amazingly, the amputation also removed her fierceness, and for the last couple of decades of her long, exemplary life, she was the sweetest, kindest soul I ever knew.

Delivering a eulogy for my grandmother in that church was the hardest thing—all I could think about was how often she'd prayed in there for all of us, even including me, and I did my usual terrible, choked-up job. (Gloria's was better.) And Lester presided over the funeral, smiling mirthlessly, leaning forward hawkishly, telling stories about Granny and her life in the nursing home. He didn't know about her other life, burying that five-year-old son, my uncle Evan, dead of pneumonia during the Dust Bowl years; or her brave trip to New York City in 1918 and her tearful dismay at losing that hat; or her endless nights when three of her surviving four sons were all off fighting World War II at the same time. She spent a lifetime of Sundays in that old church. Lester just got there in time, at the end of the run.

"She lost her leg, yes," he told us. "But that couldn't keep her down! I can see her now, up there in heaven now, having *fun*—running around on all her legs."

Me, too, Lester.

I don't know what politics the people who make up the congregation at Olive Hill have, but I suspect there's not a lot of room for meanness and intolerance—even of people like Mirecki and Dawkins—in any of it.

Religion is important to most Americans, no matter what their political point of view might be. The tradition of civic respect for religious belief has traditionally been a hallmark of red-state politics. It still is, even if it's been pushed into the margins of public life by the media, academics, cynics, and politicians. The middle of America doesn't own traditional morality, but many Kansans and Nebraskans know there's a secular tide that's been rising for the last decade or so, one that's flooding the coasts of the nation with hatred for faith and ridicule of those who try to navigate life using ethics based on religious precepts—including simple rules of respect. They know that tide of hatred threatens to drown everyone, including, to their great expense, conservatives who can't bring themselves to engage in the country's great national debates with the civility and generosity they claim as benefits of their faith.

Out here, people who feel that way are still in the majority, maybe because they have civic role models whose views still reflect a broad spectrum of midwestern people from the right and from the left. For example, Concordia's most prominent native son is Frank Carlson—a six-term representative, a former governor, a three-term U.S. senator, and one of the most popular politicians in Kansas history. Ross Doyen—another Kansas political leader from Concordia—told me Carlson was brilliant at knowing "how to do the right thing at the right time, so people thought a lot of him. But for us, the best thing about him was he never forgot where he came from."

How could he? Just to get to Concordia, you have to take the Frank Carlson Memorial Highway into town. Walk into the Frank Carlson Library and go to the Frank Carlson Room and there you'll find a cluttered and colorful record of Frank Carlson's many achievements. He was a politician in the old-fashioned Kansas mold, so the artifacts in the Carlson Room are modest and homey. He was a Republican moderate who didn't use the word as a euphemism, but to fairly describe his attention to the broad, middle way, and he was an avid, early supporter of Ike's.

The room is filled with presidential signing pens, copies of highway bills, notes about civil rights legislation from back in the days when Republicans were about the only hope African-Americans had of gaining political equality with whites. Carlson quietly lived his faith. He was proud of it, proclaimed it, and made it the basis for his views of the world.

The most ostentatious thing in the room is a tasteful display of the talk Carlson gave to a Senate breakfast group on June 19, 1968. The speech was widely quoted at the time because many people thought it was a piece of superior rhetoric. Forty years later, it still sounds about right.

> Never before have so many hated on such flimsy cause. Never have so many denounced so many with such little knowledge. Never has the dollar been as important as it is today. Never has wild pleasure or physical abandonment been considered fitting human behavior as it is today.
>
> Never before have public officials been so brazen and open in seeking the vote of the people through promises of things that are morally and spiritually wrong. Never have ministers of the Gospels turned their pulpits and their pastoral duties toward the direction of social order to the near exclusion of the salvational order as abounds in our time. . . .
>
> . . . The daily press—notoriously indifferent to religious news—reports a few lines on the inner and back pages that tells us clearly how growing numbers of Americans treat holy things with irreverence and contempt.
>
> Not only have vast numbers of Americans lost all sense of the sacred, the moral, and the ethical, but the spiritual leaders from both the laity and the priesthood are often found in the forefront of this irreligious pursuit of comfort rather than conviction—of accommodation rather than truth—of the pleasant life rather than the meaningful life. . . .
>
> You cannot pick up a paper, magazine or book that is not in and of itself critical of something or somebody, even including

among its victims almighty God Himself. In truth, the criticisms of God rank well above almost all other criticisms of the hour. More people—in more ways and on more occasions—cast doubt, hurl darts, and throw charges against God such as this country has never seen in all of its history.

To accept the doctrine of universal criticism leaves us with almost nothing that is sacred—almost nothing that is absolute—and nothing that is eternal.[11]

Nothing, that is, except wheat, weather, and common sense.

Acknowledgments

I have a lot of people to thank for their help with this book, starting with the citizens of Concordia, Kansas. There are 5.4 thousand of them—enough to fill all twenty-six pages of the *Reader's Digest*–sized local phone book. So just let me say that Concordia is a terrific town filled with lovely people, good food, lots of churches, and not enough bars, but what can you do? I am especially indebted to Marsha Doyenne, Kirk Lowell and his newspapering kinsman, Brad, and to Larry Paine, Bud Kennedy, Art Slaughter, Lawrence Uri, Everett Miller, Susan Sutton, Roy Reif, Steve Womack, Rod Imhoff, Jane Linden, Linda Palmquist at the Cloud County Historical Society Museum, and Vikki Jochems at The Citizens National Bank. Charlene Bambauer in Fairbury, Nebraska; the finely tuned members of the Beloit Community Orchestra; USD 400, home of Marla Elmquist and her remarkable school in Lindsborg; and Boo Hodges and Gia Kvaratskhelia and the fencers at the Kanza fencing club in Salina—all of these and scores of others welcomed me and my family and tried to help me write a good book. I hope they think I succeeded.

I'm also grateful to the legislators from both parties who were quite cordial to me during the 2005 special session, especially former representative Joanne Freeborn, former speaker Doug Mays, current speaker Melvin Neufeld, and house minority leader Dennis McKinney. The statehouse press corps were very collegial and great fun, but I won't embarrass any of them by thanking them (actually, in some cases I was asked to not mention them at all). However, I think I can publicly thank Martin Hawver, who has been covering the follies in Topeka for more than thirty years, and who, with his wife, Vickie, runs the Hawver News Company, an essential resource at www.hawvernews.com.

The reference staffs at the Kansas State Historical Society library and at the State Library of Kansas were extremely helpful, as was Lue Ann Snider, Research Analyst, Kansas State Department of Education, who helped me with some of the historical research. So did Karl Peterjohn, of the Kansas Taxpayers Network, and the anonymous and apparently tireless "Kansas Meadowlark," whose blog and other .alt dispatches do more to uncover money trails and conflicts of interest than a busload of sleepy reporters. I used only a tiny fraction of the data the Meadowlark organizes and makes available.

At Doubleday, Adam Bellow, Dan Feder, Kathy Trager, and Bonnie Thompson, a brilliant copyeditor, all made thoughtful suggestions useful to this project. But if I could dedicate this book twice, the other dedication would be to my great friend and occasional colleague Harry Stein. Harry is a better journalist than I am by far, and a better friend too: The help he gave me with this book was substantial, extending at one point to coming out from New York just to help me eat BBQ and get the manuscript back on track. It was his inspired idea to let the citizens of Superior speak for themselves.

Every small town in Kansas and Nebraska contains hundreds, thousands of complicated tales. In fact, the Midwest has more stories than acres. So I'm sure I got some of it all wrong, despite the efforts of Keith and Bethany Roe of Mankato, Bill and Rita Blauvelt of Superior, Tom Zoellner, formerly of Frankfort, and many others, all of whom tried to find answers for me no matter how dumb my questions were. None of them could save me from myself. The errors in this book are all mine.

Finally, I need to thank my family—not just my parents or my intelligent, pretty wife and my three clever and beautiful daughters (my daughter Hattie has read this thing so many times, she can recite it from memory, almost) but every Boyles and Boyles-in-law in Kansas and Nebraska and beyond. In obvious ways this is a personal book about a place I love not just for the subtle scenery but especially for the people who live there. That includes lots of coconspirators linked to this project by DNA, since my regional genealogy isn't just a tree, it's ground cover. There are Boyleses everywhere out there, people with good hearts and good midwestern names like Clyde and Chester and *Goldine,* my phenomenally indomitable aunt, whom I adore. I lost another aunt, Jackie, while working on this book—her boys, and I count myself among them, will miss her. In this book, I name only some of my cousins galore: Not only do I have a Pat Ann, a Deb or two, a Gloria Dale, a Glenna Jo, a Gayla Marie, a plain old Marty, and a Fabulous Baby Elaine, but someplace deep in our ancestral woodpile is a certain Napoleon Comfort Joy and a whole bunch of other Comforts and Joys, no matter what you call them. I appreciate them, every single one.

Appendix 1

Below is the full text of the speech Frank Carlson gave to a Senate breakfast group on June 19, 1968.

The subject of the text I am using is "Wanted a Man—a Man Who Will Stand." We have had men in both ancient and modern society who have had the courage to take a stand and stand firm. . . .

In Ezekiel 22:30, the Prophet says:

"And I sought for a man among them who would build up the wall and stand in the breach before me for the land that I should not destroy it."

God is searching for men who are unique, thoroughly saved, and filled to running over with His spirit. God and the world need men who will stand in the gap . . .

Modern Americans have accepted and are tolerating conditions never before permitted by any generation of our ancestors.

Never before have so many hated on such flimsy cause. Never have so many denounced so many with such little knowledge. Never has the dollar been as important as it is today. Never has wild pleasure or physical abandonment been considered fitting human behavior as it is today.

Never before have public officials been so brazen and open in seeking the vote of the people through promises of things that are morally and spiritually wrong. Never have ministers of the Gospels turned their pulpits and their pastoral duties toward the direction of the social order to the near exclusion of the salvational order as abounds in our time.

In that same 22nd chapter of Ezekiel, the Prophet speaks of Israel's leaders in these words:

"Her priests have done violence to my law and have profaned holy things; they have made no distinction between the holy and the common, neither have they taught the difference between the unclean and the clean, and they have disregarded my Sabbaths so that I am profaned among them."

Israel's religious leaders of that earlier time would be appalled to observe what is transpiring in the churches of God today. Even the daily press—notoriously indifferent to religious news—reports a few lines on the inner and back pages that tell us clearly how growing numbers of Americans treat holy things with irreverence and contempt.

Not only have vast numbers of Americans lost all sense of the sacred, the moral, and the ethical, but the spiritual leaders from both the laity and the priesthood are often found in the forefront of this irreligious pursuit of comfort rather than conviction—of accommodation rather than truth—of the pleasant life rather than the meaningful life.

If God is to have men who will stand in the gap and hold back the flood of destructive emotional and spiritual forces, we must first understand the nature of the problem, and why things are the way they are.

There are three major forces that have brought about this chaos, frustration and anti-Christian era in which we live. They touch both the philosophical and religious bases, were first voiced by the few in number whose intensity deceived millions, and have been permitted to flourish by both the unwary and the fearful.

First, we live in this age of uncertainty because we have either accepted or endured a doctrine of universal conformity.

The forces that reduce the power of an influence of God and Christ in the lives of our people are seeking to become levelers of men. It is their conviction that only through lowering mankind to a dependence upon the

ideas, ideals, and material judgments of superior people can we live together in harmony and peace.

Evidence is rampant that this kind of meddling and interference with
God's natural law brings fearful conflict, death, destruction, riots, crime
and disregard of decency and principle among our people.

Today, there is widespread devotion to the idea that nothing, absolutely
nothing, can remain the same. All things must change, and there is practically no consideration given as to whether change is good or bad—right
or wrong—easy or difficult—necessary or unnecessary.

The doctrine of change stands on just the precise idea that change is
inevitable. That is absolutely true. But irresponsible, erratic, violent
change only for the sake of making things different is as illogical and as
unreasonable as it is misguided.

No intelligent person argues against the necessity of question marks
after many of our inherited notions and preconceived ideas. But when
the question mark is turned into a totem pole or a marble altar on which
the people are supposed to lay sacrificial offerings, such people have escaped the general limit of common sense and sound judgment and have
launched off into material idolatry and a rushing toward a degree of spiritual insanity.

If human reason has so totally lost its respectability and no one is allowed to go from a major and a minor premise to some sort of orderly conclusion, then the welfare of our people is entrusted to the care of strange
and weird people.

Great changes had to take place during these recent years, and even
greater changes will have to take place in the future. But no safe and
proper change is seen in recent times—and certainly none of the irrational changes that outnumber the sane ones—can justify the wholesale
abandonment of the safe and sure principles of God and this country
which have brought us safely this far. In the face of great changes, we
Christians have to remember that we have a firm point of view and that
we operate from certain unchanging foundations.

We believe in a God who does not change—in human nature which does not change except for its accommodation and acceptance of God—in standards of right and wrong that do not change—in death and judgment which are inescapable—and we believe in a truth that is absolute, not relative, and which is forever settled in heaven and can never pass away.

The Christian today—even in the midst of the erratic and erotic commitments of its irreligious leaders—does not follow the failing steps of the priests of Israel. Christians make a clear distinction between the holy and the common. They teach the difference between the clean and unclean. They observe and keep the Sabbath and they do not profane either the name, the spirit, or the power of God.

The third cause of our uncertainties in this time is the doctrine of universal criticism. Today, man is taught not to accept anything until he has first put it under strong and critical examination. Trust nobody—believe nobody—have faith in nothing—and accept no truth until it has been proved to you with mathematical exactness and material demonstration. That is the agony of hour when the doctrine of criticism has taken over our people.

You cannot pick up a paper, magazine or book that is not in and of itself critical of something or somebody, even including among its victims almighty God Himself. In truth, the criticisms of God rank well above almost all other criticisms of the hour. More people—in more ways and on more occasions—cast doubt, hurl darts, and throw charges against God such as this country has never seen in all of its history.

To accept the doctrine of universal criticism leaves us with almost nothing that is sacred—almost nothing that is absolute—and nothing that is eternal. So real has our acceptance of the doctrine of criticism become that even the word "indoctrination" has been turned into an evil word that must be shunned like "discipline," "disciple" or "patriotism."

These three doctrines—universal conformity, universal change, and universal criticism—have left our nation without moorings or anchors.

We are being tossed in the sea of doubt and uncertainty that is about to sink the ship of God before our very eyes.

The world today is looking for:

Men who are not for sale;

Men who are honest, sound from center to circumference, true to the heart's core;

Men with consciences as steady as the needle to the pole;

Men who will stand for the right if the heavens totter and the earth reels;

Men who can tell the truth and look the world right in the eye;

Men who neither brag nor run;

Men who neither flag nor flinch;

Men who can have courage without shouting it;

Men in whom the courage of everlasting life runs still, deep, and strong;

Men who know their message and tell it;

Men who know their place and fill it;

Men who know their business and attend to it;

Men who will not lie, shirk or dodge;

Men who are not too lazy to work, nor too proud to be poor;

Men who are willing to eat what they have earned and wear what they have paid for;

Men who are not ashamed to say "No" with emphasis and not ashamed to say "I can't afford it."

God is looking for men. He wants those who can unite together around a common faith—who can join hands in a common task—and who have come to the kingdom for such a time as this. God give us men.

Appendix 2

William Allen White, "What's the Matter with Kansas?"

The following editorial ran in the <u>Emporia Gazette</u> on August 15, 1896.

Today the Kansas Department of Agriculture sent out a statement which indicates that Kansas has gained less than two thousand people in the past year. There are about two hundred and twenty-five thousand families in the state, and there were about ten thousand babies born in Kansas, and yet so many people have left the state that the natural increase is cut down to less than two thousand net.

This has been going on for eight years.

If there had been a high brick wall around the state eight years ago, and not a soul had been admitted or permitted to leave, Kansas would be a half million souls better off than she is today. And yet the nation has increased in population. In five years ten million people have been added to the national population, yet instead of gaining a share of this—say, half a million—Kansas has apparently been a plague spot and, in the very garden of the world, has lost population by ten-thousands every year.

Not only has she lost population, but she has lost money. Every moneyed man in the state who could get out without loss has gone. Every month in every community sees someone who has a little money pack up and leave the state. This has been going on for eight years. Money has been drained out all the time. In towns where ten years ago there were three or four or half a dozen money-lending concerns, stimulating industry by furnishing capital, there is now none, or one or two that are looking after the interests and principal already outstanding.

No one brings any money into Kansas any more. Which community knows over one or two men who have moved in with more than $5,000 in the past three years? And what community cannot count half a score of men in that time who have left, taking all the money they could scrape together?

Yet the nation has grown rich; other states have increased in population and wealth—other neighboring states. Missouri has gained over two million, while Kansas has been losing half a million. Nebraska has gained in wealth and population while Kansas has gone downhill. Colorado has gained every way, while Kansas has lost every way since 1888.

What's the matter with Kansas?

There is no substantial city in the state. Every big town save one has lost in population. Yet Kansas City, Omaha, Lincoln, St. Louis, Denver, Colorado Springs, Sedalia, the cities of the Dakotas, St. Paul and Minneapolis and Des Moines—all cities and towns in the West—have steadily grown.

Take up the Government Blue Book and you will see that Kansas is virtually off the map. Two or three little scrubby consular places in yellow-fever-stricken communities that do not aggregate ten thousand dollars a year is all the recognition that Kansas has. Nebraska draws about one hundred thousand dollars; little old North Dakota draws about fifty thousand dollars; Oklahoma doubles Kansas; Missouri leaves her a thousand miles behind; Colorado is almost seven times greater than Kansas— the whole west is ahead of Kansas.

Take it by any standard you please, Kansas is not in it.

Go east and you hear them laugh at Kansas; go west and they sneer at her; go south and they "cuss" her; go north and they have forgotten her. Go into any crowd of intelligent people gathered anywhere on the globe, and you will find the Kansas man on the defensive. The newspaper columns and magazines once devoted to praise of her, to boastful facts and startling figures concerning her resources, are now filled with cartoons, jibes and Pefferian speeches. Kansas just naturally isn't in it. She has traded places with Arkansas and Timbuctoo.

What's the matter with Kansas?

We all know; yet here we are at it again. We have an old mossback Jacksonian who snorts and howls because there is a bathtub in the state house; we are running that old jay for Governor. We have another shabby, wild-eyed, rattle-brained fanatic who has said openly in a dozen speeches that "the rights of the user are paramount to the rights of the owner"; we are running him for Chief Justice, so that capital will come tumbling over itself to get into the state. We have raked the old ash heap of failure in the state and found an old human hoop-skirt who has failed as a business-man, who has failed as an editor, who has failed as a preacher, and we are going to run him for Congressman-at-Large. He will help the looks of the Kansas delegation at Washington. Then we have discovered a kid without a law practice and have decided to run him for Attorney General. Then, for fear some hint that the state had become respectable might percolate through the civilized portions of the nation, we have decided to send three or four harpies out lecturing, telling the people that Kansas is rais-ing hell and letting the corn go to weeds.

Oh, this is a state to be proud of! We are a people who can hold up our heads! What we need is not more money, but less capital, fewer white shirts and brains, fewer men with business judgment, and more of those fellows who boast that they are "just ordinary clodhoppers, but they know more in a minute about finance than John Sherman"; we need more men who are "posted," who can bellow about the crime of '73, who hate pros-perity, and who think, because a man believes in national honor, he is a tool of Wall Street. We have had a few of them—some hundred fifty thousand—but we need more.

We need several thousand gibbering idiots to scream about the "Great Red Dragon" of Lombard Street. We don't need population, we don't need wealth, we don't need well-dressed men on the streets, we don't need standing in the nation, we don't need cities on the fertile prairies; you bet we don't! What we are after is the money power. Because we have become poorer and ornerier and meaner than a spavined, distempered mule, we, the people of Kansas, propose to kick; we don't care to build up, we wish to tear down.

"There are two ideas of government," said our noble Bryan at Chicago. "There are those who believe that if you just legislate to make the well-to-do prosperous, this prosperity will leak through on those below. The Democratic idea has been that if you legislate to make the masses prosperous their prosperity will find its way up and through every class which rests upon them."

That's the stuff! Give the prosperous man the dickens! Legislate the thriftless man into ease, whack the stuffings out of the creditors and tell debtors who borrowed the money five years ago when money "per capita" was greater than it is now, that the contraction of currency gives him a right to repudiate.

Whoop it up for the ragged trousers; put the lazy, greasy fizzle, who can't pay his debts, on an altar, and bow down and worship him. Let the state ideal be high. What we need is not the respect of our fellow men, but the chance to get something for nothing.

Oh, yes, Kansas is a great state. Here are people fleeing from it by the score every day, capital going out of the state by the hundreds of dollars; and every industry but farming paralysed, and that crippled, because its products have to go across the ocean before they can find a laboring man at work who can afford to buy them. Let's don't stop this year. Let's drive all the decent, self-respecting men out of the state. Let's keep the old clodhoppers who know it all. Let's encourage the man who is "posted." He can talk, and what we need is not mill hands to eat our meat, nor factory hands to eat our wheat, nor cities to oppress the farmer by consuming his butter and eggs and chickens and produce. What Kansas needs is men who can talk, who have large leisure to argue the currency question while their wives wait at home for that nickel's worth of bluing.

What's the matter with Kansas?

Nothing under the shining sun. She is losing wealth, population and standing. She has got her statesmen, and the money power is afraid of her. Kansas is all right. She has started in to raise hell, as Mrs. Lease advised, and she seems to have an over-production. But that doesn't matter. Kansas never did believe in diversified crops. Kansas is all right. There is absolutely nothing wrong with Kansas.

"Every prospect pleases and only man is vile."

Introduction: Welcome to Superior

1. See lewhunter.com and bensherwood.com. Sherwood's excellent novel, published in 2000, is being developed as a musical and, maybe, as a film.

2. It wasn't until I read his obituary in the *Superior Express* that I learned Bob's mother was from Superior. He never mentioned it.

3. It was "Sinclair green," as I found out later from Bill. "That green in the hotel lobby? It was from a shipment Sinclair Oil had sent by mistake. It was a whole *car-load*. We painted everything in town green for years. I think there's still some left."

4. This version of Wilson's speech appeared in the February 2006 issue of *Commentary* magazine.

Out Where?

1. *Daily Mirror,* November 3, 2004. Actually, the population of the United Kingdom is closer to 60 million, but the *Mirror* is perhaps allowing for the possibility that a million English people may not be *so* dumb.

2. In fact, a good deal of evidence would suggest not. For example, here's a brief report card, courtesy of Standard & Poor's:

	Nebraska	Kansas	New Jersey	New York
Average SAT score 2004	1145	1169	1015	1007
Instructional expenditure per student ($) 2003	5,151	4,413	7,424	8,213
Operating expenditure per student ($) 2003	8,074	7,454	12,568	11,961

3. Thomas Frank, *What's the Matter with Kansas? How Conservatives Won the Heart of America* (New York: Metropolitan Books, 2004), p. 248.

4. November 15, 2006. "What's the Matter with Kansas?" was the title the paper gave to a November 31, 2005, editorial. If only William Allen White, the Kansas editor who first popularized the phrase (see Appendix 2), could collect royalties.

Transcript 1: Superior People

1. It's still going strong, despite the Internet. A recent *Express* ad: "GOOD TIMES await! A subscription to *Country Connections* helps country-loving people meet new people. Reputable, confidential plan. Free details. Write Country Connections, PO Box 406, Superior, Neb. 68978."

Return of the Part-Time Native

1. At the time an annual published by Kansas State College Press, in Manhattan.

2. William A. Peffer, an often-ridiculed, extremely bearded agitator, was a Populist senator from Kansas from 1891 until 1897. He was also the editor of the *Kansas Farmer* and hence a White rival.

3. Some even attribute the defeat of William Jennings Bryan—a Nebraskan, a Democrat, and a Populist—by McKinley in 1896 to White's editorial, which was used widely by the GOP as campaign literature. Bryan's "Cross of Gold" speech was the "My Sharona" of late-nineteenth-century political oratory, his single hit, which he trotted out again and again until what had once been a rousing display of rhetorical genius was an irrelevant and dull piece of theater.

4. Frank, p. 245.

5. Some conservatives aren't convinced that Frank would want to be left out of that elite, by the way. His promo blurb for a recent issue of his magazine, the *Baffler*: "Many commentators have remarked that the United States is a nation of rank buffoons. Few, however, have carefully measured our nation's recent and steep tumble into idiocy, much less attempted a unified theory to explain it. In its sixteenth issue, 'Nascar, How Proud a Sound,' The Baffler reveals the shocking breadth of American ignorance, and argues that the nation's mental and moral decline—like that of the Roman Empire—is spreading from the better classes downward." As columnist John Altevogt, one particularly fiery target of Frank's, remarked to members of a Kansas e-mail list, it is "strange how [Frank] commu-

nicates through those great working class political organs *Le Monde Politique* and *Harpers.* Clearly the kind of magazines one finds littering the bathroom stalls of our factories."

6. Mission Hills is considered the wealthiest place in Kansas. But there's actually a town in Reno County called Willowbrook with a much higher per capita income level. The population is only thirty-six, however, so most statisticians ignore it.

7. Miner is the author of a very readable and useful new state history, *Kansas: The History of the Sunflower State, 1854–2000* (University Press of Kansas in association with the Kansas State Historical Society).

8. I don't know if the book made many converts in Kansas. (Although in fairness that may be because not even the choir bought the sermon; in my casual and incomplete survey of Kansas statehouse Democrats, I could find only one who had read the book—although a couple admitted to owning copies. Jim Ward, the assistant minority leader, who said he had read it, dismissed it as being "too negative.") Even Kansas Democrats, hearing how they should run on a platform that Kansans abandoned during the Roosevelt years, get skeptical in a hurry. A friend of mine, a hardworking Kansas Democrat, said she'd been to hear Frank give a talk, but had come away apparently disappointed with the old-left message: "The people who came had open minds, but he lost them early on." According to the *Kansas City Star's* blog, Frank was a "special guest" at Kathleen Sebelius's 2007 inauguration (January 3, 2007).

You Are Not Here

1. Richard Dooling, "Nebraska's Nostalgia Trap," *New York Times,* February 5, 2006.

2. *Main-Travelled Roads* (1891).

3. Michael Everhart's *Oceans of Kansas* (Bloomington: Indiana University Press, 2004), beautifully illustrated with charts, graphs, and a bunch of speculative paintings of the monsters that once lived in the inland sea that once divided the North American landmass, is the essential book of charts for the dryland mariner. The book grew from a fabulously detailed Web site Everhart created: oceansofkansas.com.

Midwestern Scale

1. I've always liked Richard Hugo's explanation, in his part of "The Only Bar in Dixon," for what makes a place home:

This is home because some people
go to Perma and come back
from Perma and say Perma
is no fun.

Hugo was talking about Dixon, South Dakota, but the poem works for any small town, except Perma.

2. Nebraska's a little better. Not only were settlement patterns different—resulting in vast, underpopulated western counties, where smaller ones would be as nutty as they are in Kansas—but the state has a tradition of seeking efficiency through local government reform. For the last seventy years, Nebraska has had a unicameral legislature in which everybody gets to be a senator. Nominally nonpartisan, party affiliations are nonetheless clearly understood.

3. Even so, Mike O'Neal, a Republican lawmaker from Hutchinson, and a longtime advocate of government consolidation, estimated that $1 billion could be saved "just with a moderate amount of consolidation."

4. In May 2004. That issue's cover is devoted to the "Heartland," and Jim Richardson's excellent photographs and text are well worth the trouble of finding a copy. If you want a copy of the Cuba photographs, send a note to him at the gallery he runs with his jewelry-designing wife, Kathy, at 127 North Main Street, Lindsborg, KS 67456, or e-mail him at smallworld@ks-usa.net. The day the magazine appeared, the citizens of Cuba held a daylong celebration of Richardson's enduring affection for the town. They made a video of the event, available from the Cuba museum.

The Republican River

1. New York bureaucrats, beat this: I sent my inquiry at eight-thirty on the Saturday morning of a three-day weekend. I had my reply from Mr. Knox by two P.M. on Sunday afternoon. I saw from his reply that at least two other people—Marta Ahrens and Jim Hall—had been involved in making sure I got the information I needed.

2. Self-reliance and lifeguarding the neighbors have always been the secrets to prairie survival. Sometimes, that clashes with the blue-state vision of government as your only reliable friend and neighbor, especially in a disaster. Example: 9:45 Friday night, May 4, 2007. That's when a tornado struck tiny Greensburg, Kansas, leaving at least nine dead and nearly all of the town's 1,500 residents homeless.

Within hours, locals—including Dennis McKinney, the local Democratic state representative—had been joined by volunteers from all over the area to clear the streets and move the rubble. When U.S. senator Pat Roberts arrived later that day, he surveyed the damage, called the White House to expedite aid, and asked the commander of the state's National Guard, Tod Bunting, if he had everything he needed. Bunting, a Roberts staffer told me, repeatedly said yes.

The early news out of Greensburg: A potent mixture of faith, family, friendship, and especially midwestern grit was triumphing in the face of a huge natural disaster. One story involved McKinney's own daughter, Lindy. Her father sheltered her in a basement bathtub as the twister raged. While their home disintegrated above them, the girl prayed—not for her safety, but for the mother and baby next door. They all survived. Greensburg was a story about the kind of Kansas courage Mrs. Williams would have understood.

But by the time the cameras were in place for the Monday morning news shows, that story had changed. Local volunteers were banished as Governor Kathleen Sebelius—who, it finally emerged weeks later, had been in New Orleans with Louisiana's governor Kathleen Blanco—showed up to blame the Bush Administration for what she claimed was a shortage of National Guard equipment that had gone "missing" when it was sent with state units to Iraq and Afghanistan. As she told reporters, "The real victims here will be the residents of Greensburg"—not because their town had just been erased from the Earth by a huge twister, but "because the recovery will be at a slower pace."

Sebelius's supporters in the state's press ran back-slapping editorials, but many Kansans were furious. Critics said she was exploiting Greensburg's misery to promote her run for Roberts's senate seat or the vice-presidential slot on the Democrats' 2008 ticket. The stunt certainly had "nothing to do with the people of Greensburg," Kansas house speaker Melvin Neufeld told me. It was "one hundred percent about politics."

The White House protested too and the Pentagon noted that Sebelius hadn't even asked for help. So once the story had delivered the heavy news play Sebelius needed, her press spokeswoman, Nicole Corcoran, quietly retreated: The governor hadn't actually meant *Greensburg*, Corcoran said. Greensburg was "fine." She meant *potential* problems with Guard shortages: "What the governor is talking about is down the road."

The episode left a bitterness in Greensburg. When the town went ahead with its high school commencement ceremony, it was Roberts who was invited to speak to the grads.

Exploiting tragedy for political gain is sacred strategy in blue states. As Bill

Clinton's FEMA director, James Witt, once famously observed, "Disasters are very political events." So Sebelius's story of missing Guard equipment "hampering" recovery efforts in Greensburg continued to run for weeks and weeks.

I finally asked a Pentagon spokesman if, since the start of the war in Iraq, there had *ever* been an instance anywhere of the Guard being unable to respond promptly to a mission because of "missing" equipment. Like all government agencies, the Guard's always got a hand out, but the answer from Lieutenant Colonel Michael Milord was a fairly unambiguous "No."

3. There are many accounts of the 1935 flood. Most of the towns along the Republican have a collection of flood-related documents, newspapers, photographs, or journals in their municipal museums. Mrs. Post's account is from the Nebraska genealogy Web site maintained for Franklin County by Patti Richter Simpson at http://www.rootsweb.com/~nefrankl/.

Gone with the Wind

1. P. T. Kilborn, "Bucking Trend, They Stay, Held by Family and Friends," *New York Times*, December 2, 2003.

2. In "The Great Plains: From Dust to Dust," *Planning*, December 1987.

3. Frank J. Popper, "The Buffalo Commons: Metaphor as Method," *Geographical Review*, October 1999, pp. 491–510. This passage is cited from the draft version appearing on the Great Plains Restoration Council's site at www.gprc.org.

4. Great Plains Restoration Council mission statement, www.gprc.org/about.html.

5. This affection for the plains is also nicely reflected on the Buffalo Commons book blog, maintained by two witty midwestern professors, Jim Hoy and Tom Isem, and their colleagues at www.plainsfolk.com.

6. C. J. Donlan, H. W. Greene, J. Berger, C. E. Bock, J. H. Bock, D. A. Burney, J. A. Estes, D. Forman, P. S. Martin, G. W. Roemer, F. A. Smith, M. E. Soulé, "Re-wilding North America," *Nature* 436: 913–14, [August] 2005. Naturally, the scheme was one of the *New York Times Magazine*'s "Big Ideas of 2005": "Thirteen thousand years ago, truly mega fauna, including lions, cheetahs, camels and five kinds of elephant, also walked the land—and still would today, had humans not come along to speed their extinction. Why not bring 'em back? It's a delicious idea, and the moment seems ripe." This appeared on December 11, 2005, eleven months before the 2006 elections, when camel-exterminating human Kansans once again became acceptable to the paper's editors.

7. C. Josh Donlan, "Lions and Cheetahs and Elephants, Oh My!," *Slate,* August 18, 2005, www.slate.com/id/2124714.

8. *Man Eaters Motel* (Ticknor & Fields). Highly recommended.

A Local History of Democrats

1. One, involving a secret agreement to create a partnership between Kansas University Hospital and Medical Center and Kansas City's St. Luke's Hospital, and apparently involving execs from Stowers Institute for Medical Research, has even upset some of the governor's erstwhile supporters. For example, in describing the deal to his readers, Dolph Simons Jr., the editor and publisher of the *Lawrence Journal-World,* wrote, "It is not a pretty picture, and the manner in which it has been put together allows many to question the real motives behind the action" (February 3, 2007).

2. The idea, apparently, was to give the pro-slavery faction the aura of Masonic association. However, the relationship, if any, between the pro-slavery Blue Lodge and the Masonic movement has been debated for a very long time. For an interesting survey, see the *Builder,* January 1924, available online at phoenixmasonry.org.

3. Samuel J. Crawford, *Kansas in the Sixties* (Chicago: A. C. McClurg & Co., 1911).

4. Ibid.

5. A new play, *Bleeding Kansas,* by a Women's Project playwright from Yale, opened in August 2007 in Ithaca, New York. I have neither seen nor read it, but the theater's announcement sure makes it all sound fun—like *Oklahoma!* with shooters: *"Bleeding Kansas* will take audiences back to 1856 and a hard-livin', hard-drinkin' time before Kansas became a state. As homesteading farmers fight the elements to start a new life, a violent battle over ideology explodes around them. Abolitionists and pro-slavery factions descend on the territory, and a fledgling nation takes a dangerous step towards civil war."

6. To become as smart as a Kansas schoolkid, I suggest Miner's *Kansas* (op cit.) and David Donald's *Charles Sumner and the Coming of the Civil War.* I plead guilty to grossly oversimplifying a highly complex historical period, but the bottom line here is not at all unclear—those who wanted Kansas to embrace racism, and worse, were southern Democrats, not only the Southern Democrats of 1854 but also the southern Democrats of a century later.

7. Tom Pendergast, a saloonkeeper, had started his political involvement in Kansas City's working-class Tenth Ward, but he soon came to control not just

Kansas City politics but Missouri politics as well. Introduced to politics by Pendergast's nephew, a war buddy, Truman was installed as a judge in Kansas City and in 1934 elevated to the U.S. Senate in an election rigged by the Pendergast machine. Pendergast finally died in 1945. "When Truman attended that man's funeral," Thull said, "we Kansas Democrats were just *disappointed.*"

8. Stowers effectively targeted conservative Kansas legislators he thought might pose a potential risk: One Kansas City–area legislator, Mary Pilcher Cook, was defeated by a Republican-turned-Democrat who was supported by a well-funded organization called Kansans for Lifesaving Cures, widely suspected of having ties to Stowers, but the implicating documentation was mysteriously absent from public files at the time. Besides, forget about the complications of money links. Apparently, the science itself was complicated enough for Pilcher Cook's opponent: "She keeps talking about 'nomadic stem cells,'" Pilcher Cook complained. Unfortunately for Pilcher Cook, even the Bedouin vote was not sufficient to carry the day, and she lost by 150 votes.

Meanwhile, Europeans are seen as the political opposites of most Kansans. But when the issue of embryonic stem cell research came up before the E.U. in July 2005, Germany and Austria led the effort to impose the kind of common-sense restrictions that made Kansas liberals furious. Elisabeth Gehrer, then Austria's science minister, asked if the E.U. really wanted "300–400 fertilized human embryos to be destroyed to create stem cells? This destruction of human embryos to create stem cell lines is not something we can support. We do not want community money, which includes Austrian money, to support this." The E.U.'s research commissioner agreed: The E.U. "will not pay for the destruction of embryos with E.U. money," he said. This was echoed by Germany's education and research minister, Annette Schavan, who told reporters, "The protection of human dignity, the right to life, need to be properly entrenched. There should be no financial incentives for the destruction and killing of embryos." Noble sentiments from what conservatives used to call the weasel brigade. Of course, if Kansas politicians had uttered these words, they'd be branded as right-wing wackos by liberal Republicans, Democrats, and the Kansas press. As indeed they were.

Stowers, and the money directed by organizations associated with Wichita abortion-clinic operator George Tiller, was a huge influence on the 2006 elections in Kansas. Conservative researchers, especially the indefatigable (and anonymous) blogger at the Kansas Meadowlark, were still trying to unravel the money trail long after the election, the press failing to demonstrate much of an interest.

9. Roxana Hegeman, "Petition Effort Seeks Probe of Abortion Patient's Death," *Lawrence Journal-World,* April 5, 2006.

10. Not exactly the kind of story the *Kansas City Star* would care to break. The paper's editorial board won a Maggie Award from Planned Parenthood for its "support of reproductive rights and health care issues." The citation: "In 2005, reproductive rights in Kansas were under constant attack—bids to seize confidential medical records, efforts to pass a clinic regulation bill designed to block abortion services, and ongoing legislative efforts to de-fund family planning programs. [Planned Parenthood] honors *The Kansas City Star* that through it all, championed reproductive justice, family planning, and the right to confidential health care on its editorial pages, providing a welcome antidote to the efforts of anti-choice extremists."

Like many major dailies, the *Star* artfully colors the identification of those who are pro-life to make sure they are seen as "anti-choice extremists." Recently, for instance, the paper described state senator Phil Journey as a "Republican who opposes abortion rights," apparently because he publicly worried whether inaccurate diagnoses of "mental illness" were being used to justify otherwise illegal late-term abortions.

11. John Hanna, "Committee Endorses Tiller Charges," *Lawrence Journal-World,* March 27, 2007.

12. In retaliation, the Johnson County Republicans voted Kline into Morrison's old job, their prerogative under state law. This infuriated the *Kansas City Star,* which demanded that the DA's salary be cut to punish Kline, presumably for accepting the job. But the *Star's* irritation was nothing compared to the governor's fury. After Kline accepted the Johnson County appointment, Sebelius released an unprecedented attack on his "fitness for law enforcement and his pursuit of misguided, personal priorities in public office. . . . I do not believe such a clear majority of Kansans rejected Kline's stewardship as attorney general with the intention of seeing him continue a public career in law enforcement paid for by taxpayers." (On February 13, 2007, the Kansas Supreme Court dismissed all the charges Kline had made against Tiller.)

Kline had done the unforgivable: He had turned the nation's attention on what conservatives see as the state's shame in failing to enforce its own apparently sententious laws concerning abortion and child molestation. After the Summer of Mercy, especially, abortion is an issue that divides the state just as decisively as slavery did in the days of Bleeding Kansas. To the state's liberal establishment, Kline is the enemy that must be destroyed. No doubt, he will be a target of Kansas liberals for as long as he holds any office anywhere in the state.

13. The underfunded Doug Mays; the paralytically indecisive Representative Jerry Moran, who kept everybody guessing about his gubernatorial plans until funding for other potential candidates dried up; and the unrealistically ambitious Senator Sam Brownback, who apparently thinks he can be president, if only anybody outside Kansas can learn to recognize his name.

14. Democrat Nancy Boyda was the winner of Ryun's congressional seat in 2006. One of her first acts was to join with House Democrats to withhold $300 million needed to house the families of thousands of redeployed 1st Infantry Division soldiers returning to Fort Riley. The anti-military vote was taken without hearings and left Junction City and Fort Riley blindsided. The arrival of the extra soldiers had been one of the few bright spots in the area's economy, fueling an increase in jobs in construction and related fields. Deep cuts were also made at nearby Fort Leavenworth. Both Fort Riley and Fort Leavenworth are in Boyda's district. Boyda promised angry residents the money would be found elsewhere, but months later, that still hadn't happened. Kansas's other Democratic congressman, Dennis Moore, voted with Boyda to withhold the funds.

Snapshot: Prairie Companions

1. Factually, this is an exaggeration. Emotionally and aspirationally, it's a gross understatement. The dorm actually housed one thousand women. At the same time.

2. He never lost. Although he'd won his last election by only 166 votes after outspending his opponent, Jeff Crist, by more than three to one, in 2006 he stepped down rather than face another election.

3. "Paying Respect to Democratic Values," *Dodge City Globe,* January 17, 2005.

The Modern Main Street

1. This isn't the book to read if you want to learn anything about the crazy world of ag policies. It's a huge welfare scam, not just for indolent corporate rice farmers in Louisiana or conceptual wheat producers in North Dakota but for every single American who buys the cheap food this country produces. My cousin Doug can give you a very thorough lecture on the artificially low prices Americans pay for their food. Can we fix it? Well, farms are everywhere; if France or China

or Brazil has crop subsidies or high ag tariffs, then we have to have them, too, or all our farms will blow away. Americans have no idea what it costs to grow food (not even many farmers do, for that matter). The violence all this does to a free market system that many feel if left alone could feed the world efficiently and inexpensively is the fascination of James Bovard, whose book *The Farm Fiasco* is a helpful (if somewhat dated) starting point for anyone interested in an overview of America's idiotic agriculture policies.

2. Rex's findings appeared in 2004 in his thesis written in support of his master's degree in agricultural business from Kansas State. Its full title is "Causes of Retail Pull in Nebraska Counties and Towns," and if you're an economic-development officer or a chamber of commerce director in a small Nebraska town—one with less than, say, 10,000 citizens—you really need to give Rex a call. His study excluded the urban centers, Lincoln and Omaha; he ranked Grand Island as the most vibrant retail community in Nebraska.

3. The Concordia Music Festival, as it's now called, is held the third weekend in August.

Old-Timers and Newcomers

1. The first time I went to the Brown Grand, it was to see the local theater troupe perform a great spoof on the eccentricities of the Kennedy clan. But Concordians are nothing if not open-minded. The theater is also used for visitors brought in as part of an annual lecture series. Among those either on their way to or just leaving Concordia: Thomas Frank and Kathleen Kennedy Townsend.

2. Some historians suggest that Lyons, Kansas, some thirty miles southwest, is the real turning point. Father Juan de Padilla, who accompanied Coronado, was killed there. His roadside memorial is four miles west of the town.

3. A rival claimant: Lucas, home of the Grass Roots Art Center—an impressive collection of pop-top constructions, cement models, dolls, paintings, iron cutouts, and other evidence of wit, genius, and widespread obsessive behavior. Look in the backyards as you drive through town: Behind one house is the World's Largest Collection of the World's Smallest Versions of the World's Largest Things, all jammed into a van next to a satellite dish marked "Soon to become the world's largest souvenir plate." You have been warned. There's also an alarming yellow sign leaning against the back of a house, the kind usually used to show stick men at work. This one shows a stick figure dragging another stick figure by the leg. On the other side of town, the Garden of Eden, the fab-

ulously eccentric monument to concrete and populism built by S. P. Dinsmoor, a Civil War vet (some would say casualty), whose corpse is available for viewing in his concrete mausoleum out behind the concrete house with its concrete furniture, surrounded by towering concrete constructions showing concrete bankers and concrete lawyers ripping apart the concrete common man. Rage built to last.

4. "Chess Fever Hits Lindsborg," by Lisa Gutierrez, *Kansas City Star,* September 9, 2004.

5. That would be John Donaldson, a popular international master and chess writer and the director of the Mechanics' Institute Chess Club in San Francisco. "Lindsborg? Surprising? Yes," Donaldson told me. "And even more surprising to me because I beat several grandmasters there."

6. Gutierrez, op cit.

7. For *Wall Street Journal* subscribers, Murray's November 2, 2005, account of the event is here: http://online.wsj.com/article/SB113088641320885637.html.

The News from Brahmasthan

1. Including the ex-military Brit who used to stand unsmiling in front of Buck House under a bearskin, but who moved to the border area with his wife and son on an "entrepreneurial visa" under the terms of which he must either support himself or leave. The process took the couple two years. According to the local paper, for a while he was getting by making lawn jockeys who will stand unsmiling in front of your very own house. The terms of the visa, however, required him to either invest $500,000 or create eight to ten new jobs. So he bought a small café, investing the family's entire savings, and gave it a go. When that didn't work and the family was finally penniless, the INS moved in to deport them. "People tell us we should just go to Mexico, then climb the fence and come back in," the Englishman's wife told me thirty days before they were supposed to go. "But we're law-abiding and honest. I hate giving up my home and everything, and we love it here and all these lovely people. But we're not brain surgeons or the kind of professionals America needs, and we're out of time." Locals were circulating petitions; I called the office of Jerry Moran, their congressman, and left a message but got no reply. "What can we do?" she asked. "We're making the business work slowly, but it's taking too long. I think it was a terrible mistake to do it this way." They asked not to be identified. "We don't want to cause any trouble," she said.

2. See fightincockflyer.blogspot.com.

3. Duane Schrag, "Parents Concede Lawsuit's Plaintiffs Fared Well in School," *Salina Journal,* July 3, 2005.

4. Editorial, *Salina Journal,* July 27, 2005.

5. Timothy Egan, "Vanishing Point: Amid Dying Towns of Rural Plains, One Makes a Stand," *New York Times,* December 1, 2003.

6. The group's literature explains that the "US Peace Government" isn't competing with the other U.S. government. There's no need, really, since "the US Peace Government will actually rule the country at the fundamental level of consciousness."

7. The thoroughly enjoyable George Diepenbrock of the *Lawrence Journal-World,* April 4, 2006.

8. According to Linda Baetz at the *Pioneer,* things have gone downhill for bliss in Brahmasthan since I was last there. "There's a little bit of a strain since you were last here," she told me over the phone.

"We're not sure what to think. There was supposed to be a meeting between some of the citizens in town and the T-Mers," she said, referring to the Global Country of World Peace's affection for Transcendental Meditation. "They were supposed to answer some of the questions people had, but they didn't show up. So everybody went down to their office—the T-Mers have an office in town now. It got pretty heated."

Baetz said the locals felt they hadn't been able to get clear information about what was going on. "The people here had heard talk about all the jobs, but now there are some Mexicans who came in to do that. And the Indians—well, people just can't understand what they're saying."

Baetz had tried to do a little investigative reporting but got caught. "The T-Mers were all down at the Pizza Hut in their tan suits, so I thought, Well, while they're there, I'll just go out and take a look around." But as soon as she got out to the site of the coherence creating center, "some people came out, so I had to interview them." Did she get a scoop? "Not a thing."

Mayor Archer, meanwhile, has a FOR SALE sign in front of his house. "They say he's going to Iowa," said Baetz. "I'm just not sure."

I wondered if he was going to find a quieter place to live, or if maybe he was off to take a course in levitation in Fairfield. But when I called to ask, a woman answered the phone shouting, "We're just not interested!" and hung up.

Compassionate Conservatism (the Early Years)

1. This and the other notes and comments here are from the Cloud County Museum files, except where otherwise indicated.

2. There's a very charming video of the waitress involved in this arresting story at http://www.livinghistoryfarm.org/farmingthe40s/money_04.html.

3. The band's wooden chairs are still in use at the Brown Grand Theatre.

4. Brace later wrote *The Dangerous Classes of New York and Twenty Years Work Among Them,* a good midwestern book title if ever there was one. For historical details, I consulted *The Orphan Trains: Placing Out in America,* by Marilyn Irvin Holt (University of Nebraska), and *The Story of the Orphan Trains,* by Michael Patrick et al. (Donning Company Press).

5. Annette Riley Fry, "The Children's Migration," *American Heritage,* December 1974.

6. Matt Bowers, *The Virginian-Pilot,* December 18, 1994.

7. Jeff Gammage, "For Adoptees, Racial Divide Still Wide," *Philadelphia Inquirer,* May 8, 2006.

8. The closest to what might be described as a cause cleric in Topeka is the Reverend Fred Phelps, the infamous homohysteric preacher who shows up everywhere in Kansas—and sometimes beyond—with his little army of goons holding signs that read, "God Hates Fags!" Phelps, incidentally, is a Kansas Democrat.

Learning, the Hard Way

1. Mark Bauerlein, "The Long Disengagement," *Chronicle of Higher Education,* vol. 52, no. 18, January 2006, p. B6.

2. Full disclosure: "Beyond" would mean my living room in France, since my three children are enrolled there. These days, I pay my taxes in Kansas.

3. Louisiana's education department studied all the available research relating to school size and performance and was unable to find a single instance of performance improving as school size increased. The conclusion: If you send a kid from a small school to a larger school, he'll get a worse education every time. "Small School Districts and Economies of Scale," Louisiana Department of Education, May 2003.

Of course, with so much at stake there is an ongoing effort to use statistics and studies to buttress one view or another of the government's role in children's education. Like everything else in twenty-first-century America, education is just another political tool, and both the Bush administration, with its No Child Left Behind farce, and the Democratic establishment, with its reliance on "education" as a way of growing government, have a great deal at stake, so it's unsurprising that so many assessments are configured to reveal desired outcomes.

The release of one recent National Education Advancement Programs study, for example, was given the predictable headline in the July 15, 2006, *New York Times,* where the editors oppose school choice: "Public Schools Perform Near Private Ones in Study." The *Times* report said, "Children in public schools generally performed as well or better in reading and mathematics than comparable children in private schools."

The actual study said, "In grades 4 and 8 [the only grades included in the study] for both reading and mathematics, students in private schools achieved at higher levels than students in public schools."

The only similar outcomes in the study were for poor public school kids and poor private school kids. That cohort may be an unreliable sample, since, sadly, school choice does not exist for most poor parents, so there just aren't very many poor private school kids.

4. All this legwork is courtesy of Michael Strand, who reported it for the *Salina Journal* on February 11, 2004.

5. One favorite tactic, according to Dale: across-the-board pay raises. If a superintendent offers, say, a 10 percent pay raise across the board, that means $3,000 or so for every teacher—"everybody likes that"—but it also means another ten grand for the superintendent, who's already making three teachers' salaries.

Currently, Kansas spends less than 60 cents of every education dollar in the classroom—on teachers, supplies, and the like—and so far Sebelius has dodged legislation that would increase this. The state ranks forty-first in the nation. Nebraska, ranked ninth, spends almost 64 cents of each education dollar in the classroom.

6. Olive Sullivan, "USD 250 Leaders Closely Following Education Funding Lawsuit," *Morning Sun,* January 28, 2003.

7. *Salina Journal,* August 25, 2005.

8. There's also the fact that the French system's no better than the American one. In February 2005, the Ministry of Education's man in charge of instruction, Patrick Gérard, told the *International Herald Tribune* that French education was a "failure." About 15 percent of French kids drop out of school every year. Of those who stay to graduate, three-quarters lack basic skills in reading, writing, and arithmetic—about average, Gérard said, for most of Europe (March 14, 2005).

9. More about the board of education later, but here's an example of the *Salina Journal*'s sense of editorial fair play: On June 26, 2006, the paper lumped the conservatives who served on the state board of education together with Dennis Rader, the "BTK" serial killer of Wichita, as "characters [who] give our state

the unsavory reputation." The paper's attacks on Corkins were also angry, bitterly personal ones.

Judging and Politics

1. Megan Brown, *State Court Docket Watch,* August 2004.

2. *Topeka Capital-Journal,* April 17, 2003.

3. *Topeka Capital-Journal,* May 12, 2005.

4. June 22, 2005.

5. The coverage was self-parodying at times. For example, one Associated Press story that appeared statewide was headlined "Schools in Crisis" and cited nine sources, eight of whom supported, one way or another, the narrative that conservatives were going to close the state's schools. One citation, two sentences from a blunt, right-wing legislator, fed the warnings of the other eight. June 11, 2005.

6. Scott Rothschild and Terry Rombeck, "Budget Favors Higher Education," *Lawrence Journal-World,* January 12, 2005.

7. Ibid.

8. Vratil is a partner in Lathrop & Gage, one of the state's largest and most powerful litigators, with an active specialty in representing school boards. Lathrop & Gage, oddly, represented the state in *Montoy*—although I often heard that the state's case had been presented inadequately. One high-ranking member of the house leadership even took me aside and, after asking for anonymity, said, "You really need to look into that" and hinted darkly of scandal—an allegation Kline's office instantly dismissed.

9. It was the second time he had recused himself, actually. The first time was soon after he came to the court. He apparently un-recused himself, however, since, until caught with his spreadsheet down, he played an active role in the court's deliberations.

10. Chris Moon, "State Pays Court Costs," *Topeka Capital-Journal,* May 30, 2005. By way of contrast, here's the *Wichita Eagle*'s headline a year later: "School Suit Cost Kline Nearly $191,000 in '05."

11. Or for a prayer: The statehouse prayer group meets upstairs at the Celtic Fox.

12. It actually took two years. A gaming bill passed in 2007 with no opportunity for hearings or any other legislative consideration. As with school funding, the moderates and Democrats used their now-familiar tactics to pass the bill Sebelius wanted.

Descent of the Straw Man

1. Justin Kendall, *Kansas City Pitch,* August 18, 2005.

2. *From the Darkness: One Woman's Rise to Nobility,* 2002. "I hate that subtitle," she said. "The publisher chose it, but it's embarrassing!" I agreed, but then I don't think much of mine, either.

3. At http://www.ksde.org/ last I checked.

4. I suppose I should note the obvious: Maggie's theory of creation, roughly anticipated by Saint Thomas Aquinas, does not at all exclude those theories cited by Dawkins. His doesn't leave much room for Maggie's, though.

5. According to the National Institute for Literacy, the mean prose literacy scores of U.S. high school grads ranked eighteenth out of nineteen countries. If the kids had two to three years of college, they went all the way up to fifteenth place.

6. That would include a large number of politically correct science types, by the way, who completely shut down the discussion of evolution when a University of Chicago scientist said he had found evidence that some brains evolved and others didn't and in doing so crossed the live wires of intelligence and race (Antonio Regalado, "Head Examined: Scientist's Study of Brain Genes Sparks a Backlash," *Wall Street Journal,* June 16, 2006).

7. The Associated Press, invested in the narrative that held that Mirecki was the victim of religious "fundies," reported the news this way: "A University of Kansas professor who drew criticism for e-mails he wrote deriding Christian fundamentalists resigned Wednesday as chairman of the Department of Religious Studies."

This abbreviation of the facts so offended the University of Kansas that a spokeswoman told me she had called the AP to protest and explain that it was Mirecki's views about Christians in general and Catholics in particular that had caused him grief. "If it had just been one group"—i.e., the "fundies"—"this would not be as much of an issue," she told me.

The AP flatly refused her request to correct the story, however, and the newspapers of Kansas and around the world carried the tale that "Christian fundamentalists" had driven Mirecki from his chairmanship. A few weeks later, Mirecki claimed he had been followed through morning darkness by thugs in a pickup truck and when he pulled over, he said, they gave him a black eye while angrily denouncing his proposed class. That too was carried by the AP, despite the fact that the local police told me they were unable to shed any light on the alleged incident, or even ascertain if it had happened as Mirecki described.

8. Ruth Gledhill, "Societies Worse Off 'When They Have God on Their Side,' " *Times* (London), September 27, 2005. There should be a warning slapped on British journalists who cover religion. The BBC's "religious affairs" correspondent once was caught rattling away on the radio about the "American Episcopalian" church and its "same-sex bishops."

9. Gregory Paul, "The Great Scandal: Christianity's Role in the Rise of the Nazis," *Free Inquiry,* vol. 3, no. 24. *Free Inquiry* is published by the Council for Secular Humanism, an organization dedicated to advancing "the secular humanist eupraxophy as an alternative naturalistic life-stance." The Council is a resource for those who need experts to speak about the evils of intelligent design. According to the organization's Web site, Paul is one such "expert": "His book, *Beyond Humanity,* discusses the impact of intelligent cybertechnology on religion, further equipping him to speak on the role of religion in society. Because of his scientific background, Paul is also able to speak on broad debate issues, such as evolution v. creationism and the like." www.secularhumanism.org.

10. Of course, if Paul's "study" had been about how "atheistic belief" had been responsible for 80 to 100 million deaths in the twentieth century—as communism was—nobody would have noticed because it would never have been published anywhere. When I called the editor of the *Journal* to ask what he was thinking when he ran the article, he nervously repeated over and over that the journal was "peer-reviewed"—which, of course, may have been the problem.

11. The full text is reprinted in Appendix 1.

Index